This book is dedicated to:

Donald R. Levi, DREI

Whose book "How to Teach Adults"
has been under our arms and in our heads for 20 years

And to

Mark Barker, DREI

Without whose tireless efforts and dedication to the
process of educating adults, we would all be lesser instructors

With Special Thanks to Past REEA President, Philip Schoewe, who acted
as our sounding board and was an invaluable resource in the assembly of
these ideas.

To everyone who has ever attempted and succeeded at teaching someone else something new.

About YOU!

Since you are holding this book in your hands you have my admiration and respect. Not because you bought it, in fact I truly hope that someone cared enough about you to place this in your hands. You have my respect because in the simple act of opening this book you have demonstrated a commitment to the advancement of education and you have taken a positive step forward toward attempting to improve the level of your instruction.

As a Distinguished Real Estate Instructor (DREI) I long ago abandoned any thought or belief that one day we reach the magic pinnacle of perfection. DREI's are committed, as are you, to the continual pursuit of excellence and they know full well that the next class will reveal another flaw, another misstep, another inadequacy which we will have to focus on and rectify before the next. I do not pretend to know all of the answers or the perfect way of doing things anymore than you. I have learned a lot in the decades I have spent in front of people trying to help them understand some new fact, information or concept. I am honored to share those experiences with you.

May you find delight and a sense of fulfillment out of the continual journey that leads to self-improvement. Those who are at least aware of the need for constant and continual improvement such as you will always get from me a standing Ovation!

About the Author
Len Elder, J.D., B.A., DREI

"Len Elder is a powerful, passionate and persuasive speaker, and his ability to ignite any audience into action is remarkable. He did his homework and was well versed on what the rules were in Oklahoma. The presentation was diverse and encompassed many techniques to hold the audience's interest but most of all he connected with the audience on an emotional level. The participants were very impressed and the feedback was extremely positive overall. I personally would recommend him to anyone wanting a brilliant and inspiring presentation."

Patricia Wheeler, Director of Education
Oklahoma Real Estate Commission

Educational classes and events should leave students excited, energized, inspired and knowledgeable. Len has a B.A. degree in Speech Communications and a Juris Doctorate in Law. He was a nationally recognized intercollegiate debate award winner and was the Speech Forensics Debate Coach for Capital University. He is the youngest recipient ever of the John J. Getgey Memorial Award for Academic Excellence and Achievement in the practice of law. As an attorney, Len was undefeated in court of appeals proceedings and in arbitration hearings. The National Real Estate Educators Association (REEA) has recognized Len as a Distinguished Real Estate Instructor (DREI). He has been published as the author of law journal articles, cover stories for the National Real Estate Educators Association Journal and his books titled, **"UnRandom Thoughts"** and **"A Treasonous Season"** are published on Amazon.com.

This book would not have its power and reach were it not for the gracious and insightful contributions of the collaborative authors. All of them are well respected in their fields and they have given freely of their time, inspiration and efforts to make this project a more beneficial resource for you. One thing that they have in common; they all believe it is about the students. Some of their stories will make you laugh, some will make you think, some will inspire you, but all of them will add to your understanding and education in the art and science of presenting.

Thank You, Applause & Standing Ovation to:

Ryan Adair
Dan Adler
Tony Ray Baker
Mark Barker
Lucy Barraza
George Bell
Cindy Chandler
Amy Chorew
Doug Devitre
Roseann Farrow
Bill Gallagher
Julie Garton-Good
Rhonda Hamilton
Joe McClary
Beverly McCormick
Sharon Montague
Annalisa Moreno
Bruce Moyer
Karel Murray
Dana Rhodes
Marcie Roggow
Philip Schoewe
Sharleen Smith
Marie Spodek
Terry Wilson

Back to School by nuttakit
FreeDigitalPhotos.net

"There is great irony in writing a textbook on the education of adult learners when all of the theoretical, empirical and statistical research indicates that there are much better ways to learn."

"Standing Ovation" for the CE course creation and instruction of MREA and SHIFT, the CE Courses, Tucson, AZ

The Author

OVATION
TABLE OF CONTENTS

What A Lot of Things There Are to Learn!

As the curtain opens the scene is a large tree in the middle of a forest. Moonlight shines through the branches and illuminates an elderly Wizard who is telling a tale to a young boy beneath the tree.

And Merlin the Wizard said to the young boy named Arthur who would become King...

"The best thing for being sad," replied Merlin, beginning to puff and blow, "Is to learn something. That's the only thing that never fails. You may grow old and trembling in your anatomies, you may lie awake at night listening to the disorder of your veins, you may miss your only love, you may see the world about you devastated by evil lunatics, or know your honour trampled in the sewers of baser minds. There is only one thing for it then – to learn. Learn why the world wags and what wags it. That is the only thing which the mind can never exhaust, never alienate, never be tortured by, never fear or distrust, and never dream of regretting. Learning is the only thing for you. Look at what a lot of things there are to learn."

T.H. White, The Once and Future King

Prologue
Backstage
Before the Show

The Impact of a Teacher
Personal Experiences from the Early Classroom

Somewhere way back there in your memory was the teacher. The teacher who made a difference and that you remember to this day. We tend to undervalue teachers in our society. I find that a little strange since I have never met anyone who did not have a teacher somewhere in their past who made a huge impact on their life and quite possibly even changed the direction of it.

I'm willing to bet that in most instances the teacher at that time didn't even know the impact of what was occurring. They were just doing their job, but they knew it had merit. They knew it had worth. That's why they were there. That's what they believed in and what they probably most wished for occurred and in all likelihood went completely unnoticed by them.

If you ever get the opportunity to let them know the impact which they had please take the time to do it. I guarantee you it will be a worthwhile effort for both of you.

"It's All My Teacher's Fault"

It was 10th grade, Sophomore year, English literature class. I wasn't there because I chose to be. The course was required. When Martha McCallum, our teacher, walked into the room, she didn't say, "Welcome to English literature class." She didn't tell us we were going to have to "work" our way through the classics of English literature. She didn't command us to pay attention because there would be a final at the end of the year. She just smiled. She laughed and she said, "In this class we are going to go on some grand adventures and we're going to learn what those adventures mean to us." Okay, now I was listening.

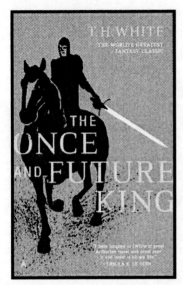

Go on grand adventures we did. We learned together through *A Tale of Two Cities* by Charles Dickens, *Romeo and Juliet* by Shakespeare and oh yeah, the adventure that has defined my life since that classroom, *The Once and Future King,* by T.H. White. *The Once and Future King* is the tale of King Arthur and the Knights of the Roundtable. It was about as far removed from our lives as you could get. None of us lived in castles or even a country with a King. We had never seen a knight and who cared about a roundtable? How old was this book anyway? Then Martha McCallum made us care and changed everything. She made us care because she took the material and made the story relevant to us. She didn't make us memorize the characters or the plot (she made us want to get to know them) because she simply wanted to know, "What were the lessons from the story *for us*?"

- She wanted to know if we thought that a world where kings used their power for good rather than conquest was an important goal;

- She wanted to know if we thought that people should work together like Knights at a Roundtable and if so, what things could we work on with other people that would make the world a better place;

- She asked us how we wanted to be remembered and she had us do activities where we had to talk about the legacy we wanted to leave and what we wanted people to remember us by.

What do you know? It wasn't a dusty old inapplicable tale like I thought. The story made us think and the way she engaged us as students and involved us in applying it to our lives, has stayed with me forever. I guess I never escaped that 10th grade classroom.

In 1976 she even incorporated videos. One of our assignments was to watch the Lerner and Loewe musical, *Camelot,* based on the book we were reading. In the final scene King Arthur is on the eve of battle and a young boy comes to help him fight. The boy explains he wants to be a Knight. Richard Chamberlain playing the role of King Arthur turns to the boy and says:

> *From the stories that people tell you, you wish to be a Knight? Now tell me what you think you know of the Knights of the Roundtable?*

> *I know everything me Lord,* the boy replies. *Might for right. Right for right. Justice for all. A roundtable where all Knights would sit. Everything.*

> *Now listen to me, Tom from Warrick. You will not fight in the battle, do you understand? You will run behind the lines until it is over. Then you will return home to England to grow up and grow old. You will remember what I, the King, told you and do as I command. Each evening from December to December before you drift asleep upon your cot, think back on all the tales that you remember of Camelot. Ask every person if he has heard the story and tell it strong and clear if he has not; that once there was that fleeting wisp of glory called Camelot. Now say it out with love and joy...don't let it be forgot that once there was a spot for one brief shining moment that was known as Camelot.*

King Arthur then "knights" the boy a member of the Roundtable and the King's page reminds Arthur that a great battle is about to begin to which the King replies:

> *I have won my battle. This is my victory. What we did will be remembered...you'll see. He is one of what we all are; less than drops in the great blue ocean of the sunlit seas, but it seems that some of the drops sparkle.some of them do sparkle.*

I didn't know it then, but McCallum's way of touching us emotionally with the story, causing us to connect with it, engaging us to apply the moral and the meaning to our own lives was implanted forever. There in that classroom was created everything I was to be, become and believe in:

- *Might for right. Right for right. Justice for all* = before I knew it I was enrolled in law school

- *A roundtable where all knights would sit* = a lifetime of trying to assemble a collaborative group, a team, pull people together, in order to accomplish things bigger than ourselves

- *Think back on all the tales and tell the story strong and clear* = an unending love affair with storytelling and the sharing of tales with others

- *Don't let it be forgot* = a desire and a fire to understand heritage and past contributions of others and a desire to make certain that others remember and build on everything that they know. Heck it will even make you write a book about it all

- *Less than drops in the great blue ocean* = a humility and a repetitive admission that individually we are less than we all are collectively

- *Some of the drops sparkle* = a commitment to try and at least sparkle in everything I do and try and help others to shine and sparkle too

- *My battle, my victory. What we did will be remembered* = a lifelong commitment of trying to have memorable impact…on my clients…on my students…on readers of this book

So now you know where we are coming from in the writing of this book. You know why we simply cannot identify with comments like, "*It's just a course*" "*Teaching doesn't matter that much*" or "*Teaching is dull and boring.*" They just don't resonate with us. Instead, we believe that teaching, storytelling, relating material to learners personally, engaging them in thought and dialogue can change lives. It's not a theory that teaching can have impact. Camelot is not a dream. It happens. I know. I have proof. It happened to me. In the back of my mind there is still this 10th grade teacher and her story, begging me to go and tell the tale.

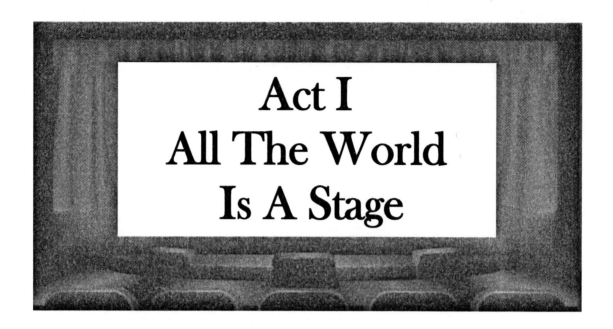

Act I
All The World
Is A Stage

A Brief History of Theatrics in Educating Adults

Let's face it, education, training and speaking is a lot like the theater. It's always a show. That is not to say that it is "made-up" "fake" or "pretend". It is to say that the profession of teaching, training and speaking is a production that must engage, entertain and enlighten the audience and we are the actors playing the leading roles in that process.

All the world's a stage,
And all the men and women merely players;
They have their exits and their entrances,
And one man in his time plays many parts...

Shakespeare, As You Like It, Act II, Scene 7

You have looked at an email, a flyer, or a promotional movie trailer and decided then and there that an upcoming production was one you had to see, much like our students choose their classes. Knowing how to promote and market a presentation is every bit as important as the production itself and it is something we explore more in Act XI. Then there was the content of the production. You observed its elements; sound, lighting, the visuals, the environment. They all contributed to your experience and we will discuss their importance in Acts IV and VII. The presenter or actor had a lot to do with that experience. You sized up their skills and abilities and all of it had an impact; the timing of their lines, the way they appeared, the techniques they used, all of which will be discussed in Acts V and VI. The quality of your experience also depended on the strength of the script and its content. We will discuss the art of Screenwriting in Act III. We live in a technologically advancing multi-media world. Proper utilization of those tools has been included in Acts VII and XI. Then there is the audience and the uniqueness of each member in it. We will learn more about our audience and how to appeal to each of those members in Act II. The combination of all of these things resulted in your review of the production and the comments you wrote or made, but mostly you were commenting on the collective experience and integration of all of these items.

It is that collective experience concept we want you to grasp most of all as you read this book. Education, classrooms and presentations of all nature and sorts results in an experience for the student. How we approach each of these elements dictates the end result. We have all been lured in by a great script or story only to be disappointed by the performance of the actors and while it is true that a great actor can sometimes carry a bad script, it is only when both are at their zenith; great script, excellent acting that we nominate those productions for academy awards. Reading this book will help you realize the importance of all of the elements that contribute to the experience from a good opening scene to the final act.

Greek Performances in an Olive Grove

We would all benefit by a better understanding of how we arrived at the theater of education today and there are lessons to be learned from understanding some concepts given to us by the greatest teachers of the past. In trying to pinpoint the origin of our profession seems no one really knows where the first classroom occurred or when it popped into existence. Its actual origins have been washed over by eons of time and lost in the subsequent revolutions of the earth. We are left with little but a few scattered fragments from the great teachers and legends of the past.

So let's begin with Socrates. We don't expect you to actually remember him. His bones have been buried for over 2,400 years. He is often held out as the world's first great teacher from Athens in the City State of Greece (469-399 BC). Although his classroom was simply a gathering of young Grecian men among a grove of olive trees, we presume that there were teachers before him. We say this because we have never known of a single teacher who did not have teachers. Nonetheless, there is not a single record left behind by Socrates; no teacher's manual, no student handouts, not even a cob-webbed  PowerPoint. He preferred a conversational engaging style of teaching and all we know about him today we know only through his student, Plato. How fitting that a teacher should be known only through the eyes of his students.

Those students tell us that Socrates was married to Xanthippe. She is said to have resented the fact that he charged no fees for his teaching, which just proves that some things despite 2,400 years of history haven't changed much in our profession. Admiration and knowledge of Socrates was honed during law school years. It has long been and still is the practice of most law professors to teach their students by way of the Socratic Method. What was that method? Well, in essence, questioning. If we were to bump into Socrates in a classroom today the discussion might very well go like this:

Student: What are we going to learn today?

Socrates: What would you like to learn today?

Student: Something important.

Socrates: And what is important to you?

Student: Knowing how to be a better teacher.

Socrates: What do you think makes someone a good teacher?

Student: Someone who causes me to know more than I currently know.

Socrates: So you admit that there are things you do not know?

Student: There are lots of things I do not know.

Socrates: Do you want to learn new things?

Student: Yes. But, are we going to learn anything today or not?

Socrates: What did you just learn?

At age 70 Socrates was brought to trial on charges that he was an atheist and a corrupter of youth. He was found guilty and was sentenced to death. On the order of his judges, Socrates drank poison hemlock and died. The trial, the last days and the death of Socrates are described by Plato in the dialogues; Apology, Crito and Phaedo. All of that simply reminds us that this entire business of teaching and educating adults can be a killer. It seems that rocking the boat was a bad idea even in ancient Athens.

Steve Jobs once said that he would trade all of his technology for an afternoon with Socrates. We wonder what you would give for the privilege of being in the teaching presence of the legend.

Socrates would have been pleased we think, that his student Plato absorbed so much and sought to bring more order and structure into the world of education. It was Plato who founded the Academy of Athens in 387 B.C. Don't spend a lot of time searching for the registration office or the dormitory. The Academy existed as a loose gathering of individuals schooled in a garden to the west of Athens. Plato, employing the skills he gathered from Socrates, wrote the dialogues. The dialogues posed a series of questions about life, morality and politics and Plato sought to draw his audience in much like Socrates through the asking of questions to provoke and encourage thought. Interesting! The world's first class outline was just a series of questions for Plato to ask his students.

Plato's most famous student was Aristotle (384-322 BC). Aristotle studied at Plato's Academy for twenty years (367-347 BC) before founding his own school, The Lyceum. We guess there is nothing new about competition in the education industry from the very people we may be teaching. The Lyceum was founded upon Aristotle's return from Macedon and his tutoring of the young prince Alexander (later to be known as Alexander the Great). Aristotle's students went on to achieve great things. Do you know what your students have gone on to achieve? Do you think that should be the true measure of an instructor?

After 150 years of archeological efforts, construction workers excavating a parking lot area for a Museum of Modern Art at Constitutional Square in Athens, accidentally unearthed the original site of the Lyceum. We share this with you just to prove that what you are reading is based on historical fact, not fantasy.

At the Lyceum Aristotle and his students became known as the peripatetics. The word "peripatetic" means one who walks and travels about and Aristotle had a habit of walking in and among his students while discussing philosophy. Hey, turns out Aristotle was a pacer. He taught and developed theories in the Lyceum for eleven years. Today we have less than 20% of Aristotle's work that survived the ages, still much praise has been lauded upon Aristotle over the years.

A tireless scholar, whose scientific explorations were as wide-ranging as his philosophical speculations were profound; a teacher who inspired - and who continues to inspire - generations of pupils; a controversial public figure who lived a turbulent life in a turbulent world. He bestrode antiquity like an intellectual colossus. No man before him had contributed so much to learning. No man after could hope to rival his achievement

Jonathan Barnes (1982) *Aristotle*, Oxford: OUP.

Only fragments of Aristotle's treatise *On Education* are still in existence. We thus know of his philosophy of education primarily through brief passages in other works. Aristotle considered repetition to be a key tool to develop good habits. He believed that the teacher was to lead the student systematically. This differed, for example, from Socrates' emphasis on questioning his listeners to bring out their own ideas. He also placed great emphasis on the practical applications of everything he taught, believing that we learn most through doing and that we only learn when we can see the practical applications for what it is we are being taught. He also mentioned the importance of play.

Eventually Aristotle was charged with impiety (the same charge which had led to the execution of Socrates) and was forced to live in exile in Macedon. He died a year later. Teachers after all, cannot live without their students you know. This famous trio of Socrates, Plato and Aristotle forms the bedrock of the principles, concepts and methods that are utilized in this book. Knowing them better helps us all to be better educators, understanding their techniques, philosophies and perceptions helps us to become great instructors. That is true so long as we remember the most fundamental of their principles: true success all lies in the application of what we know.

Here is what they left with us that we can employ in the classroom today:

- **Asking questions causes reflection and advances thought**

- **Wisdom is based in humbleness and admitting our own ignorance**

- **We learn best by doing**

- **We must see the practical applications for the knowledge we are imparting**

- **Education is an experiential journey for the learner who must play along the way**

Clearly Socrates, Plato and Aristotle learned some things about the way that most adult learners digest and process information. How then did we end up with lecture style deliveries that often tend to almost take the students and interaction out of the equation? Where do our stereotypical perceptions of a teacher at the front of the room lecturing and presenting a canned presentation come from? They certainly do not come from these ancient masters.

The Teachers Take Center Stage

In the Middle Ages of Europe (800-1200), education primarily became the role of the church. Prior to their formal establishment, many universities were monasteries and church operated places of education. In that world most beings were regarded as evil, not good, and it was up to the knowledgeable teacher to instruct and "save" them. It was accepted that the teacher would need to control and dictate the conduct of the students, but it was also expected that they would keep the learning environment strict and in many ways non-creative and uninspired. The domination of teacher focused learning is sometimes tracked back to the Calvinists. In direct contrast to our Greek ancestors, the Calvinists believed that wisdom was evil. They espoused that adults direct, control and ultimately limit children's learning to keep them innocent.

Schools and universities developing in this period were organized to prepare young boys for the priesthood. They preached indoctrination, memorization and rote repetition as an effective approach to instill beliefs, faith and ritual. It was the casting of an image and approach in education that we are still trying to shed off centuries later.

In the United States, the learning and education paradigm mirrored that of early Europe in both its secular nature, the elevated role of the professor and its purpose. Harvard University, founded in 1636 is regarded by many as the oldest university in the United States. Samuel Eliot Morrison was its founder (the name Harvard was attached from John Harvard, an English pastor and the first benefactor of the college).

The original purpose and goal of one of our most historical educational centers was about as far from the engaging enlightening of Socrates as one can get. The reason that Samuel Eliot Morrison and John Harvard were interested in forming the educational beacon that would become Harvard University is often omitted from the history books. Kenneth Davis in his book, *America's Hidden History* reminds us that Harvard's story really began in the cold darkness of a late winter in New England when Hannah Emerson Dustin was kidnapped by Abernaki Indians. She and her friends killed her "savage" captors and escaped. Her eventual escape and the massacre of her captors was detailed by Henry David Thoreau in *A Week on the Concord and Merrimack Rivers*, (1849*):*

> *Early this morning the deed was performed, and now,*
> *perchance, these tired women and this boy, their*
> *clothes stained with blood, and their minds*
> *racked with alternate resolution and fear killed*
> *their captors and escaped."*

The founders of Harvard College (later to become Harvard University) enlisted the support of Puritan leaders such as Increase Mather and his son, Cotton Mather in the original formation of the College. The Mathers had gained notoriety for their writings on witchcraft and their roles in the Salem Witch Trials. They used the story of Hannah Dustin and her deeds to gather support for the formation of the College. They argued that the colonies needed an educational institution in order to triumph over the perils of evil and native savagery. When Harvard College was officially founded in 1635, its charter was to "Educate the English and Indian youth of the country in knowledge and godliness." As far as the Puritans were concerned, the best thing they could do for savages was to convert them to Christianity. Therein were laid the cornerstones of an educational system that believed the teachers knew all and the students knew nothing. As we said, about as far from the enlightening student and instructor discourse of Socrates as you could get.

Today we are still engaged in a battle to define and shape the purpose and the outcome of education and the battle has taken us nearly full circle. Today, entities like the Real Estate Educators Association (REEA) and the Distinguished Real Estate Instructors (DREI) espouse an educational philosophy that sounds a lot more like the ancient Greeks than the Calvinists or the Puritans. It was the Grecian principles, not the Calvinists or Cotton Mather's which have become the focal point of the Generally Accepted Principles of Education (GAPE)

Old School by Carlos Porto
FreeDigitalPhotos.net

which we will explore in the next chapter. How those principles were developed and created was a long road through a history of education that takes us from Socrates to today. Many have contributed much so that we might teach a few.

In fact, we could fill this book with nothing but highlights from the centuries of great educators who have gone before, but that kind of information would not engage you in the questioning, thought provoking dialogue that was advocated by the distinguished Greeks of long ago and we doubt whether we would immediately perceive from further narrative the practical applications of that knowledge. So that is not the best way for us to learn together. Instead here are a few names of other great teachers of the past. By no means is this list complete, but we think it will give you some insight into teaching and as educators we should recognize these names. Can you see the factors of their success applied to presentations today?

The Academy Award List of Teachers

Confucius (551-479 BC) Socrates of the East and founder of the Ru School of Chinese thought, a teacher who emphasized teaching and study. Made an impact not by long diatribes and presentations, but because people remembered his aphorisms. An aphorism is a short statement delivered in memorable form. *"He who learns, but does not think is lost. He who thinks but does not learn is in grave danger."*

Martin Luther (1483-1546) Leader of the great religious revolt of the 16th Century in Germany. Founder of the Lutheran Church and denounced by the Catholic Church for transcribing the Bible. He believed that education and understanding ought to be available to everyone, not just priests and archbishops.

Johann Amos Coménius (1592-1670) This educator challenged the traditional schools of the 1600s, saying they crushed a person's innate desire to learn. He was an advocate of natural learning and an opponent of education limited to books and classrooms. He felt that all children deserved an education and also believed a person is a student for the entirety of his life, not just during the traditional years of school.

Jesus (5 BC - 30 AD) Considered by many to be the Master Teacher, he made teaching and learning a part of daily life. His brief, informal lessons, which often made use of parables and proverbs, challenged the pupil to think or take action.

Friedrich Fröbel (1782-1852) He founded the first Kindergarten (in German, "garden of children") which focused on growing young minds through self-expression and creativity, while using manipulative materials to learn mathematical concepts such as geometry, shape, color, structure, and pattern.

Horace Mann (1796-1859) Mann was a Massachusetts lawyer and legislator who, having been raised in poverty and hardship, came to believe in social harmony and the need to win "some victory for Humanity." Thus, though self-educated himself, he became "the Father of the American Common School" which he intended to be "the great equalizer of men." Many would say that we have public education and a public school system in America because of Horace Mann.

Ralph Waldo Emerson (1803-1882) Emerson addressed a radical rethinking of the relationship between education and culture, viewing knowledge not as the end product of a preexisting truth, but seeing learning as a continuous process—a perpetual journey relating the self to the world.

Henry David Thoreau (1817-1862) Thoreau may be best known for his writings, but he was a teacher first. As a schoolteacher he believed that children should not have to study exclusively from texts. He created a curriculum that included journal writing (rather than just memorization and recitation) and field trips (to the countryside for nature study, as well as to the local newspaper office, gunsmith, etc.). Although he ended his classroom career early to spend the rest of his life learning and writing, he continued to reflect on the process of teaching and was a pioneer in adult education.

Anne Sullivan (1866-1936) Sullivan was a devoted teacher who, despite her own handicap, demonstrated a tireless commitment to a student (Helen Keller) who had severe learning disabilities. She developed a method of touch teaching, using direct experience rather than attempting to explain a concept; and she reasoned that children learn by imitation and repetition, working out their own understanding of the subject.

Maria Montessori (1870-1952) Montessori believed that each child is born with a unique potential to be revealed, rather than a "blank slate" to be written upon; that learning requires a stimulating environment which engages all the senses; and that the teacher's role is primarily in organizing materials and establishing a general classroom culture.

Robert Frost (1874-1963) Frost the famous American poet, was a college teacher who taught his own children at home. He believed that education should both delight and instruct. His approach favored involvement and enjoyment rather than scholarship and criticism.

Jean Piaget (1896-1980) Piaget brought the theory of knowledge out of the realm of philosophy and made it into a science, by observing that children's logic and modes of thinking are entirely different from those of adults; that they are constantly creating and testing their own theories of the world.

John Holt (1923-1985) Holt was a schoolteacher and educational reformer who coined the term "unschooling," believing that children do not need to be coerced into learning. He thought they do so naturally if given freedom to follow their own interests and provided with a rich assortment of resources.

Somewhere in your past lies your favorite teacher. They made an impact and a difference that has remained with you until today. Chances are that the reason the teacher had an impact is because they employed some techniques or philosophies which differentiated them from all of the others. Do you have that person in mind? Then answer the following questions.

1. Who was your favorite teacher?

2. What made them memorable to you?

3. Were they more like the Greeks or the Calvinists? Why?

4. What principles that we have discussed from history did they employ?

5. From the list of famous teachers who would you say they most resembled?

Curtain Call

"What Real Estate Agents Need From Education Today: Making Rain"

By Lucy Barraza & Tony Ray Baker, Real Estate Professionals, Tucson, Arizona

Lucy Barraza and Tony Ray Baker are practicing real estate professionals in Tucson, Arizona. They are admired by their clients, operate a successful practice and are on the leading edge of the real estate industry. They have attended a vast number of real estate education courses from a wide variety of instructors. They hold multiple real estate professional designations including ABR, CRS and GRI. They also operate multiple web and social media sites. You can reach Tony and Lucy at MyGreenTucson.com or BuyandSellTucsonRealEstate.com

We met at a coffee shop in front of a large mall just off Broadway. Lucy and I didn't know why we were meeting Len, but when he sent the message through Facebook requesting our presence, we could only say, "Yes." Lucy and I would do anything for Len and Theresa; we had followed them around from the start of their education company. If they were teaching a class, we were taking it. Besides, I really wanted a hot mocha, even though it was 100 degrees in Tucson that day.

Len arrived, we all ordered drinks and then sat down and got reacquainted. Len told us that he was very excited because he and Theresa were writing this book you are reading now. The book was all about being a great presenter and at the end of each chapter they had something called a *Curtain Call* where famous speakers wrote a few words about the art of presenting. But that's not why we were there. Oh, they did want us to write a *Curtain Call*, but from a very different angle. They thought that Lucy and I, both being full time REALTORS®, could share our thoughts on what we want from educational courses and the people who present them.

A few minutes later we found ourselves looking at Len's laptop and he was showing us how to create videos. Using a free video program that anyone could download free of charge, Len proceeded to take a video, cut it up and add a soundtrack. He threw in a few transitions and some titles and in just a few minutes, we had a whole new video. More importantly, I knew exactly how to do something I had never tried before. We left the coffee shop, promised Len that we would write and went back to the office very excited about the whole video experience and a little nervous about what we had just committed to.

Lucy and I discussed what we should write about for this *Curtain Call*. What are we looking for in education and presenters? We discussed personality traits of the instructor. We want the instructor to be flexible, get to know their audience and speak to that group's knowledge and questions. We learn best when the instructor is enthusiastic about the material and able to teach it in different ways. After all, we all learn differently. We appreciate it when the instructor is engaging and can show us the benefits of the material they are teaching.

We also discussed the different subjects we want to learn. As most business owners, we need to know how to bring in more consumers. We realize that marketing and advertising have become a big part of our schedule and we either turn it over to an agency who will charge us a fortune or we do it ourselves. In the current economy, it only makes sense to conserve a little money, especially with all of the free venues for bringing in new business.

So Lucy and I discussed websites, social media, syndication, blogging, online classified ads, pay per click campaigns, search engine optimization and the list went on. Yes, we all need to learn some of it, or all of it, and yes it's all a little overwhelming. By the end of the day, we were a little confused about what we need from education and more confused about what to write for this *Curtain Call*.

That night I was home watching a popular sitcom. One of the characters, we'll call him Tom, wanted to stop the girl of his dreams from going on a camping trip. She would be going with male a co-worker who wanted to get to know her better. After trying many different things, Tom sought out an expert instructor well versed in Indian culture. Tom asked the instructor to teach him to make rain. The instructor spent hours with Tom, patiently teaching him the same information in different ways until he was convinced that he knew what he was doing. With faith, perseverance and a lot of singing and dancing on a roof top, Tom literally made it rain and the camping trip was cancelled.

That's when it hit me; we all want to know how to make it rain. No matter what business we are in or reason we seek new information, we are all looking for some bit of information that will help us complete some goal and most likely the instructor will never know what that goal is. For Tom, making rain would give him a chance to work on a relationship.

The day Lucy and I met Len at the coffee shop, he taught us how to make rain. He was so enthusiastic about showing us how to create videos that it probably never even dawned on him that he was teaching us something that would bring new clients to our business for years to come.

Now, with clarity, we can say: If the instructor really knows the material, has a passion about presenting it and has the flexibility to teach it the way each individual audience needs, rain will be made. We are all just looking for a little rain.

Curtain Call

"What My First Few Years Taught Me About Instructing: Getting Started"

By Bruce Moyer, Ed.S., Instructor, Charlotte, North Carolina

Bruce Moyer, Ed.S., has a Bachelor of Arts as well as an Educational Specialists Degree (Masters +30) from the University of South Carolina. With over 10 years in counseling as a Licensed Professional Counselor, Bruce entered the real estate teaching profession with a wealth of knowledge about education. As a practicing professional at Keller Williams Southpark in Charlotte, Bruce is a member of the North Carolina Real Estate Educators Association (NCREEA) and teaches at Superior School of Real Estate. You can reach Bruce by email and contact him at BruceMoyer@KWCharlotte.com.

Most of us remember the teachers in our lives that believed in us, pushed us, and encouraged us to do our very best. They seemed to know what we were capable of before we ourselves knew. I am lucky to have had several of these teachers that changed my life that way. One was Mrs. Fitzner who taught me Spanish at South Aiken High School, SC for three years and was the first to tell me "You can do anything you set your mind to Bruce!" She helped me decide to go to college. Dr. Burgraff and Dr. McFadden at the University of South Carolina, Columbia, SC taught me during my graduate studies program and provided further examples of great teaching. My degree as an Educational Specialist emphasized connection with others, listening, reflecting what I heard, mirroring what others said, and understanding a person's life and their own uniqueness. I learned to help them make a change when *they* were ready. This training as a counselor combined with an examination of good teachers (e.g. Mrs. Fitzner, Dr. Burgraff, and Dr.

McFadden) helped me to develop an approach that I have found works well with adult learners.

First, as a counselor learns early in their training, watching verbal and nonverbal messages is critical to understanding others. I have found this equally true in teaching. I have learned to be a keen observer of my students when I am in front of them. I look for verbal and nonverbal cues that tell me I am on target and have their attention, or tell me they are tired and need something different from me. So, I always have a "Plan B" to every segment of instruction. Being able to adapt to every class keeps me engaged, alert, and ready to deal with whatever they need from me. No two classes are ever alike and keeping this skill is an important essential element of instruction.

When I teach, I am reminded of the parallel that being a counselor is not about telling them what to do to fix their problems, but instead to get them to learn something because they will benefit from the change in their way of thinking. I want them to understand and then incorporate knowledge as they chose. I remind students that they will make the biggest change in entering real estate by learning new, current, and relevant information that changes their life, as well as the life of their client.

Likewise teaching keeps me "on my toes". Being an effective teacher means that multiple methods of learning must be employed because everyone learns in different ways. Teaching with relevant, personal, relatable materials and exercises gives students understanding of the materials and the necessary tools to use once away from the classroom environment. Keeping aware of the student helps me to know where they are and allows me to monitor and adjust the class room environment accordingly.

I have also incorporated social media, videos and music in the classroom. Video vignettes that illustrate real estate principles are readily available on the internet and I have had a lot of laughs with my students as a result. For example, "Closing Costs Explained Visually" is a great cartoon on a dry erase board that I have played multiple times throughout several key points of the closing process discussion. Sources such as YouTube are critical to this method. I use several videos from television series, movies, and advertisements to relate to students in a nontraditional method. At break intervals, I ask students to tell me of a musician they would like to listen to and/or watch their music video. Many state that this addition alone made them more relaxed, energized, and connected them more to me and the learning process.

Another activity I have developed is a Jeopardy game. Students are divided into teams, I get to play Alex Trebeck, I state the answer, and they must reply with the question. The first team to raise their hands and answer correctly gets the dollar value of the card. The team with the most points gets to take home a quiz instead of taking it in class. This kind of activity allows learning to be fun, less intimidating and allows them to relate to something we have all had in our lives like the game show Jeopardy.

Just as in counseling, respecting students, relating to them, knowing what is happening in their lives, and knowing what they bring to the class from their vast experiences and lives has given me far more success in classroom management. Extrapolating from their experiences, painful as they are sometimes, connects them to the learning process and to one another. Being dismayed by their experiences, verbally showing them and articulating my surprise to their experience lets me connect with them and joins them to the classroom materials. Like anyone, students want to know you respect them regardless of their knowledge.

In ten years of counseling I never stopped learning and growing. Viewing my clients as a teacher helps me see my world from a broader perspective. If you take the time to look in someone's baggage you will find something that will enrich you. I feel the same about teaching. The real art of being a good teacher is the willingness to see what you can learn from a person and a class. The best teachers are the ones most open to learning. I usually have three goals when I teach. One, I want them to learn something that affirms what they already know. I believe people learn more when truly some of the material is familiar and known. They are less overwhelmed. Secondly, I want them to learn things that they used to know, but don't use anymore. We are all lifelong learners who need to be reminded of things we knew. Finally, of course, I want them to learn new things and that's where I try to channel those wonderful teachers from the past and use all my skills from being a learner and a listener.

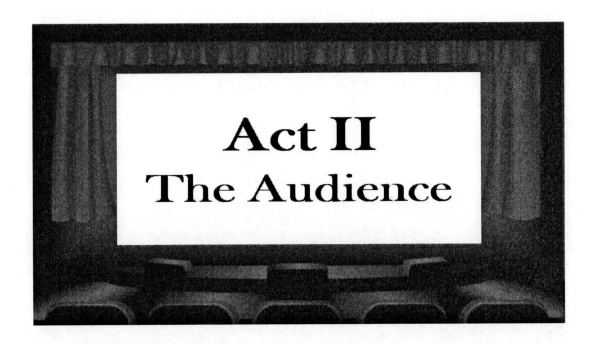

Understanding Today's Adult Learner Audience

Today we do not have the luxury of being a Socrates, the lone standout in a grove of olive trees and the only show in town. We compete for our audiences every day against a myriad of factors and the audience itself is distracted and fragmented. Information is simply generated at an absolutely astounding rate. We live in an ever increasing information age and all one needs do is to look at some of the statistics:

- **There are approximately 130 billion Google searches every month**
- **Wikipedia has over 15 million articles (78% of them are non-English)**
- **More information is generated each year than was generated in the previous 5000 years combined**
- **By age 65 the average person will have seen over two million television commercials**
- **One issue of the New York Times contains more information than a person would have seen in a lifetime in the 18th century**
- **YouTube videos receive two billion views a day (Double the audience of all three major U.S. networks combined)**
- **More videos are uploaded to YouTube in 60 days than all three of the major networks created in 60 years**
- **There have been close to a 150 million blogs created since 2002**

All of this has led many observers to say we live in the age of information overload. We disagree. We live in an age of data overload. In order for that data to become information it must be collected, digested, interpreted and explained in an understandable fashion. Enter the evolution revolution where as teachers we are constantly having to collect, distill and format all of this data, translate it into information and turn it into education.

Entertainment by digitalart
FreeDigitalPhotos.net

But people are distracted and fragmented by more than just the sheer volume of data available. They are inundated with an assault on their senses; movies, social media, text messages, rock concerts, streaming videos, email all competing for their attention. Students who walk in to a classroom or a presentation today are not comparing you to other classrooms and live presentations. They are comparing this experience to the last experience they had: the one on the internet, the rock concert last night, the latest movie they attended. Therefore, our job is to ensure that the classroom experience is exciting, upbeat and inspiring.

So as instructors, we live not in an olive grove of tranquil serenity, but in a world filled with an overwhelming amount of stimuli. It was easy for Socrates, we think, because he had less competition and less challenges. After all, where else was there to go besides the olive grove? It's not like the students were listening to someone else's podcasts online. Our world of teaching is more foreboding. ("MORE foreboding?" screams Socrates from the grave, "Did you already forget that they killed ME.")

What Socrates seemed to understand was the way in which adults learn. He clearly was using some techniques and teaching strategies that left his students "hooked." All of the Greek instructors had loyal students who were willing to risk it all in the quest for knowledge. It makes us wonder, what the instructors did to cause that? It turns out that thousands of years later we are just beginning to understand the ways that people perceive, take-in and digest information. There have been piles of abstracts, books and articles spent on this topic. Researchers have spent years on it...enter Stage Left... Malcolm Knowles.

The Legacy of Malcolm Knowles

The central figure in U.S. adult education in the 20th century has been Malcolm Knowles. In the 1950's he was the Executive Director of the Adult Education Association of the United States of America. Knowles was a Harvard graduate who worked with YMCA groups in Boston and Massachusetts directing their adult education programs. He was also a University Professor associated with Boston University and North Carolina State University. He wrote several books including *The Modern Practice of Adult Education* (1970) and *The Adult Learner* (1973).

Until Malcolm Knowles there was not a clear discernible model for understanding the needs and objectives of adult students. Much work had been done in the field of pedagogy, the science and art of teaching children. Knowles labeled learning strategies focused on adults, andragogy. It is the process of engaging adult learners with the structure of the learning experience and Knowles believed very much in fostering the experience of the adult learners. He believed that teaching and educating adults had to incorporate some basic principles. He outlined characteristics that defined the learning experience. They can be summed up in 6 overriding needs and objectives surrounding the way that adults learn:

1. **Need to Know**. Adults need to know the reason for learning something.

2. **Need for Foundation**. Experience provides the basis for learning activities.

3. **Need for Self**. Adults need to be responsible for their decisions on education; involvement in the planning and evaluation of their instruction.

4. **Need for Readiness**. Adults are most interested in learning subjects having immediate relevance to their work and/or personal lives.

5. **Need for Orientation**. Adult learning is problem centered rather than content oriented.

6. **Need for Motivation**. Adults respond better to internal versus external motivators.

The Principles of Andragogy

In his book, *The Modern Practice of Adult Education*, Knowles elaborates on each of these fundamental needs and developed more detailed concepts and outlines the for the goals of adult education. It really is the work that most of modern adult education rests upon and we would encourage everyone to buy a copy and read it. The book talks about the following concepts:

Adults should acquire a mature understanding of themselves. They should understand their needs, motivations, interests, capacities, and goals. They should be able to look at themselves objectively and maturely. They should accept themselves and respect themselves for what they are, while striving earnestly to become better.

Adults should develop an attitude of acceptance, love, and respect toward others. This is the attitude on which all human relations depend. Adults must learn to distinguish between people and ideas, and to challenge ideas without threatening people. Ideally, this attitude will go beyond acceptance, love, and respect, to empathy and the sincere desire to help others.

Adults should develop a dynamic attitude toward life. They should accept the fact of change and should think of themselves as always changing. They should acquire the habit of looking at every experience as an opportunity to learn and should become skillful in learning from it.

Adults should learn to react to the causes, not the symptoms, of behavior. Solutions to problems lie in their causes, not in their symptoms.

Adults should acquire the skills necessary to achieve the potentials of their personalities. Every person has capacities that, if realized, will contribute to the well-being of himself and of society. To achieve these potentials requires skills of many kinds—vocational, social, recreational, civic, artistic, and the like. It should be a goal of education to give each individual those skills necessary for the student to make full use of his capacities.

Adults should understand the essential values in the capital of human experience. They should be familiar with the heritage of knowledge, the great ideas and the great traditions of the world in which they live. They should understand and respect the values that bind men together.

Adults should understand their society and should be skillful in directing social change. In a democracy the people participate in making decisions that affect the entire social order. It is imperative, therefore, that every factory worker, every salesman, every politician, every housewife, know enough about government, economics, international affairs, and other aspects of the social order to be able to take part in them intelligently.

As the Real Estate Educators Association (REEA) worked with the principles and theories of andragogy, the question still lingered as to how these theories and principles could be turned into practical classroom applications. Distinguished real estate instructors (DREI's) led by Mark Barker took the work of Malcolm Knowles and developed some standardized practical tactics that could be used in the classroom. They are called the Generally Accepted Principles of Education (GAPE) and form the foundation for instructors who would like to obtain one of the highest certifications our profession offers, the Distinguished Real Estate Instructor (DREI). In order to become a DREI, an instructor must pass a written test regarding their knowledge of GAPE, attend a GAPE focused Instructor Development Workshop (IDW) and then demonstrate those skills in a videotaped or live presentation that is judged by a panel of outstanding instructors.

Many of the instructors who contributed to this book are DREI instructors and they are widely recognized as some of the most influential adult real estate educators in the country. We firmly believe that nothing will improve your teaching more than going through the DREI process. We are even more certain that having your DREI and being associated with members or the Real Estate Educators Association will assist you in forming lifelong bonds, friendships and support that you will be able to rely on every day of your teaching career.

The GAPE standards are aspirational and practical guidelines that elevate the level of professionalism in the world of adult education. As you find out throughout this book, they are sound principles, backed by educational and psychological research and proven and tested in more classrooms than we can count. On the following pages are the practical applications spread across five categories: knowledge, andragogy, speech, teaching aids and learning environment.

Generally Accepted Principles of Education
(Adopted By the Real Estate Educators Association)

Category: KNOWLEDGE
Instructors should:

1. Provide current information.

2. Present alternative viewpoints on material when there is not a single position that is accepted industry-wide.

3. Clearly identify opinions as the instructor's opinion.

4. Build a proper foundation for each major element of a subject.

5. Deal with all key elements of a subject.

6. Cover the material adequately in the allotted time.

7. Answer all questions logically and concisely.

8. Be informed enough to handle a variety of questions on the subject being taught.

9. Admit when he/she does not know the answer to a question and volunteer to obtain that information.

"It is the supreme art of the teacher to awaken joy in creative expression and knowledge."

Albert Einstein

The category of Knowledge carries with it a dedication to the ethics of the teaching profession. The ethics of instruction require an instructor to constantly be updating course material and to be well enough informed to handle a variety of questions on the subject being taught. The execution of these principles requires diligence and a commitment to constantly grow and aspire to learn more.

Category: ANDRAGOGY

Instructors should:

1. Present new ideas by relating them to pre-existing knowledge held by the learners.

2. Teach at the learner's level.

3. Show in a specific way how new material will benefit learners.

4. Encourage questions and motivate involvement.

5. Show tolerance – both to ignorance and disagreement thus avoiding arguments and confrontation.

6. Build learner's self-esteem.

7. Call learners by name.

8. Involve learners in the learning process through planned activities.

9. Use a variety of teaching methods.

10. Teach to all participants, not just those who show interest.

11. Present key points by using examples as illustrations.

"My heart is singing for joy this morning. A miracle has happened! The light of understanding has shone upon my little pupil's mind, and behold, all things are changed."

Anne Sullivan

It is the category of Andragogy which attempts to infuse Malcolm Knowles' philosophies of adult education principles into teaching. The heart of these elements always centers around a showing of respect for the adult learner. It is the job of an excellent instructor, through a variety of teaching methods to inspire and draw out the opinions of the students and requires the instructor to treat each contribution in the classroom as valuable and important. Andragogy teaches us that our true value as instructors is measured by what we bring out of our students.

Category: SPEECH
Instructors should:

1. Use concise, simple, and normal speech patterns; use simple terminology.

2. Do not read to the class.

3. Keep the presentation on pace thus finishing the material in the allotted time.

4. Keep the topic flowing.

5. Speak loudly enough to be heard by all.

6. Enunciate clearly without being overdone.

7. Restate an individual learner's question to the group as a whole prior to attempting to answer the question.

8. Use humor when appropriate to make a point.

"It usually takes me more than three weeks to prepare a good impromptu speech."

Mark Twain

As you review the elements in the category of Speech you are probably thinking that of all the categories, this section carries the most common sense rules that everyone should know, yet we would propose that these skills are some of the most difficult to master. They require a degree of ease and comfort in public speaking that simply does not come naturally, but which is honed over time by practice, repetition and experience. The ability to flow easily from topic to question to answer to point sounds effortless when done correctly and appears as pure torture when it is not.

Category: TEACHING AIDS

Instructors should:

1. Make sure materials are legible, correctly spelled, properly numbered and mechanically produced using readable typeface.

2. Use visual imagery when possible to enhance written words.

3. Use written words when possible to enhance oral speech. NOTE: Written is better than oral; visual is better than written.

4. Follow the prepared outline.

5. Make sure that all material on the outline will be covered in the class and none of it is extraneous.

6. Deviate from prepared material only to meet specific needs.

7. Arrange the classroom so that learners do not have to look through physical objects.

8. Use modern presentation equipment such as overhead projector or computer projection.

9. Use equipment that enables the instructor to remain looking at the learners rather than turning their back to the class to write.

10. Make sure that the physical stature of the instructor does not block the view of the learners toward the projected material.

11. Make sure that the projector screen is easily visible to the group as a whole.

12. Use color.

13. Use large images for projected material.

14. Turn the projected image off when not in use and turn it on to call attention to the material.

15. Never block the image by walking between the projector and the screen with the projector on.

 *"There can be infinite uses of the computer and of new age technology, but if the teachers themselves are not able to bring it into the classroom and make it work, then it fails."*

Nancy Kasselbaum, U.S. Senator

We think Senator Kasselbaum has said it well. Enough said.

Category: LEARNING ENVIRONMENT

Instructors should:

1. Be positive toward the subject matter.

2. Refrain from ridiculing either the learners or others.

3. Wear professional attire.

4. Attend to personal grooming.

5. Set up the room to accommodate the approximate number of learners expected to attend.

6. Make sure empty seats are kept to a minimum.

7. Make sure that lectern or table at front of room is unobtrusive.

8. Provide writing surfaces for learners.

9. Make sure that learners have ample space between them.

10. Not stand behind physical objects for more than a short time period.

11. Use gestures during the presentation.

12. Use physical movement during the presentation to minimize the physical distance between the instructor and learners and try to involve all learners equally.

"Education is the most powerful weapon which you can use to change the world."

Nelson Mandela

Understand that every second of every minute that you are in front of a classroom that opinions are being formed about you. Those opinions and impressions will impact the effectiveness and responsiveness to your message. Understanding that the educational experience is about much more than the words that you have to share is to come to understand the category of Learning Environment.

The concepts of GAPE are not difficult to understand, but their application in the classroom is a matter which requires constant attention and focus. Just think of it as the return to the days of Socrates, Plato and Aristotle where the instruction was very much focused on the student and their involvement, rather than focused on the teacher. Psychology teaches us that we learn what we do in our own way and experience is the adult learners living textbook.

What the concepts of GAPE, Malcolm Knowles and the andragogic principles teach us is that we must constantly strive to:

1. Let learners know why something is important to learn

2. Show learners how to direct themselves through information

3. Relate the topic to the learners experiences

4. Accept that people will not learn until they are ready and inspired to learn and that it is our role as educators to ignite that inspiration

5. Help them overcome inhibitions, fears, behaviors and beliefs that they may already hold as preconceptions about learning

Business Man Standing by Ambro
FreeDigitalPhotos.net

Understanding Different Types of Learners

The concepts of Malcolm Knowles, andragogy and GAPE certainly identified that adult learners as a group are different. We now know that even within the broad category of adult learners, not every adult learner learns in the same manner. Let us say this as kindly as possible, not all adult students are equal. They come from different backgrounds, different mindsets and different beliefs. While we realize the futility in fitting any given student into a predefined box of characteristics, there are some fundamental characteristics that we can assign to learners based on their learning type.

A full understanding of learning types allows us as instructors to meet students where they are, appreciate their manner of learning and then craft presentations and courses that appeal to various groups of students. Much can be gained by understanding our audiences better.

For years researchers have been aware that aptitude tests, school grades, standardized tests and classroom performance are not always accurate indicators and fail to identify real ability. In attempting to explain this phenomenon, Robert J. Sternberg listed various cognitive dimensions in his book *Thinking Styles* (1997). Several other models are also often used when researching learning styles. This includes the Myers Briggs Type Indicator (MBTI), Howard Gardner's Multiple Intelligence Model and the DISC Assessment.

Rest Time by Meiklejohn
FreeDigitalPhotos.net

Indeed, lots of models have been proposed and the whole process of putting learners in a few select boxes has been heavily criticized and challenged.

Even though the validity of various learning styles has come under fire in recent years, most instructors and educators still believe there is something to be learned from understanding these different styles and many would vehemently argue their accuracy, validity and usefulness in the classroom.

The VAK Model of Learning Types

The most widely used model is the VAK model created by Fleming. Neil Fleming is a New Zealand teacher who has been teaching and researching in the field of education for nearly half a decade. He simplified the models and divided learners into just three categories:

LEARNING STYLE	DESCRIPTION
Visual	Seeing and Reading
Auditory	Listening and Speaking
Kinaesthetic	Touching and Doing

- **Visual Learners (THE GAZER)**

- **Auditory Learners (THE LISTENER)**

- **Kinesthetic Learners (THE DOER)**

It is one thing to talk about these concepts in the abstract and another to understand their application in presentations. So let's first of all apply it outside of the classroom and then turn to examples of applying it inside the classroom. On a Saturday afternoon three individuals go to a movie. They all sit in the middle of the theater. If we were to closely watch those three people we would notice that they are all taking in the information or the experience in very different ways:

THE GAZER – Visual Learner

- Never takes his eyes off the screen
- Can converse with his friends because they are taking the movie in visually by watching the screen
- Pays attention to special effects and film editing for a possible academy award

In the Classroom:

- Keeps asking what page of the handout we are on
- Wants to see numerous detailed notes
- Tends to sit in the front of the room so that they can see better
- Comments on the quality of our PowerPoint
- Wants to know if you can draw them a picture of the concept

THE LISTENER – Auditory Learner

- Keeps telling others to stop talking so they can hear the movie
- Can hum the soundtrack of the movie on the way out of the theater
- Leans back in their seat, closes their eyes and listens to the dialogue

In the Classroom:
- Asks you if you can turn up the microphone volume
- Wants to know if you can repeat the questions that other students ask
- Would like for you to have the people around them pay attention and quit talking

THE DOER – Kinesthetic Learner

- Didn't go to the theater, bought the DVD
- Their favorite part of the DVD is the interactive director feedback
- Watched the movie at home so they can do other things during the movie
- Has already made multiple trips to the kitchen for popcorn

In the Classroom

- Asks when we are going to get to the classroom group discussions

- Has already started making a to do list on the back of the student handout
- Wants to know if there are other resources that they can refer to after class
- Took time during the class to write a detailed critique of your student materials and hands it back to you at the end of class with all the corrections marked

Expanded Learning Type Models (LTM's)

Today, most educators analyze learning styles in more complex fashion than Fleming's VAK model did. There are lots of tools, quizzes and resources to allow us and our students to asses our learning styles. One of the best we have seen is the Learning Type Measure (LTM) developed by Bernice McCarthy. McCarthy's 4MAT Model is heavily researched and documented. It is an extraordinary tool for assessing learning styles and it is promoted and sold at AboutLearning.com.

With the LTM's graphical overlay, you'll construct easily interpreted representations of your personal strengths and weaknesses as a learner. It's designed to help managers, trainers and communicators map out strategies for improving individual potential, motivating learners with strategies crafted to their unique learning style and identifying situations in which different people function most effectively. The Learning Type Measure's 26-point self report questionnaire measures individual preferences for selecting, organizing, prioritizing and presenting knowledge. The LTM is an invaluable tool for designing instruction, managing human systems, parenting and improving personal relations.

Most of the contemporary work done on learning styles categorizes learners across four planes as compared with Fleming's 3 part approach of visual, auditory and kinesthetic. This reflects a more thorough understanding about the way that students take in and process information rather than simply whether they see it, hear it or do it. The four categories most widely used are:

EXPERIENTIAL – where students are exposed to new concepts and experience new information that may be delivered to them in a variety of formats. At this point, it is information, not yet turned into knowledge

PROCESSING – where students learn by absorbing expert opinions, reviewing studies and statistics and analyzing data

CONCEPTUAL – where students draw conclusions or meanings, theorize on the relevance and determine truths or trends within the material

APPLICATION – where students learn by relating the material to actual situations and or case studies and try to use the knowledge to solve problems

What all of this means is that knowledge is seen as being transferred through a four part process or cycle:

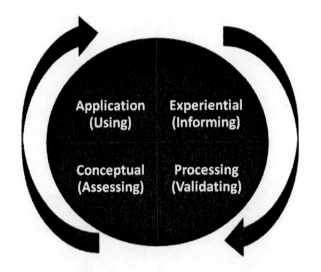

THE LEARNING CYCLE

For knowledge to be complete and transferred to the student, the instructor must take the learner through the complete learning cycle.

1. **Informing.** The student goes through a process of experiencing. The instructor is delivering new material, ideas and concepts.

2. **Validating.** The student begins processing the information. They are examining the source of the information and searching for experts, studies and research that supports the information.

3. **Assessing.** The student conceptualizes the material They are attempting to fit it into their pre-existing framework and determining the impact of the new information.

4. **Using.** The student begins application of the material. They are applying it to real world examples and case studies to solve existing problems.

Ideally an instructor leads the students through all four phases of the learning cycle in order to adequately convey the knowledge to the students. In the classroom, look at this way:

1. Here is what you need to know...
2. This is the source of the information...
3. This information means that...
4. Here is how you use it...

Knowledge is conveyed easier to all of the learning styles when it is taught in this cycle. Some of us as instructors are better with facts and statistics, (Processing/Validating). Others of us are better at theories or drawing conclusions and analysis based on facts (Conceptual/Assessing). When we skip steps in the learning cycle hands start to go up or minds start to turn off. The students who have learning styles in particular quadrants have begun to say:

- I don't know what you are trying to say? (Experiential)
- How do you know that? (Processing)
- So what does it mean? (Conceptual)
- What do we do with that? (Application)

This is precisely why we believe we do not live in an information overload age, we live in data overload age. It is also why so much of the current delivery of information really never gets turned into knowledge or education. For example, an association makes available to its members MLS statistics. Despite access to the data, it has not become knowledge to the members. Not because they didn't see it, but because it was simply statistical data that didn't take the recipient through an entire learning cycle to turn the information into knowledge. A brokerage sends out a memo informing licensees of a statutory law change. The memo never made it past the experiential quadrant of the cycle. Only those students who have a learning style conducive to that quadrant are going to effectively digest the information.

We strongly recommend that you invest the time and effort to at least complete your own learning assessment as an educator. You can do this online at AboutLearning.com for less than $15.00. We recommend this approach because the biggest mistake we make as instructors is that we tend to teach to whatever learning style we personally possess. This results in us ignoring or overlooking the contrasting learning styles that our students might possess. Having a firmer understanding of our own personal bias and tendencies for where we operate strongest in the cycle and broadening our approaches to teach to all students will improve our presentations.

In today's world we advance to a higher level of understanding our audience if we sub-categorize them one more time. Enter Stage Right…generational teaching.

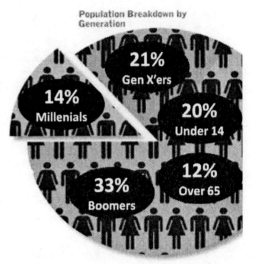

The Art & Science of Generational Teaching

Today we are asked to instruct, train and educate individuals across the widest generational spread that has ever existed. Sometimes as instructors it sort of has to hit us over the head before we get it and that happened about 4 years ago in a continuing education class. We were discussing at the time the topic of text messaging. There were many in the class who hated text messaging and there was also the opposing viewpoint. Here is how it unfolded on that insightful day. It is a true story.

Len: *How many of you hate text messaging?* (Lots of hands go up and I am feeling good about my role as instructor, so onward I went)

Len: *I am with you. I never understood how punching a bunch of letters and numbers in on my phone's keypad ever became more efficient than pushing speed dial #3 and just talking to the person.* (That's when a 24 year old student in the middle of the room stood up. Just to give you some insight, it is usually not a good thing when a student decides to stand up in the middle of a classroom).

Student: *That's what I would expect someone in your generation to say.* Yes, there were gasps from the others! (But having the heart of an instructor and trying my best to apply the GAPE concepts and not fall back into the Calvinist approach of saying "sit down" I invited further comment).

Len: *What makes you say that?*

Student: *You are a baby-boomer and you learned to communicate in big long narrative sentences and paragraphs. I have read your text messages. They all begin the same, "Hello, I just had a few moments and so I thought I would take a few moments to text you and let you know that...." and if I texted like that I would hate it too. Communication is not about big long sentences and paragraphs. It's not even about correct spelling. It's about communicating a thought, idea or piece of information as quickly and efficiently as possible."* I wanted to ask the student if they knew they were saying this to an instructor with a degree in communications, but the voice of Socrates was shouting in my ear.

Len: *Can you give us an example in real estate?*

Student: *Sure. If I am your client and we just wrote an offer and it gets accepted, you could just text me one word "accepted" and I would have received the information, read it on my phone and we would have been done. But not you, because you are Mr. Efficiency with speed dialing, so you called me and you had to leave a message. By the way your phone messages sound a lot like your texts, "Hello, I just had a few moments and so I thought I would take a few moments to call you and let you know that...." So I listened to your message and at the end the stunning piece of information you gave me was that I needed to call you back. So I did. I got your voice message because apparently you are busy too. Then we proceeded to exchange voice messages throughout the day*

Len: *But we did communicate and you got the information, right?*

Student: *From my standpoint as your client I was adding up the entire time we wasted. We spent 20 minutes throughout the day, calling each other and exchanging voice messages. When you finally got me on the phone you spent another 10 minutes telling me my offer got accepted. All in all you wasted 30* *minutes of my time and I found out at 5:00 PM rather than at 8:00 AM. what I needed to know.*

Len: *Thank you.* (I was just trying to practice the art of thanking the student in accordance with the GAPE concepts, but just before he sat down the student shoved the knife through my heart).

Student: *Maybe as my broker you have that kind of time to waste, but as your client, I don't!"* Now a hushed silence fell over the room.

The exchange changed our viewpoint of text messaging forever. It also made it very clear to us that in the classroom we are teaching adults across a wide range of generations and Malcolm Knowles would remind us that they are all bringing into that classroom their own experiences and backgrounds which we have to take into account. It means that everything we knew about different learning styles is complicated by another layer of generational differences that must be recognized if our presentations are going to have appeal to all students and we are to have a true appreciation of what is occurring around us in the classroom.

Much has been written about different generations and the varying perspectives that they may bring into a classroom. This is the first time in history that classrooms have contained people from all four distinct generations. It challenges our presentations and our skills to be able to reach across multiple generations and still have meaningful impact. Again, while no one ever fits neatly into one box and while we all know older people who are very tech savvy and younger people who think more like those of the mature or civic generation, they are the exception and not the norm. There are common generational characteristics of individuals and with each of them come some baggage and ideas unique to the times in which they lived.

For simplicity and ease of reference we created this table of generational differences and the impact that it has on education. It appears on the next page:

Generation	Years	Core Values	View of Education	Communication & Philosophies
Mature Civics	1922 -1945	Respect for authority, conformers, discipline	A dream	One on one, write a memo
Baby Boomers	1946 -1964	Optimism, involvement	A birthright	Phone me anytime, emails
Generation X	1965 - 1980	Skepticism, fun, informality	A way to get there	Cell phones, technology, laptops
Generation Y	1981 - 2000	Realism, confidence, social	An incredible expense	Social media, videos, internet, hand-held devices

To appreciate the impact of these generational backgrounds in the classroom just imagine making a casual reference to a supporting website during your presentation. The baby-boomer raises their hand and wants to know if you could email them the link after class. The Gen X'er wants to know why you can't just go to the link right now, the Gen Y'er has already looked up the link and is reading from that website to the rest of class and the Mature/Civic is simply appalled that it all so out of control since the other students have lost total respect for the instructor.

In much the same way that our learning methods and tools must be adapted to account for different types of learners, so too must they now be adapted to account for the generational differences in the classroom. The beauty of students is that they are always thinking. I would like for you to imagine for a moment making the following statement. Then read what is likely to be going through the heads of your students based on their generational influences.

Instructor: We have to do what is best for our industry to elevate the education of our members and to increase the level of professionalism.

Family Lying In Circle by photostock
FreeDigitalPhotos.net

Mature/Civic: I already did my part in the military. The United States is the greatest country in the world and we need to focus on what is best for America.

Baby-boomer: Yeah, right. The instructor is probably just trying to get us to join the professional association so that we pay them dues.

Generation X: I can't do my part until I get my career going. I need money to be able to do this effectively. Are you going to teach us how to be successful?

Generation Y: It's about time. We all have something to contribute to the overall good of society. I want to be part of that.

The real challenge is how do we adapt our teaching to account for the different generations in the classroom? The real answer is to simply be aware. That awareness means that we have to overcome the most fundamental fact of teaching and that is that we tend to teach primarily from our own background and knowledge.

How did we get all of the way from GAPE to generations in one act of this play? Well, GAPE sets forth standards for us to teach at the learner's level and today that level is impacted by much more than subject matter knowledge. Teaching to the learner's level also means delivering material to the learning style by which they best can absorb new information. Teaching to the learner's level means being able to reach them regardless of the generation of which they are a part. How do we do that? We get there by knowing our audience, being conscious of the styles of learning we are teaching and being knowledgeable about generational differences.

All of this is why we are so fascinated with the principles of GAPE. It looks easy. The concepts look too simple, but the more you learn about teaching the more you will come to appreciate their depth.

The very first time we ever read through the GAPE list of concepts we remember thinking…"No kidding, teach to the learner's level. Who wouldn't do that?" Now we know that in order to do that we have to understand our audience. We have to know something about their background, makeup and preconceived beliefs. We have to be able to apply different learning styles and understand how they operate in the classroom. We have to utilize different techniques if we are really going to meet these people where they are. We will need to understand a learning cycle and then make certain that each time we introduce new concepts and information that we are systematically leading the students through each quadrant in a four part circle. We are going to need to know about different generations, how they think, what they believe and the baggage and preconceived notions that they bring into the classroom.

We think we liked it better when we thought that teaching to the learner's level just meant not talking over their heads. Now you really know why Merlin is sitting in the front pages of this book saying "What a lot of things there are to learn."

The best instructors will tell you that after years of teaching and thousands of students we are all still learning.

Curtain Call

"What is the Big Deal About GAPE'

By Philip Schoewe, DREI, Past REEA President, 2001 REEA Instructor of the Year

Philip Schoewe is the past president of the National Real Estate Educators Association and the Southwest Central Educators Group. He was the recipient of REEA's coveted Jack Wiedemer Distinguished Career Award in 2010. He is also a distinguished Real Estate Instructor (DREI) and was recognized as 2011's National Real Estate Instructor of the Year. He has a law background and multiple teaching certifications. He teaches across the country, but lives in Lubbock, Texas where he serves as the Senior Instructor and Curriculum Advisor to TARREC, a West Texas Real Estate School. You can contact or reach Phil at TARREC.com or at (806) 797-0769.

I am honored to be asked to reflect on GAPE, Generally Accepted Principles of Education. GAPE was primarily the work of Mark Barker, DREI, as noted in the last publication of a hand book on "How To Teach Adults" by Don R. Levi, DREI. Mr. Barker remains a maven in real estate education. He accepts that today's research indicates GAPE applies to both children and adults alike. Portions of GAPE even apply to the animal kingdom. GAPE offers a hand in grasping key components of CORE competency for teaching in synchronous or asynchronous environments in both live and technologically enabled or hybrid deliveries. The teaching hand book you are reading, *Ovation*, explores and expands delivery applications of GAPE. It moves teaching principles forward, expands the grasp of a teacher's inward and outward control of a teaching environment and in doing so, it facilitates learning something new, something just beyond the reach of what is already known. GAPE creates and musters a learning environment for each learner who discovers a seemingly easier grasp of something new. Adept use of GAPE principles bridge what is known with what is to be learned. GAPE's primary author, Mr. Barker, earned an ovation from this commentator. Your goal is to earn ovations from your learners each and every time you teach. You start by exploring what other teacher's learned and are willing to share about teaching. This is one reason why you are reading this primer.

Another reason for reading *Ovation* is that you might believe that you were born with a natural talent to teach. That's a nice thought. When you have completed reading this teaching primer, your knowledge about teaching will have changed. You may discover that what you know about teaching is not all that there is to learn about it. And like those who have gone before you, a new understanding leaps off the pages in the form of a quiet, persistent and quite personal question. "Can I really improve what I know about *How To Teach Adults*? The answer lies in the reader's heart. When the reader has the heart of a teacher, a true teacher, the answer is a resounding "Yes"! The true teacher reads *Ovation* and accepts a simple truth that emerges from the pages ~ those who teach and teach well were born with a desire, not a talent, to teach. Great teachers learn how to teach. Look at the name of this hand book, *Ovation*. You receive the title's meaning only after you teach and teach well.

How do you learn to teach well? It takes an artful number of years to develop even the appearance of a so-called natural talent to teach. This handbook is a great primer. So let's wonder about something close to that idea. Let's put aside this handbook for a time and discuss what is found in a book of hands. Let's visit primates and their hands. This quick side bar will help anyone get a handle ~ a grip ~ a firm but delicate hand around a group of learners or even a gentle hand around one learner if you tutor, as I do and have done for over 30 years. Remember, desiring to teach is the dream, the goal. Building the steps to get up there is the handiwork. This is where apes and humans have a common characteristic. When each wants to hold something, each reaches to get a hand around it. If the goal is beyond reach, each develops tools to build a means to reach the goal. If you desire to attain the respect of those who come to you to learn, you first have to get a hand around the topic that is to be learned along with what controls, assists and guides the learning process. You need to master GAPE. Where does it all begin? Let's start with ourselves. Look at one of your hands and notice it resembles the hand of an ape. Look now just at your left hand.

On your left open hand, starting at the left, you see your thumb. Moving to the right of your thumb, eye your index finger, followed by your middle finger, then your ring finger and finally, on the far right, your little finger. Get a washable black marking pen. On the pad of the thumb print in CAPITAL letters print the letter "K"; continuing in CAPITAL letters on the pad of the index finger print an "A"; on the middle finger print an "S"; on the ring finger print a "T"; and finally, on the little finger print an "L". Look at your hand. From left to right, on the inside pads of the five fingers of your left hand you should see "KASTL". Pronounce it like and equate it with the word and the importance of the protective nature of a "castle". Perceive a "castle" as representing your classroom environment, a safe haven for the learning environment. It needs to be the same safe place, a place where every learner is protected and respected just like someone who enters a castle for shelter and protection from what is outside the walls of the castle. Remember, each learner first traversed a trusted drawbridge symbolized by your marketing. Each chose to cross a moat of distractors in their busy lives to enter into your environment symbolized by registering for the course and scheduling their time to focus with you, their knight, a symbol of trust. Look again at your left hand, never forget, "KASTL". It is your reminder to control, assist and guide those who have come for shelter and protection from what awaits outside the protective walls of your learning environment. Every teacher's classroom is their KASTL. Memorize the new word on your left hand. You will use it to guide you to an ovation. Let's explore "KASTL".

"KASTL" is your mnemonic tool guide used to coordinate the efficacy of each of the five finger tips, each symbolizing one of the five areas of GAPE:

"K"knowledge ~
"A"androgogy ~
"S"speech ~
"T"teaching aids ~
"L"learning environment.

First, focus on your thumb, see the letter "K". All primates have a similar thumb ~ an opposing thumb ~ and it is what makes primates distinctly competitive, even as a teacher. In teaching any topic, "k"nowledge is by analogy the opposing thumb. The other four touch pads of teaching; androgogy, speech, teaching aids and learning environment connect with the opposing thumb of knowledge in order to control, assist and guide the learning process. Artfully applied, what a learner already knows bridges to what is not yet known by simple extension of knowledge. This knowledge transfer occurs by adept use of a combination of the opposing thumb of knowledge as it touches and combines with the other 4 skill sets. Look at your left hand and after knowledge see, androgogy, speech, teaching aids and finally learning environment. Together, the first letters spell KASTL, the analogical control mechanism to implement the principles of GAPE.

GAPE is the collective *skillset(sic)*, the plan, the grip to control the delivery of any topic, the applied mindset of a visual hand tool of teaching in synchronous or asynchronous environments in both live and technologically enabled or hybrid deliveries.

What is a *skillset*? It is the commentator's definition that a *skillset* is a clearly defined statement of the collective skills and knowledge required by an individual to meet a performance requirement. Note that skills are joined with knowledge in this commentator's definition, "...skills and knowledge...". Without the opposing thumb of "k"knowledge, no amount of strength applied by the other four skills compensates for a loss of the efficacy, the power of the opposing thumb grip on the teaching delivery, just like in your hand. Imagine holding anything without your opposing thumb. All (5) skill sets require mastery in fluid and adept application, like the movement of the hand and fingers when grasping a delicate item or holding concretely onto something heavy. Collectively, the teacher's grasp over the learning process appears to be and is in reality only one *skillset*; one word, not two; a singular word, not plural. This *skillset* labeled "KASTL" defines the master teacher's delivery ability, a strong yet flexibly delicate hand over and around the learning environment, anchored with the strong opposing thumb of "K"knowledge.

Mankind, womankind have an opposing thumb, like the ape, yet humans differ in numerous ways from all other primates. Whether arguably relatives or not, humans differ greatly in performance output even from the closest primate relative, the chimpanzee. Look at your left hand again. Do it now. One particularly notable difference is the infinite and delicate control advantage of the human's opposing thumb. Your hand is the most dextrous of primate hands due to the high pad-to-pad contact, which is the finest, the most precisely adaptable of the opposing-thumbs-characteristic of the entire primate family. And so it is also with the human mind. Your adaptable mind can create mental projections of ideas that can seemingly touch and affect your surrounding physical environment, your teaching environment. And your mind can further imagine controlling your teaching delivery by analogy to the grip and touch of your left hand. Your hand is capable of firm yet delicate control and this ability can mentally extend to the learning environment for the benefit of all your learners, a critical first step in the learning process from the side of the teacher. This first step moves you in the direction towards receiving the tenets of this primer, *Ovation*. Never forget this first step: "Understanding and then believing that the shared delivery of your knowledge is for the benefit of the learner."

True teachers recognize the learner as the most important asset in synchronous or asynchronous environments whether teaching in live classrooms or in technologically enabled or hybrid delivery methods. True teachers know the importance of a smooth delivery of knowledge from their hand to hands of the learner. And to ensure a skilled delivery with ever changing groups of learners and learning environments, the true teacher must also be a continuous learner.

Are you beginning to see how an ape or human's hand, your hand, is related to GAPE? Do you see the simple strength in visualizing the mnemonic mental tool of "KASTL"? Do you sense the power in leading the learner handily to the next learning objective by perfecting your delivery of the knowledge? What is the importance, the shear gravity of the relation of the opposing thumb of "K"knowledge to learning? I submit it leads us to recognize that all true teachers are consistently true learners. To a true teacher, learning never ends. I submit that all true teachers and learners alike either consciously or unconsciously relearn repetitive thought or action and are avoiders of thinking and acting out of habit alone. They analyze, self-critique and relearn a finer way to think or act bridging the improved thought or action from off what they already know, then stepping higher to include what they are wanting to know. This is a base primate attribute and we can apply it to the finer aspects of GAPE.

GAPE is all about learning. And relearning. And relearning yet again because relearning can lead to exceptionalism, only one of many hidden treasures in the primer, *Ovation*. Exceptionalism is a byproduct of bridging desired goals with the steps in a staircase to reach yet higher goals and to repeat the process all the while getting more knowingly proficient. Relearning the topic taught gives the teacher a stronger opposing thumb in the grip of the learning environment. Relearning a knowledge topic can lead to re-teaching the topic in a better way, in an exceptional way that leads to a prolonged, sustained appreciation by the learners, which is the basic definition of the word, "ovation." Isn't that one reason why you are reading this primer? You want to improve yourself! Take a bow! Exceptionalism is not apologetic. Take yet another bow!

Improving oneself is not new to this commentator. A favorite saying of mine overlays a plaque displaying a rainbow amongst some lofty clouds. The plaque was given to me in 1973 by a USAF T-38 Instructor Pilot, Capt. John Massey. He was an exceptional pilot, an exceptional instructor and without exception, John cleverly disguised his relearning personality by portraying himself and allowing others to identify him as a habitual perfectionist. He was simply an addicted re-learner. The saying that inspires me reads as follows: "You have built your dreams among clouds in the sky, now build the stairways to reach them." I still have the faded plaque and on it the vivid, living memory of my dreams in those lofty clouds; in my hand, tightly grasped, I still have the readied hammer and nails. And, I have a plan next to the pile of wood. John never knew that I hand-painted a small, climbing jet onto the picture with a trailing contrail indicating upward movement. That climb reflected his teaching objectives, not always my flying ability.

Capt. Massey never allowed for a restful landing here or there on those long, winding, climbing learning stairways in the sky over Lubbock, Texas, unless of course, it was a returning jet he was referring to in which case a perfect landing was the declared and unapologetic objective. He allowed no time to settle for "half-rate, second best or almost made-its" in the learning process…no time, whatsoever. Re-teach, relearn, apply, perfect and relearn again. No time was allowed for anything else, that is, except for…exceptionalism itself. And he required that you, his learner, keep climbing towards exceptionalism which meant that you were two steps or more but never a restful landing behind him. He was about being exceptional. He was selectively deaf to the saying that "perfectionism is the enemy of good enough." Instead, John Massey selectively heard an inner voice say, "I can do better next time. I know why. I know what to do. I know how to do it better because I just learned something new while doing what I thought I already mastered."

EXCEPTIONALISM ~ It's all about EXCEPTIONALISM, an eventual byproduct of bridging all learning modules based on what one already knows or perceives one knows and then linking that experience to something slightly out of reach, something new which is not yet incorporated into the learner's knowledge base. It's like building the stairway to those ever changing dreams amongst lofty clouds. Building any stairway takes a hammer and some nails and a pile wood. And it takes a plan. In teaching, we call it a lesson plan. When we create a lesson plan we ask several key questions. Why have we declared these particular objectives as the goals to learn? What tools will we use to reach the goals? How do we use the tools in the teaching process? What if we do what we plan to do? What will happen to the learners' careers if they successfully reach the lesson plan goals, learn the objectives and then apply the newly learned knowledge as tools in their trade? Why? What? How? What if?

These 4 questions require that teachers actually "thimpk", more than think, both in preparation of a logical lesson plan and then in a GAPE Standard delivery that actually follows the plan. Almost anyone with a little stage presence can perform habitual tasks disguised as teaching. How often do we see today an instructor whose thumb of knowledge has been supplied by someone else's packaged PowerPoints and prewritten materials? How often today under the banner of "edu-tainment" do we witness clever speech deliveries of learning objectives, stippled with packaged humor and coupled with other entertaining teaching aids? How often today do we find that the teacher is instructing the learner in an area for which the teacher has never achieved mastery, except that is, in a veneered delivery of the information. These teachers frequently do not possess any successful experiential foundation for the topic at hand. Instead, they are artful in avoidance where answering learners' questions is concerned. They have no foundation of topic knowledge to truly address the questions at hand. They do not have to "thimpk" during delivery. They present with polished, yet sophomoric depth on the topic at hand and only think in a behavioral habit sense in order to get to the end of the course objectives during the allotted time. Artful and polished as they are, they remain mere presenters, not true teachers, and the learners know it.

True teachers, on the other hand, "thimpk" about it, whatever they do, as my 6th grade English teacher used to say. Because of her, I wonder if my "thimpking", if not my spelling, is better today. What is in that English teacher's word, "thimpk" that is not in the word, "think"? And what does any difference between any words really matter if the meanings are close? True teachers do not merely present, they are "thimpking" about what they present as they present it. Think or "thimpk"? Two words to ponder.

I submit that the first word, think, means that you more likely than not behaviorally act out and more times than not, act out without really "thimpking" about it at all, especially if you are performing a well-rehearsed presentation. The second word, "thimpk", an intentional misspelling of the first word, creates a slight momentary wonderment and that is perhaps one of the most powerful elements of learning for anyone, the act of wondering why, or how, or what or finally, what if. Use of the misspelled word "thimpk" makes you actually stop and, however briefly, think more effectively because "thimpking" encourages your mind to wonder, not wander into behavioral repetition. Words, after all, direct your thought even as they come from your thought.

Today, start "thinking" less" and start "thimpking" more. Then, when you next begin to ask these 4 lesson plan questions, really "thimpk" about each of them. Why? Because the following four words reflect differing learning styles found in all learning environments.

Why?
What?
How?
What if?

"Thimpk' about them. You will be glad you did and so will your learners!

Let's begin to summarize this commentary on GAPE with a few select words that apply to the topic of words that we have a choice to use when we speak and write about learning and teaching. Far too often these words are used interchangeably. As you will see, they are not interchangeable without unconsciously affecting learning outcomes as they alter the attitude within a learning environment. What is the difference between the word student and learner?

Words have meanings creating unique ideas, all of which have a different set of consequences. Students 'have to be' learning something. I submit that learners, on the other hand, 'want to learn' something, something that puts another extension in the learning stairway to help them reach a higher goal, the vivid dream that is in their mind, the reason for 'wanting' not just 'needing' to learn something. It is why the learner attends your delivery of knowledge. They will learn to expect EXCEPTIONALISM when you teach any topic because they know, as you now know, that you never teach a topic without the opposing thumb of subject matter mastery. They trust you, like the knight in the castle! Students can be converted to learners through your exceptionalism in teaching. Is this not a worthwhile to goal to end this commentary on "GAPE" in the primer, *Ovation*?

EXCEPTIONALISM ~ what a great and performance output goal to climb towards. More likely than not, it is just beyond your current reach and if not, it is time to set a higher goal and stretch your reach to that higher level. Perhaps we should remember a second mnemonic, a personal challenge disguised in the meaning of GAPE ~ Go And Practice Exceptionalism! Why not do this in all that you do, in all that you learn and above all, friends and fellow teachers, true teachers, in all that you teach! That, I submit, will bring you an "OVATION," in which Mr. Barker and Don Levi, both an exceptional DREI, would be proud to participate.

This commentator thanks the authors of *Ovation*, Len Elder, DREI, JD and Theresa Barnabei who join with me, Mark Barker and Don Levi in saying to each and all of you who would strive to be a true teacher:

"GAPE! Go And Practice Exceptionalism in all that you teach and with humble pride, hear your learners' "OVATION!" Then, take a bow! You have earned it!

Curtain Call

"You Are What You Teach;
The Truth About Learning Styles."

By Sharleen Smith, Senior Director of the Alabama Training Institute, Auburn University at Montgomery

Sharleen Smith is the Senior Director of the Alabama Training Institute. Sharleen has over 25 years of experience in motivational speaking, training, curriculum development and organizational consulting. Prior to coming to Auburn Montgomery she served as the State of Alabama Training Director. She has conducted extensive work and research on the topics of personality profiles and learning styles. You can reach Sharleen at ssmith@ati.aum.edu

Learning. Whether you are a motivational keynote speaker or a computer program instructor, learning is important. After all, most presentations are judged by the return on investment. Return on investment is usually based on the participants' application of knowledge or motivation as derived from training. So with that in mind, is learning a responsibility of the speaker, trainer and/or instructor? Or, is learning a responsibility of the audience member or training participant? Though debatable, this article will focus on the responsibility of the presenter, assuming that the participants are willing and able to learn. In order to fulfill this responsibility, trainers and presenters need to examine how people learn. With this focus, trainers are able to modify their presentations and deliveries to various learning styles, thus, maximizing the chance that the participant will learn or take away the information for application.

While many people adopt Neil D. Fleming's concept of learning styles which has a focus on whether training participants are visual, auditory or kinesthetic learners, it goes much deeper. The VAK theory, as called by Fleming is a great beginning. However, a presenter needs to look at two more profound aspects of learning. First, how does a learner take in information? How does someone naturally approach the information being provided by a presenter? The 4MAT system, as discussed below, teaches us that there are two ways to take in information: by direct experience or abstract conceptualization. Second, once a learner has taken in the information, what do they do with it? How do participants "work" with the information in order to understand and acquire the content of the presentation? The 4MAT system, suggests that we approach information in one of two ways: reflective observation or active experimentation. With these possible combinations, the 4MAT system divides learners into four learning types or styles.

Type One learners learn best when sharing and discussing ideas after the presentations. They tend to learn by integrating their experiences and trusting their perceptions about the topic or content. They tend to be highly imaginative and insightful and have an exceptional ability to see ideas from many perspectives.

Type Two learners learn best by listening, examining details, thinking through the ideas and taking time to reflect on the concepts taught. They tend to seek the facts from the experts and judge the accuracy of the information by this standard. Type two learners tend to learn best by lecture and systematic environments that are free from subjectivity and discussions of others' ideas. They dissect problems prior to coming to conclusions when presented with them.

Type Three learners seek the usability of the information. They like common sense and hands-on learning experiences; thereby, applying and mastering the new information. They have a need to know how things work and they solve problems based on the information imparted by the trainer. On-the-job training and skills practice appeals to Type Three learners.

Type Four learners learn by dynamically doing and feeling through self-discovery and exploration. They learn by trial and error and look for the hidden possibilities. They enjoy synthesizing the information and adapting it to their own use even if it involves risk-taking and challenges in order to learn.

Herein lies the dilemma for an instructor who wants a standing ovation. Instructors tend to teach and/or present in their preferred learning style. For an example, a Type Four instructor will normally teach in a way that is most engaging for those with a Type Four learning style. Thus, the instructor alienates the participants with the other three styles. The responsibility of a presenter or trainer is to take all learning styles into consideration when delivering a presentation. How can a presenter deliberately incorporate all four styles into their delivery?

A Type One instructor can reach a Type Two, Three and Four learner by focusing more on outcomes and procedures, spending more time on the implementation of ideas and how to make them workable, and taking more time to strategically plan the presentation to include other learners. A Type One instructor will be stretched by allowing flexibility even if it is uncomfortable to teach or train under this pressure. It will also be beneficial to a variety of learners if the Type One instructor incorporates an element of risk into the training through the use of experiential activities.

In order to reach a Type One, Three and Four learner, Type Two instructors need to work on their creativity instead of spouting facts. They need to allow the participants to take the topic in a direction for which they have not planned. If the Type Two instructors will use their instinct when presenting, they will be more open to mid-presentation changes. Additionally, they can reach other type learners by being more inspirational.

Type Three instructors need to change their delivery in the following ways in order to reach learners who are Type One, Two and Four. Because they tend to focus on the practical use of information when learning, a Type Three instructor's presentation will be enhanced by taking time to chat with audience members, pay attention to the participants' needs and consider all ideas presented by the audience members.

A Type Four instructor needs to focus more on structure, strategy and specifics in order to reach Type One, Two and Three learners. For example, a Type Four instructor needs to be more cognizant of participants who have a lower tolerance for chaos and innovative techniques. A Type Four instructor needs to realize that lecture, "how to" exercises and discussion groups are very useful to some learners.

So where can you find more information on the 4MAT Learning System? It was developed by Bernice McCarthy who is a world renowned educational theorist. The assessment tool, the Learning Type Measure, may be used to assess learning types thereby allowing you to adjust your delivery and presentation to an audience or class with a plethora of learning methods.

As instructors, presenters and educators, we need to truly seek the best for our audience. This means that we may need to change our mono-style of teaching to a quad-style of instruction. Does this take more on the presenter's part? Absolutely. However, as professionals who believe in education and learning, presenters need to stretch themselves in order to reach each participant. As Denis Waitley says, "Never become so much of an expert that you stop gaining expertise. View life as a continuous learning experience."

Act III
The Art of
Screenwriting

How to Develop & Craft Winning Presentations

Success of the presentation always depends on a good script. Today a number of instructors teach classes and professional designation courses from content created and developed by others. Many instructors have never written or created a course. At Course Creators we have written hundreds of courses. Some of those courses are for the purposes of continuing education in various professions, including real estate. They also include technology courses, business planning courses and topics such as negotiation.

We believe that courses ought to take into account all of the concepts of adult education that we discussed surrounding GAPE, types of learners and generational teaching that we presented in the last chapter. In this chapter we will lay out the basic step by step process utilized to create a course. Our hope would be that the presentation of the course development process in a step by step fashion will help you overcome the paralysis that keeps many people from writing their own courses. It is the equivalent of overcoming writer's block, where we sit and stare at our computer screen wondering just what we should do and how we should do it.

Before we can take you through that step by step process, we cannot emphasize enough that it is all tied intricately to the art of storytelling. We are going to explore all of the concepts discussed below in much more detail in subsequent chapters, but let's start with a basic understanding and appreciation of the art of storytelling.

The Art of Storytelling

In 1678, four brothers, our distant ancestors, left the islands of Scotland, traveled through Ireland, and boarded a vessel for America. They left behind a culture, family, roots, and long lost Gaelic traditions of the *shanachies* (pronounced *shawn-a-kees*). Shanachies were the traditional storytellers of Scotland and Ireland who used a variety of storytelling conventions, styles of speech and gestures, as they wandered the greenish hills conveying legends, facts, and folk tales to the peoples of those lands. They became the custodians of knowledge, and they were teachers who went from community to community, spreading their stories and lessons.

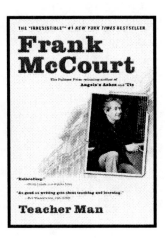

Some things haven't changed very much. In the area of adult education, we are all really shanachies at heart, passing along lessons using our particular craft and skills. It seems, however, that our educational processes may have diminished rather than improved. We could have learned from these village storytellers. The more time we spend in a classroom and the more we study REEA's Generally Accepted Principles of Education (GAPE), the more we realize that our success on any given day is strangely tied in parallel fashion to how closely we practice this lost art of the shanachies. In his book, *Teacher Man*, Pulitzer prizewinning author and former New York City schoolteacher Frank McCourt, wrote:

> *Instead of teaching, I told stories.*
> *Anything to keep them quiet and in their seats.*
> *They thought I was teaching.*
> *I thought I was teaching.*
> *I was learning.*

In a later passage, McCourt adds:

> *I was more than a teacher. And less.*
> *In the classroom, you are a drill sergeant, a rabbi, a shoulder to cry on,*
> *a disciplinarian, a singer, a low level scholar,*
> *a clerk, a referee, a clown, a counselor, a dress code enforcer,*
> *a conductor, an apologist, a philosopher, a collaborator, a tap dancer,*
> *a politician, a therapist, a fool,*
> *a traffic cop, a priest, a mother, father, brother, sister, uncle, aunt,*
> *a bookkeeper, a critic, a psychologist,*
> *the last straw.*

If you haven't read McCourt's book you really should pick it up. McCourt is an amazing storyteller and he reminds us that all great teachers are shanachies. Learn to tell a story.

The shanachies were masters of the art of storytelling. When we are at our best as instructors we have all received the student evaluations which read: "Great examples," "Appreciated seeing the principles put to practical application," and "Good practical course." Those comments come from the fact that we have taken information we know and have woven a story around it. Cold hard facts and theories recited from real estate regulations or statutes have little meaning or impact on students until they are taken and applied to concrete real world examples through the presentation  of a compelling story. It is why GAPE urges us to present key points by using examples as illustrations. Stories hold our interest and give us application for the principles or theories. A good story always has a beginning, middle, and an end. Courses and classes can also have plots.

In its simplest rendition, a class on agency concepts can simply be a series of case studies, agency rules and statutes. Or better yet, an agency class can begin as a story where the historical evolution of agency began, then advance through its development and conclude with the way things are today. Teaching classes in a plot type framework holds the students' interest better and makes the material easier to digest.

An excellent story is tied together with a theme, apt analogies, and impassioned delivery. Themes can greatly increase the attention and interest in the tale we are telling. There is no limit to the number of themes that can be tied into your courses. A risk management class could be themed as an adventure in mountain climbing, with numerous analogies comparing the rope to E&O (errors and omissions insurance) coverage, crevasses to the problems we face, and the summit as the place we are trying to end up. Can you imagine yourself in the role of a shanachie starting a class out not by saying "Welcome to Risk Management" but instead, "Today I want to share with you a grand adventure about trying to get to the top of a mountain and all the perils we will face along the way." Now, you are storytelling, and, more importantly, the students are listening.

Stories must also be contextualized. Contextualization is the process of tying what we are teaching to things that the student may already know and explaining how different concepts fit together. Malcolm Knowles, the father of the adult education theory of andragogy, that we met in previous chapters would remind us that adults learn better and easier this way. Having put together analytical and theoretical constructs in their heads, adults come to class with anything but a clean slate. Their understanding of information is directly linked to our ability to tie it into an existing framework. Can you show in a specific way how new material will benefit the learners? A shanachie would have said, "The things I'm about to share with you are lessons you will need to teach your children in order to keep them from harm's way." Amazingly such a statement is not too unlike the things that a broker must do in order to protect their licensees.

Excellent storytellers provide bridges to new material because they understand on an intuitive level the need to tie material together in a seamless web so that each aspect of the class builds on and expands earlier portions. Changing our vernacular from "Okay, let's next talk about…" to "We just finished learning this: now if that makes sense can we build on that to understand the following…" facilitates better learning. If you are telling a story, then the entire storyline should flow throughout the class. I guess that's why GAPE suggests that we keep the topic flowing and build proper foundations for each major element of a subject.

Storytellers have a way of drawing listeners in from the very beginning of the presentation. A good story is a wonderful sandwich built between two slices of bread. If you are teaching a contract class, for example, you might begin with the story of the Louisiana Purchase and tell how Monroe and Livingston traveled to France for the largest land purchase in the history of the world. The ending could be shaped with what people thought about that purchase at the time—France didn't really own the land, American Indians did and all France was really selling was the right of the United States to exercise eminent domain over it free from France's potential claim. History is a great source from which to build great beginnings and great endings that tie into real estate. Sometimes a great beginning can be developed around a song, a PowerPoint presentation, or a class exercise. Just remember, it is imperative that the beginning and ending have application and relevance to the material being covered.

In a recent airing of TV's *American Idol,* judge Randy Jackson was explaining to one of the performers what it means to be a pro. He claimed that the difference was that a pro doesn't just say or sing the words; a pro understands the words, gives their own interpretation, breathes life into them, lives, experiences, and feels them. We should all aspire to be such pros in the classroom. No greater vehicle opens the door to someone's mind than the aspect of emotion. GAPE criteria remind us to use gestures, use physical movement, and remove boundaries between the students and the instructor. These principles stress the need for the instructor to connect to the students. Before the ages of PowerPoint, recorded sound, and television's exciting and colorful vivid images, all that shanachies had were their bodies and their voices. With nothing else to hold the audience's attention; their animation, voice inflection and emotion would have been critical to their success. It is still paramount to our success in the classroom today.

Learn to talk with and not at your audience. There are ways to draw the audience into the presentation. Practice the three P's. Be Playful, Probing and Provocative. One of the best comments that a student can write is "The instructor made me think." That is what we are there for, isn't it? Don't be afraid to ask the probing questions or to play the devil's advocate. We are certain that the shanachies would occasionally have paused and while staring someone directly in the eye would have asked, "Can you imagine that?" They may even have asked if anyone had any questions and I can almost hear them say, "Laddie, that is an excellent question, but you're not goin' to like the answer much." The three top things that instructors can do to elevate classroom involvement and enhance their performance are 1) call the students by name, 2) repeat students' questions, and 3) thank them for their questions.

Develop a moral to your story. The Brothers Grimm and Hans Christian Andersen recognized that the true power in a tale was in the overall message that it communicated. Maybe they learned some things from the shanachies. Whether we realize it or not, students draw an overall message from our tales. Do we portray real estate in class as a part-time job or as a profession?" The shanachies had a way of leaving behind a message that would endure long after the storytelling stopped. We would all do well to ask ourselves, "What overall  message do I want the students to come away with at the end of this presentation?" If your answer is longer than a sentence, then you have some editing to do.

We don't think it is really right or proper to talk about the shanachies as being extinct – We don't really believe that they ever abandoned us. They have been masquerading as lawyers, politicians, teachers, real estate instructors, and news anchors. Tom Brokaw once said,' "It's all storytelling, you know, that's what journalism is all about." The next time you walk into a classroom, imagine a group of small villagers gathered around an evening fire, waiting to hear your tale. Take them on a grand adventure. If each of us approached the classroom in that fashion then we assure you that your storytelling days will be greener than the hills of Loch Lomond.

A Step by Step Guide to Presentation Development

We have experimented with dozens of different processes in creating stories and our courses, but have found the following to work the best.

1. **Generation of an idea or concept**
2. **Information chunking the idea or concept into an outline based on the time allotments**
3. **Creation of an overall theme for the course**
4. **Creation of the course PowerPoint**
5. **Insertion of multi-media portions of the course**
6. **Drafting of the student manual**
7. **Drafting of an instructor manual**

We will deal with steps 4 and 5 in later chapters which have to do with the creation and use of PowerPoint and the insertion of multi-media. For now the starting point has to be the generation of an idea. In many states across many professions there are set guideline topics and categories for mandatory education courses, but those hardly inspire us to pick up a pen or open a laptop and begin writing. As instructors we are motivated by the needs of our students and their interests. So we utilize certain tools to draw from our students insights and desires to motivate us to create certain courses.

If you are struggling with coming up with ideas for a course then here is a real world application that will help you generate new course ideas and concepts.

How to Generate Powerful Course Ideas

1. Add to your existing course evaluations a question which asks your students what additional courses they would like to attend

2. Create a post on your facebook page and invite students to add their ideas for additional courses and topics

3. Take a few minutes and survey your class asking them what else they need or have an interest in learning

4. Review your industry's magazines and periodicals for the hot topics of the moment

5. Schedule regular meetings with industry experts and subject matter experts (SME's) about what needs to be communicated

Getting Started With Information Chunking

If it appears from the above list that we place great emphasis on student feedback and involvement in the process, then you are correct. We simply believe that therein lies application of one of key points of andragogy; that adult learners take more interest in topics that are relevant to them. We have found all of the above tools to be great yielders of course ideas and topics.

Let's presume that we have received numerous student comments requesting a course on learning to negotiate. Based on that feedback we have decided to create a course on negotiation. The traditional approach would have us creating a detailed multi-level outline of the aspects of the course. Our brains do not think in terms of detailed multi-level outlines, and such outlines are not the way that we would present a course in a classroom or online setting. We tend to think more in chunks of information. So we engage in a process we call *"Information Chunking"* and break the information into major "chunks" predicated on the time allotments for the course. If we settled on a course title, "Learning to Negotiate Effectively" for a 3 hour course then by design that course should have 3 major sections. It has been our experience that this formulaic approach to course writing works well. Based on the number of hours you have, break your course down into one basic concept per hour. Our negotiation course breakdown may end up looking like this:

Hour 1 – The Basics of Negotiation
Hour 2 – Learning Negotiation Skill Sets
Hour 3 – Practical Negotiation Applications

We will then *"information chunk"* each hour into only three or four major parts. Let's face it, in a typical classroom presentation a few major points that follow in sequential order are the true goal of what you want to accomplish. It might end up looking like this:

Hour 1 – The Basics of Negotiation

- Preparing for a Negotiation
- Identifying the Right Decision Makers
- Identifying the Objectives of the Parties

Hour 2 – Learning Negotiation Skills & Techniques

- Top Skills That Negotiators Possess
- Top Mistakes Negotiators Make
- Different Negotiating Strategies

Hour 3 – Practical Negotiation Applications

- How to Start an Effective Negotiation
- How to Conduct and Effective Negotiation
- How to Conclude an Effective Negotiation

In both student processing of information and in the organized delivery of material you will find power in the rhythm and blocking of "three." Even if you may be teaching in modules different from 3 hours, sill try to think of your course in sets of three. It is no accident that we design courses whenever possible to capitalize on the power of three rhythm. Three major topics, three subsets each. The Power of Three is indoctrinated into our culture and utilized in so many venues that for us to not recognize it as course writers would be a serious omission. The emphasis on triplet thinking is embedded in storytelling "Beginning, Middle and End" or in the movies, "Lights, Camera, Action," or in taking action, "Ready, Set, Go."

Syd Field is an American writer who has become one of the most popular screenwriting gurus in the movie industry. He has written several books on the subject of screenwriting and holds workshops and seminars around the world. One of his most important contributions has been the touted advantages of the three act structure in crafting a story. Comedians also learn to utilize the series of three to create a progression in which the tension is created, then built up, and finally released. So when chunking and crafting our basic outline guide we recommend that you utilize the power of three.

The Art & Science of Course Themeing

We are big believers in the process of "themeing" a course. Themeing a course involves finding a topic or storyline that can hold the entire course together. The theme for your course can be just about anything. We have used mountain climbing themes, transportation themes, movies themes and historical themes to tie a class together. Here are just a few examples:

Learning to Negotiate Effectively – "Getting to the Summit"

The Closing Process – "A Road Trip Toward Success"

Becoming a Professional – "Ingredients for Success"

Utilizing Social Media – "Catch the Social Media Wave"

Short Sales & REO's – "Hitting Home Runs"

What these additional themes do is to allow us to create an experiential journey for the learner in line with the GAPE concepts. Elaborating on the above examples, the negotiation theme of "Getting to the Summit" will allow us to analogize everything to climbing a mountain. "A Road Trip Toward Success" will allow us to build everything in the course around a road trip theme. "Ingredients for Success" lends itself to a cooking theme. "Catch the Social Media Wave" will interlace the course with surfing pictures and allow us to analogize to surfing topics. "Hitting Home Runs" will become a baseball theme.

An Easy Way to Begin to Develop Themes

In picking themes, we would recommend starting with your hobbies, interests and activities. We always teach best from what we know best. So if you are an avid skier, then skiing seems to us to be a good theme for you. If you are a diehard NASCAR fan then creating a theme of racing seems like the best bet. You will find your own hobbies and interests to be an unending fountain of possible themes for your courses. So here is a chance for you to open up your creative mind and start interjecting and interweaving themes into the courses you have been teaching or marrying them to the new ideas you have just gathered. Make a list of the courses that you currently teach or would like to teach and start developing some possible themes around those ideas.

Course Topic / Title   **Possible Theme**

_____   _____

_____   _____

_____   _____

_____   _____

_____   _____

The benefits to underlying your course with a theme are numerous. They will certainly help you to get the creative juices following and result in a much more interesting and entertaining presentation. In practice the themes help accomplish all of the following:

- Course cohesion
- Holding interest
- Creating powerful analogies
- Facilitating the use and integration of images and videos
- Building easier segues and bridges
- Creating better beginnings and endings

So let's continue by developing further our Negotiation outline and embedding the theme into it.

Hour 1 – The Basics of Negotiation
        "Before You Climb the Mountain"

- Preparing for a Negotiation
- Identifying the Right Decision Makers
- Identifying the Objectives of the Parties

Hour 2 – Learning Negotiation Skills &
        Techniques
        "The Mountain Climbers Tools"

- Top Skills That Negotiators Possess
- Top Mistakes Negotiators Make
- Different Negotiating Strategies

Hour 3 – Practical Negotiation Applications
        "Navigating the Climb"

- How to Start an Effective Negotiation
- How to Conduct and Effective Negotiation
- How to Conclude an Effective Negotiation

Can you begin to see how the creation and integration of a theme for your course immediately adds to the interest and begins tying together the information that you are teaching? You should also begin to see how much easier it is to uncover images to accompany your presentation and create segues and bridges between the various topics. This is truly the cornerstone of course creation which will allow your creative energies and imaginations to soar.

Adding Depth to Theme Development

Go ahead, let the ideas flow. In regard to the themes you chose earlier, jot down some additional ideas that you might use to leverage the theme and bring it to life in the classroom.

Images That Can Be Used

_____

_____

_____

What multi-media (videos) Come to Mind

_____

_____

_____

What Would Classroom Activities Look Like

_____

_____

_____

What GREAT Stores or History Are Connected to This Theme

_____

_____

_____

As we mentioned, our next step would be to begin to layout these component pieces into our PowerPoint presentation. These are topics we will cover in great depth in Act VII. However, you should understand how we arrived at the order of doing the PowerPoint presentation prior to building the student and instructor manual. The reason that we believe it is more productive to create the PowerPoint presentation first is because we can then easily incorporate images and slides that we develop for the PowerPoint presentation into the course material.

Crafting Great Beginnings & Endings

What do you remember most about some of the movies and books that you have read. We're willing to bet it's the opening and closing scenes. Every good director and author knows that the best tales are told when bookended by powerful openings and closings. The goals and objectives of the beginning and ending should relate back to the PALM Principle that we discussed earlier: Be Prepared, Get Their Attention, Make them Laugh (or Feel) and Make a Point.

Our great beginnings and endings tend to be stories told in two parts. Think Paul Harvey and the Rest of the Story. Paul Harvey Aurandt (better known as Paul Harvey 1918-2009) was an American radio broadcaster for the ABC radio networks. He broadcasted news and comment twice a day, six days a week and was carried on over 1200 radio stations. His famous *Rest of the Story* segments carried an audience of over 24 million people a week and his broadcasts and newspaper columns have been reprinted in the Congressional Record more than those of any other commentator. He was a storyteller.

If you are too young to remember Paul Harvey's broadcasts or not familiar with his work, it really is worth your time as an instructor to uncover some of these gems. They are a wealth of classroom inspiration. His books are still available on Amazon.Com and PodBean.Com has a number of the Paul Harvey clips archived that you can listen to on the internet.

Great beginnings and endings can come from a number of places. We find our strongest ones coming from history and related to the theme which we have tied to the course. Want to tell a story about your favorite role model, a historical figure, a historic event, or a landmark sporting achievement, then tie it to your theme and go find the story to tell that sets the whole theme in motion.

In creating and developing out our example of the Learning to Negotiate Effectively Course – Getting to the Summit, we might employ the following two stories as the Great Beginning and Great Ending. Let's do the great beginning first.

This is a picture of the Khumbu Icefall at the base of Mount Everest. It's where every person who has stood on the top of that summit begins their journey. The icefall is a moving glacier with continually changing crevices that expand and contract. Always present is the sound and feel of falling ice and moving ground beneath your feet. The hardest part is that the crevices are crossed by tying together aluminum ladders and using them as a bridge. To many it is the most terrifying part of the Everest climb. Standing on the ladders a lot of people panic. All they can think about is falling, the vast void beneath them, the distractions that take away from their goal of crossing the crevice. It is not a difficult physical barrier. If we were to bring an aluminum ladder into the classroom (Hey not a bad idea) and lay it on the floor every one of you in this room would be able to walk across the ladder's rungs without falling over. However, put the ladder over a spacious canyon with a 500 foot drop and instantly the challenge becomes intimidating, not because the task got any more demanding physically, but because it's a head game and the distractions and the fear will paralyze you. That's what happens in negotiations. People become personally involved, focus on the distractions and become paralyzed. Today we will teach you how to keep your focus and get across the ladder safely.

This type of great beginning has built into it fundamental principles of GAPE. The students can all relate from their personal experience the act of crossing the ladder, even if they have never been on Everest. We have captured their attention, we have invoked emotion and we have made a point and are set up with a nice segue into the negotiation course. Much more effective wouldn't you say than beginning with "Today we are going to learn about negotiation!" More importantly, long after they leave the classroom the students will remember the story that started them on their journey. If they remember the story they often remember the point of the story and they always remember the storyteller.

So what about the ending. We would likely craft something of this nature:

On May 29, 1953 Sir Edmund Hillary reached the summit of Mount Everest with his Sherpa guide, Tenzing Norgay. Today they are regarded as the first men to have submitted Everest, despite evidence to the contrary. At the time Hillary suspected that his predecessor Mallory had also reached the summit of Everest but had died on his descent down. Historical research has now proven that Hillary's suspicions were correct. He was not the first person to summit Everest, Mallory was. He is, however, the first to summit Everest and return to tell about it. With that knowledge in his head, on the day that he and Norgay reached the summit, Norgay is reported to have said to Hillary, "Sir, we have made it." Recalling the fate of his predecessor, Mallory, Hillary's response was "No, we are only half way!"

Negotiation is like that. Despite all of the work we did today and everything you have learned about crafting an effective negotiation the parties are still left to carry out the terms of the contract. The negotiation only gets you half way. You have to execute on the rest.

We know that if course creation were creating detailed outlines without the stories and the themes we would be much less excited about course creation. So explore themes, play with stories and relate them and their lessons to the material that you are trying to convey. It is then that you will find yourself where we tell so many of your students that they are, "In a place limited only by your imagination and creativity."

Developing the Course Material for the Learners

We think it unfortunate that often times the student material that is distributed in the classroom appears to get the least attention from presenting instructors. It's too tempting to say, "I'll just print my PowerPoint slides," or "I'll just give them a copy of my outline." The course material is the only physical thing with which the students will leave the classroom. It is your opportunity to leave a lasting impression. We have no idea why we have continued for so many years to call things by names which don't inspire and interest our students. When we say the word "Manual" you say "Yuck!" When we say the words "handout", "exercise" and "materials" You think "boring" "work" and "dull". We would much rather our students came to class expecting to play, be entertained and be given step by step instructions to succeed, so we call everything in the students' hands a playbook.

It should go without saying that the playbook we place in the students hands should meet the basic requirements set forth in GAPE and that all of the information contained in the playbooks should be:

- **Correctly spelled**
- **Properly numbered**
- **Produced using a readable typeface, and**
- **Organized according to the flow of the course**

In addition we have created a checklist of items that we believe are mandatory in the students' playbook, a set of guidelines that we think facilitate and further our objectives in creating it in the first place.

The Ultimate PlayBook Checklist

✓ Your bio information, the PlayBook should contain your photo and your background which makes you qualified to convey the information in the course. Months from now, having your photo in the bio will help the student recall who the instructor was that taught the course;

✓ A footer on each page. It is really difficult to teach a course when the instructor is unable to refer to the page number in the student PlayBook, so every page needs to be numbered. The footer also includes the instructors name and email or phone number. You want them to be able to contact you if there is a desire to have the course taught again or if someone else picks up the PlayBook and decides they would like to offer or attend the course;

✓ A bibliography or links to sites for additional information. We already know that adult learners are self directed, so include in the PlayBook the additional internet links or resources that can help them learn more about whatever it is that you are teaching. Making your student Playbook a resource gives it a life beyond the classroom so that students will not simply file it away and forget it;

✓ Inclusion of SOME of the PowerPoint slides from your presentation. They will help to embed your presentation into the mind of the student and further the GAPE principles of using color and using visual imagery to enhance written words;

✓ Include spaces throughout the PlayBook for the students to take NOTES. Enable their collaborative participation in the course;

✓ Use the final pages of the Playbook to preview future and additional courses that you may be offering. The PlayBook can become your best promotional material.

Inserting Your PowerPoint Images Into Your PlayBook

One of the reasons that we create the PowerPoint presentation prior to the PlayBook is because we said it makes it easier to insert the PowerPoint slides into the playbook. If you did not realize that you could turn your slides into JPEG images, then here are the instructions for doing so.

1. Open your PowerPoint presentation

2. Begin to save the PowerPoint presentation as you always have

3. Click on "Other formats"

4. From the drop down menu "Save As Type" select "JPEG File Interchange Format

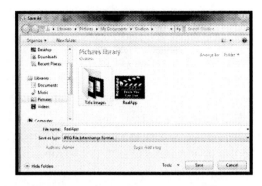

5. PowerPoint will then ask if you want to save the entire PowerPoint or just the selected slide, and it will create a folder and place the PowerPoint images you have selected in it.

6. Copy and paste the JPEG images into your PlayBook

While we agree with the GAPE principle that student materials should not have extraneous information and should follow the presentation given by the instructor we are also aware that we teach in an era of internet activity and self directed learners who appreciate additional information and resources. We believe that part of our obligations as instructors ought to be the gathering of relevant links and information for further study.

We tend to reference a lot of additional information in class that we do not have time to fully cover or explain, but we believe it still belongs in the PlayBook as additional resources for the student. This is particularly true when the information causes the students to visit your blog, website, social media pages or YouTube channel. These are all tools we will discuss in subsequent Acts of this book, but we refer to these tools in the PlayBook so they are mentioned here as well.

Creative Branding of Your Materials

We also believe that throughout the PlayBook you should try to creatively brand the material you are creating. For example "Tips for Technology" becomes "Course Creators' Tech Tips." You see evidence of that throughout this book. The contributions at the end of the chapters became "Curtain Calls," the checklists and practical guides became "RealApps – Tools You Can Use." It's a matter of owning what you create and a little creativity and thought in crafting your PlayBook will enable you to do that.

The Creation of Instructor PlayBooks

A lot of courses contain both an instructor and a student manual. One of our pet peeves is when the student manual and the instructor manual are paginated differently. It means that the instructor's page numbers are different because of the insertion of instructor's notes and materials. The second issue is that when corrections, changes and updates are made we are left trying to correct two sets of material and keep them identical. We have attempted to simplify that process.

In regard to the creation of a set of instructor materials we have found the following process to be easier and more convenient and also assure that the page numbers and format mirror the student PlayBook.

1. **First create the Student PlayBook**
2. **Then insert the instructor Notes and save as the Instructor PlayBook**
3. **Re-open the document and replace the Instructor Notes with a place for the Student to take notes**
4. **Then save this version at the Student PlayBook**

 When distributing materials to course sponsors and others to reproduce for class you also may want to take the final version of your PlayBook and publish it into a PDF format. The advantages of reproducing a PDF version is that it better maintains the page breaks, spacing and fonts that most word files do. Word files are always subject to the version of Word which is being used and when fonts aren't downloaded the final product may appear much differently than it did on your computer. Creating and printing from a PDF version solves these formatting and font issues.

Curtain Call

"Making Education More Enjoyable for the Students"

By Bill Gallagher, DREI and Owner of Superior School of Real Estate

Bill Gallagher is the owner of Superior School of Real Estate in Charlotte, North Carolina. In a single year Bill has taught as many as 26,000 students. He is a much sought after speaker, has received numerous awards and served on various committees at the forefront of our industry. He has been the recipient of Instructor of the Year awards. His students are loyal and appreciative. Everyone who has ever seen Bill present knows that he is one of the best at getting students to "laugh and learn." You can contact Bill at Superiorschoolnc.com.

Educating adult learners can be rewarding and challenging. In order to create the most conducive learning environment, the instructor needs preparation for the topic, practice in presenting the material, adding a brief video segment, and providing humor and fun in the classroom. Most instructors far exceed expectations in the first two items. So, let's discuss video next.

PowerPoint presentations over the years have developed into an effective learning tool; however, many instructors have too much information on the screen and sometimes read directly from the screen. When this situation exists, students comment they cannot read the information on the screen, students get lost between the screen and the student manual, and they get "bored" because of the repetitious nature of reading screen after screen. In my opinion, a PowerPoint screen should never have more than 6 lines of information along with a bold title at the top with numbered bulleted points, colored coordinated background to create student interest, and references to the page number in the student manual on the bottom right corner of the screen.

In my opinion, PowerPoint should be visuals and video. We've heard a picture tells a thousand words so let's do it in the classroom. Video clips can create excitement and fun in the classroom, so long as the video pertains to the subject matter at that time. A video with humor and fun can add to content as well as maintain excitement in the classroom. I think we've discussed the basic principles in order to create a learning environment where students can have fun and enjoy the material and presentation. We've heard that students "don't want to be bored" and "don't waste my time". These techniques can help.

Some instructors don't feel comfortable with humor in the classroom; however, instructors who have added some humor to their presentation have received outstanding reviews from their students. Some instructors are known for "entertaining" their students while "educating" them at the same time. This principal is a key factor for adult learners today. A combination of both "entertaining" and "educating" can be challenging, but it can be most rewarding.

In my opinion, "entertaining" can be accomplished by both students and instructors. Students sometimes share "war stories" with the class which can be hilarious. It also enables other students to feel comfortable and share with the class. The goal is to maintain control of the classroom but allow discussion and conversation. At the beginning of the class for an icebreaker, students can share in groups of 3 or 4 their funniest experience in real estate. I've found some of the "funniest" stories come from students in the field. Students are "entertaining" themselves in the classroom with the instructor leading the discussion.

When instructors think "humor" in the classroom, immediately some instructors say "I'm not a good joke teller" or "My jokes would come off stupid". "Humor" does not have to be jokes; moreover, an instructor can share a situation or real life story to the class bits of humor throughout to create an interesting and exciting presentation. Role play or scripted skits by students in a class on real estate principles can be fun and entertaining. The instructor needs to write the script, pertaining to the real estate topic, select students to participate and practice, and then present to the class. The most effective role plays I've used involve life estates, writing an offer to purchase for a buyer, loan officer qualifying a buyer, loan assumptions with release of liability and environmental issues. In addition, students usually add more items which can be entertaining while educating.

Humor can also be added by games in the classroom. Jeopardy is the best example for involving the entire class. With 5 categories of real estate topics, along with specific items under each category with money rewards, the students are challenging, are entertained, and are learning. Everyone wants to be a winner and this type of competition can be fun and rewarding. If an instructor uses jokes in the classroom, I would make sure there are no religious or political references. In addition, I would ask other instructors and previous students if the joke is appropriate. Too many jokes can be very distracting to the students; however, a limited number pertaining to classroom material can be effective.

In conclusion, some instructors do a great job in combining fun and education into a fantastic learning environment for students. Your students will definitely let you know if you are successful in balancing fun and education in your presentation.

Curtain Call

"Why Research is No Substitute for Experience"

**By Marcie Roggow, DREI and Owner
Of Creative Learning Concepts, LLC**

Marcie Roggow, DREI, ABR/M, CCIM, CRB, CRS, GRI, SRS, is a noted speaker and trainer, concentrating in the area of license law, political affairs and risk management. She works closely with REALTOR® associations at the local, state and regional level. You can't name a committee Marcie has not served on. She's received numerous CRS awards, has taught REBAC and GRI classes and has authored the best selling CRB training products. She knows how to communicate complex material so that students find it enjoyable and memorable. You can reach Marcie at Marcie Roggow.com

Years ago I was asked to teach a course on Fair Housing in a GRI caravan. Of course I knew all about Fair Housing - I'd been a REALTOR® since 1972! They gave me an outline, I researched the material, I memorized the laws, created transparency slides and off I went to teach the material. I was teaching outside of my home state of Iowa and looking forward to the opportunity of a national presence. Unfortunately, I fell flat on my face when it came to execution. I hadn't ever lived with discrimination or housing issues - other than rowdy college student tenants - so was completely caught off guard by the questions that were flying at me! Fortunately, we were traveling as a team of instructors and a local expert saved the day! I vowed I would NEVER teach any material with which I did not have an in-depth, personal, relationship! I have NEVER broken that rule and as a result have always achieved my goal of 'creating a creative learning environment'! How do you do that?

If you want a 'curtain call' and a repeat invitation to speak again, in my opinion you have to have the three C's: Confidence, Competence, and Compassion! Confidence that you know the audience and their needs; Competence to teach the topic with a complete understanding of it from every possible perspective; and Compassion for the fact that the learner may not have as complete of an understanding of the topic as you so you need to teach to an audience of every level and every learning style. The adult learner wants to be engaged! They want to know what does this mean to ME! You need to speak to each participant in a way that will help them IMPLEMENT the training you have provided. No amount of research will do that. It's the experience YOU and you alone bring to that environment; having said that, each of us will bring a different perspective to the classroom depending upon our personal involvement in the real estate business. A real estate attorney, Bless their heart, will approach law from the legal 'this is what it says' perspective. The educator who has been a broker/manager will teach from the perspective of what to watch for in the transaction and how to deal with the issue at hand. And then the agent educator will teach from the perspective of storytelling 'this is how that happened to me'. Each of them brings the 'experience' to the room. But unless you KNOW the law, have experienced what it felt like to see it broken, or had it 'done to you' you cannot bring the same feeling to the learning environment. Then you revert to teaching from research!

New educators always ask me 'What does it take to do what you do? I always thought I'd like to teach and want to know how to start!" The first thing I would always ask is "Why do you want to teach?" You know the old saying, "Those that can – do. Those that can't - teach." Don't try to teach sales if you were miserable at sales and couldn't put a deal together if your life depended upon it! It won't work. While not necessarily what they were looking to hear, when that comment is supported with examples of great educators who walk the walk and talk the talk and they share their success, it finally sinks in. Not everyone can be a movie star, or opera singer or a comedian! Not everyone should be a real estate educator. So the next question is how do you determine whether you have those 3 C's.

Confidence: If you can't speak in front of a crowd, this gig is not for you! If you look at the floor/ceiling and read from the material…no research, no experience, nothing will help you become a better trainer other than a few years in Dale Carnegie or Toastmasters. You have to have the confidence to present. It will show immediately if you do not. Practice, practice, practice! Know the set up, know the equipment, know what you know and for sure know what you don't know and get someone else to do that. Your presence alone can be what sets you apart from someone else. Let me also share that even if you are the most knowledgeable person on the planet for your topic and you have no confidence in presenting the material you will fail. No doubt about it! I have watched audiences where the material would have been great if the presentation had any spark at all. But the presenter didn't have the confidence to s-t-r-e-t-c-h themselves to be the best they could be.

Competence: I love the expression "Edutainer". My definition is "Someone who isn't competent in the topic they were hired to teach so they tell jokes and entertain the crowd until the time period has passed, they get the standing ovation and feel good, and as people leave the room they all of sudden realize they learned nothing!" Those people have made a lot of money over the years to be sure. But they aren't Competent in their field! They also don't last long in the business. So what defines competency? If I were to say a competent person is one that when asked a question in any environment would know the answer without having to look it up, would you agree that they are pretty competent? That's how prepared you should be before you hit the stage. I listened to tape after tape of Don Harlan and Gail Lyons before I ever dreamed of teaching agency. Their examples were phenomenal and I needed their level of competence before I could do what they did. They worked with me. They were my mentors for which I am eternally grateful! They weren't edutainers by any stretch of the imagination. I love to add 'entertainment' to material to make it more fun in class, which is entirely different. There is absolutely no excuse for not being prepared and totally competent in your chosen field.

Compassionate: Because I teach law, ethics and risk management topics the agents are always saying things like "When did they change this? Or.."What were they thinking?" to which I sometimes have to agree! But, I know the frustration of practicing a trade to get it right only to find out that the way you are doing it is not right. So what is necessary is to have empathy for the participant and be a coach to help them through. I remember teaching an open house class for Indiana GRI once. I was showing them how to be successful at open houses from planning to execution to follow-thru! Half the class was really into the material the other half sat with their arms folded. (BTW, that's not a good sign) So I divided the room into groups and put half of the happy folks in with a group of unhappy folks so that the happy folks could do the teaching. Obviously the unhappy people disliked open houses and really didn't ever plan on doing one until they heard how the happy folks were having success and then they finally got it! Well…except for this one girl who said none of her listings were safe enough to hold an open house, and then we had to have a different lesson on how to choose the listings you take. Always a learning experience somewhere!

Once I learned that law was my venue I settled in and learned almost every state's agency laws, which was so necessary when I was teaching the ABR courses across the country. My state matrix was always as close as my fingertips and because I had helped write some of those laws and created forms to match them I had that necessary background to address any agency question no matter the state. I use that same matrix today when I teach the Seller's Representative Specialist across the US! That knowledge just needs a yearly update and I am good to go. I have watched trainers grab on to the newest, hottest topic and write a course around it-social media as an example! I could no more teach the 'how to' on social media then I could teach Fair Housing. BUT, I can teach the law/ethics side! When I see agents violating their state's advertising law as well as the Code of Ethics on line I immediately hop into my training mode and send a gentle reminder to be careful out there. Experience is what tells me when something is wrong….not research. I don't have to look up the Article of the Code…I know it…it's Article 12 by the way! That's what you want in your belly! You want the 'I know this inside out upside down' feeling when you walk onto that stage.

I have the Confidence to walk into any environment and present the material that I know is Mine! I have the Competence to be able to apply those state laws that I know by heart and the NAR Code of Ethics and apply them to any topic. And, most of all, because I am a REALTOR® and I live the life these agents live, feel their frustrations in whatever the market is, and can relate to the frustrations of the business…I have the Compassion to approach the legal material in what's best for them and their license instead of spitting out a 'recital of law'. How is their business and the way they choose to do business going to be affected by the information you are sharing? No amount of RESEARCH could ever have prepared me for living the material that I teach. Experience has been the most fabulous education I have ever received and I only hope that when the participants walk out of my learning environment they feel that they are much better prepared to be the best that they can be and that I can feel confident that I can take a bow with pride that I gave them everything I had!

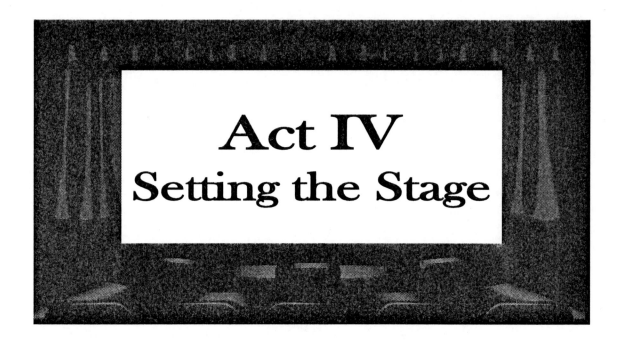

Arranging The Adult Learning Environment

Every good performer will tell you that the performance begins at the edge of the curtain. Every GREAT performer will tell you that the performance begins before the curtain is ever raised. Long before the presentation starts, opinions have already begun to form about what is going to take place. The learner took in the environment, surveyed the surroundings and began forming an impression. That impression is going to affect how well the message is received and the starting point of the learners and their mindset at the beginning of your presentation.

Even professional football, baseball and basketball players try and get some practice time on the field before the opening kickoff, pitch or tip-off and they have the luxury of knowing that the playing field has the same dimensions and perimeters each time they play. They have learned though that the turf can be different, the bounce of the ball affected and their footing altered. As a professional presenter you have all of those challenges amplified.

The furniture in your classroom isn't just a bunch of meaningless wood, metal, and plastic. In fact, how you arrange the desks in your room says a lot to students and learners about what you want to accomplish and even what you believe about student interactions and learning. There are two component parts of setting up an effective presentation theater: the effect on the students when they enter the room and the ability you will have with the space once they are in it. In this Act we will deal with them both.

Setting the Stage for Maximum Student Impact

You have experienced the effect yourself. You walked into the movie theater because you heard that the movie was great. The line outside of the theater was long and inside the flashy posters and brightly lit lights of the lobby heightened your excitement. You got your popcorn and soda and walked down the thick lush carpet toward theater number 12. Once inside you settled into a comfortable chair at just the right eye level for you. Entertained by the music playing and the running stream of previews you picked out the next movie you would like to see. Then the lights began to dim. Your attention became focused and as the dolby sound swept through the theater your mind and your heart raced. This was going to be fun. You remember how you felt don't you?

Now we want you to imagine a different scene. You walk into a room with bright lights and no one is interacting. The room is wrapped in deathly silence. A small projector screen is set up in one corner of the room. Immediately you wish you had brought a jacket because it was cold in the room. Around the space are about 30 chairs haphazardly set up. You squirm for a few minutes on the uncomfortable metal folding chairs wondering why the show hasn't started yet. A guy appears in the doorway and yells at the crowd, "Get in your seats, we will get started in a few minutes."

Cinema by Salvatore Vuono
FreeDigitalPhotos.net

The exact same presentation is about to be shown, same content, same movie, but I am willing to bet that the audience's expectations, moods and mindsets are entirely different and were formed long before the presentation even began. This is what we so often miss as instructors. This is why so many presentations start out with an uphill climb to gain the audience's attention, trust and loyalty. We don't always have the luxury of importing theater seats into our classrooms, but there are many things that we can do to change the first impressions of our learners.

Fundamental Classroom Set Up Concerns

There are some fundamental functional concerns that all instructors should have about the space in which their presentation will occur. This is the reason that we show up early and survey the turf. So here is a fundamental checklist of things to always keep in mind and you must leave yourself time to be able to do these things prior to the start of any class or presentation. After hours of presentations we can tell you that you can skip these steps, but you will have to deal with all of those omissions during your presentation. Best to check it out before the class ever begins. We have developed a one hour habit of showing up in a classroom or presentation space before the delivery and here is our mental checklist. If you have ever seen us wandering around a classroom prior to a presentation this is what we are doing.

Elemental Choices In Classroom Layout

✓ Where is the screen? Is it unobstructed and will it be visible to all students? Wander the classroom and look at the screen from different vantage points. Will everyone be able to see it? We found it amazing that in his book *How To Teach Adults* over two decades ago that Donald Levi talked about projecting the image on the wall. We do this often when the space permits. Smaller portable screens just don't give us the image presences we would like to have in the classroom. Where a blank or light colored wall exists you will find us removing the screen and projecting the image on the wall. We operate here under the principle that bigger is better.

✓ What does our presentation stage look like? Are we able to move freely in the front of the room and reach the students without obstruction? We often are pushing podiums and other tables aside. We want to be able to travel the full length of the front of the room unobstructed and we want to be able to approach the students individually. Where are the aisle ways? Are they conducive to free movement?

✓ Where is the thermostat? We have found that the most comfortable temperature setting for most environments is 72 degrees. But if we need to change it as the presentation progresses or on a break we want to know how to access it.

✓ What does the lighting look like particularly when we are playing videos or have a detailed PowerPoint slide? Is it visible? We don't know who designs most classrooms, but we are astounded that for some reason those designers always put a bank of lights up that illuminate the screen. Turn them off. We are notorious in rooms lit with fluorescent bulbs for loosening and turning off those directly above the screen because it washes out the screen image. Yes, risk manager, that was us, standing on top of a table loosening bulbs over the screen prior to a presentation.

✓ How many seats are set? As close as possible we want the number of chairs in the room to meet the number of attendees plus about 10%. We remove the exra chairs and get the junk out of the room. You don't go to a movie theater and see a stack of unwanted furniture in the corner do you? We know that students are going to survey that room and when it appears cluttered, they'll begin to form impressions about the presentation.

✓ Is the room set up conducive to the type of class and the exercises we will be conducting? There are lots of choices on room set up. But it is important to understand that the choices on classroom set up impact the experience and reaction of the students.

Arrangement Impacts on Teaching & Instruction

We operate off of a couple of fundamental concepts in configuring room set-up. Typically we regard the front of the room as being opposite the doorway entrances to the classroom. This is not an accident, it results in minimal distractions to the class from people entering or exiting during instruction. We also want to assure that all students have an unobstructed view of both the instructor and any visual material that will be displayed. Finally, we usually want to configure a room so as to facilitate the connection and proximity between instructor and the students. The final consideration has to do with making the space conducive to the exercises or type of classes which will be conducted. With all of these fundamental concepts in mind, let's review some basic room configurations.

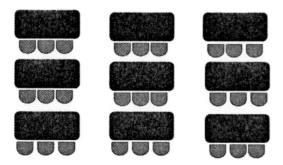

Typical classroom configurations leave one aisle down the center. More aisles mean better student interaction. So when possible create multiple aisles to facilitate the proximity between the instructor and the students. We also believe that wide classrooms work better than deep ones, again it is often better visually and in terms of interaction for the students.

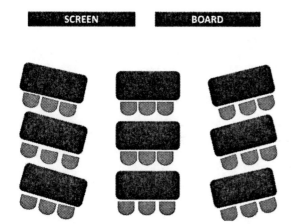

Today's classrooms often involve both a whiteboard and a screen. When possible we separate these two media presentation areas to allow for better flow with the presentation. Often times the board is not portable and there is a tendency to set the screen up in the middle of the room in a fashion that blocks the board. We are often relocating the screen to the right or left side so that we can employ both tools in seamless fashion.

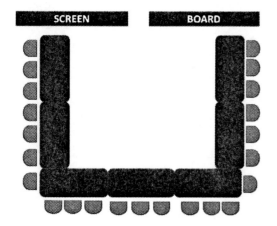

Certain types of classes require more student interaction than others. When classes call for heavy student interaction a u-type arrangement will facilitate better interaction and camaraderie between the class participants. Students tend to contribute more when they can clearly see the faces of the other students and can more easily hear and participate in the discussions.

Interactive & Group Configurations

When educational presentations call for students to do group activity or break out sessions it is best to have the students in those seating arrangements prior to the start of class. Consider doubling up tables and forget about the linear layout of the room. It is more important that the tables and chairs be angled and arranged for student comfort and visibility than that the tables are arranged in a straight line.

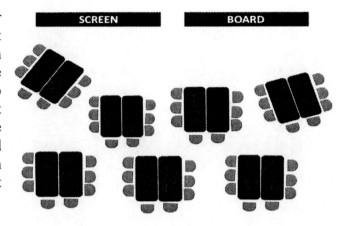

Many venues still use round tables. The most common error made is to set the chairs full circle leaving several members of the audience with their back to everything. Remove the chairs in the front of the table and push the tables closer together to achieve the same number of seats. You will be able to do this because without the front chairs the tables can be in closer proximity to each other.

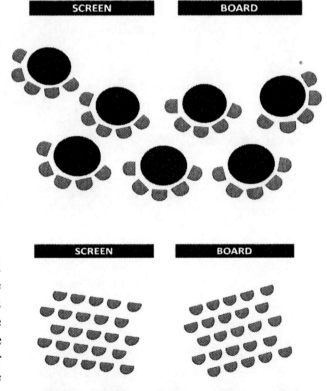

Some classes are a mixture of lecture and then subsequent breakout sessions. Here is a 50 person classroom setup that has two components. There are chairs for the lecture part and then breakout tables at the rear of the room. Notice that the chair arrangements are offset to increase visibility instead of being in linear alignment.

Contemporary Technology Considerations

Often times today there are additional technology considerations superimposed on the traditional classroom setting. Students are bringing a number of electrical communication devices into the classroom from cell phones and ipads to laptops. We believe that such trends will simply continue to increase and that as instructors we should

be encouraging their use and incorporating it into the classes rather than taking the position that such devices have no role in the classroom. However, given the fact that such technology can be disruptive, not only to the learner's attention, but also to others in the class, we think that instructors should have a technology Code of Conduct. Include it in student manuals and discuss it prior to class. Here are some things to consider for inclusion into your technology Code of Conduct:

✓ Everyone agrees that all sound on such devices including laptops and cell phones shall be turned off.

✓ Everyone agrees that any use of such devices shall be limited to classroom activities and focus. While it may be perfectly fine to look up a referenced website or take notes on an electronic device, it is not okay to be text messaging outside of class or responding to email messages.

✓ Consider building some set and directed exercises in class that allow students to utilize their electronic devices. It might be a trip to a website. We will discuss other uses of technology to engage and interact with students in a later Act of this book.

✓ Consider setting up a technology section where the students who do want to take notes or access a discussed website can operate free from the distraction of others. We have seen instructors do this very well by seating those with laptops in the back of the room, because the presence of the screens is distracting to students sitting behind them that are not using a computer.

✓ All of this heightens the need for the physical presence of the instructor in all areas of the classroom to monitor the students' use of electrical devices. So you may want to include a provision in the Code of Conduct that simply says, "If I as the instructor tap on your device while I am presenting, then it means that you have violated the policy by the website I saw that you are on or the fact that you were working on your email. If the instructor taps on your device for such a violation then you agree that you will turn the device off for the remainder of the class.

Knowing that laptops and electrical devices are becoming more prominent in classrooms also means that depending on the course the instructor may need to run additional electrical cords or power strips for the students and also often needs to know the availability of WIFI in the classroom. It may mean taping or covering electrical cords so as not to create a hazard for the students. All of these considerations are ones which are becoming more necessary and all are items which need to be addressed prior to the presentation if technology is going to be utilized.

The important point is that there is nothing standard any longer about classroom preparation and set-up, demands change as the needs and wants of the student and instructor changes. If you teach a lot in remote locations then we recommend that it is worth your time and effort to create a model floor plan diagram of the ideal set-up of the room taking all of the preceding issues into account. It is much easier to communicate with the facility or venue through a picture diagram and you will come closer to uniformly getting the room to your specifications before you arrive. Today we cannot afford to make the assumption that just because the facility has held classes before that the organizers know what room set up will work best for you and your students.

Pre-Class Tricks & Tools of the Trade

Experience has taught us that there are other pre-class preparations that will also enhance the classroom environment. Playing music or videos prior to class is a great elevator of the mood in the room. If you have not tried this, we encourage you to experiment with playing music prior to class. It's another reason that we are in the presentation space ahead of the students. We want the experience to look and sound different the very moment that

Music Notes by Renjith Krishnan
FreeDigitalPhotos.net

they walk into the room. You will notice an immediate increase in the level of energy in the room if you use music. Wouldn't you rather start your presentation in a high energy space than a low one? Experiment with different types of music. You will notice a difference.

If we could take the introductory music one step further, then as instructors we would utilize that time at the beginning of class to further prepare the student for the experience they are about to enjoy. Think about it. We have a captive audience, waiting on a presentation, staring at the front of the room toward a blank wall or screen. This would be an opportune time to create a video loop or slide presentation that promotes whatever you would like. Sounds sort of like the previews at the movies doesn't it?

These pre-class loops or videos could focus on music or material that would be tied to the class. They could feature products you have available or stand out as previews of coming attractions for other great classes that are coming up. If nothing else, why not promote some inspirational quotes that fit with the class and put some background music behind it. In the movie, *The Emperor's Club*, Kevin Kline says, "As their teacher I was willing to try anything to reach them." No matter how you look at it, this is valuable presentation time and it is often wasted in silence, when we could be setting the stage, the emotion and the tenor for what is to come.

The GAPE concepts urge us to utilize student names in the classroom. In case you were wondering it was Dale Carnegie in his classic book, *How to Win Friends and Influence People* who said, "The sweetest sound that someone can hear is the sound of their own name."

Impromptu Student Placards

For all of these reasons we believe in the use of student placards at student seats. They are much more preferable and visible than name tags and if done correctly they can help you build rapport with the students even before the class begins. We are not talking about expensive printing, assigned seating or a lot of time required. We are simply talking about what is an easy and immediate was to connect and allow you to continue to connect with the students.

✓ Go get some white cardboard stock 8 ½ by 11 inches. Fold it lengthwise. Get a bold Sharpie or magic marker.

✓ Greet the students as they come into the room. Let them sit where they would like then take a piece of the cardstock and write their name as large as you can on both the front and the back.

There is great psychology and teaching techniques behind all of this and the benefits of this brief little exercise before class even begins are immeasurable. You will already have connected and spoken personally to each of the students. Regardless of their given name you will know what they prefer to be called and whether they prefer a nickname. You will be able to refer to the names of the students easily throughout class and you will feel more at ease at the beginning of the presentation. It makes it feel like you are starting a presentation among friends you already know rather than a bunch of strangers. Try it. You'll use it.

We all have huge advantages over Socrates and Aristotle, we are not confined to a grove of olive trees. That means we are not subject to the available sunlight, the distraction of outside stimuli and the prevailing weather. We have the ability to craft and control the learning environment long before the presentation even begins. One final look around the classroom just to check the lighting, the ability of the students to see, the removal of all things distracting, the level of the sound.

We can't help but think sometimes how much was accomplished by those teaching greats in environments that today we can scarcely imagine. We have so many more tools, techniques and controls. I assure you that somewhere prior to your class one of those greats, maybe your best mentor, is just checking in, looking over your shoulder and seeing if you are really utilizing everything at your disposal. If you are I am sure Socrates would smile. The secret is that he is smiling, not because of all the little details that you may have altered, added or removed....he is smiling because as a teacher you simply cared enough to do so.

Do whatever it takes so that when students walk into the room there is visual and auditory evidence that you care. Wow! What if every class was that way? The advantage is that they are not and we have an amazing opportunity to leverage that to our advantage. Doing so will already being to differentiate you as a professional presenter before the presentation even begins.

Curtain Call

"Creating Atmospheres That Are Conducive to Learning"

By Roseann Farrow, President Elect of the of the National Real Estate Educators Association (REEA)

Roseann Farrow, President-Elect of the national Real Estate Educators Association is a highly skilled leader, communicator, motivator and coach with over 25 years in real estate sales, training, management and consulting. She personally has trained and coached thousands of real estate agents, managers and brokers who are lifted by her passion, humor, high energy and dedication to the industry. A NY State Real Estate Broker and National REBAC trainer, she provides independent training, coaching and consulting nationwide as Roseann Farrow Seminars and can be reached at roseann@rfseminars.com.

I suppose the 3 most important words I can offer in "Setting the Stage" are <u>Get There Early</u>! Let's face it. Most often the room set-up isn't what you want even when you've discussed it in advance with the program planner. I find that 2 hours early is optimum….. one hour to personally create half-rounds, create aisles, chevron long tables, set up and try out my equipment and sound (I always carry my own power strip just in case), and mess around with the lighting which includes unscrewing glaring bulbs. (Yes, I have climbed on tables or called in a taller helper!) Turning on motivational music to which I have rights stimulates me during set-up and creates a lively and welcoming touch for the attendees. I like to set up my materials/props/books on a table stage right since I tend to present from that position when I'm not walking around. Then I still have an hour to put my jacket and heels back on, freshen up and feel prepared to greet the attendees in a comfortable and stress-free manner! Invariably a few participants arrive 30 minutes early so I like to be ready for them.

When I present at an out of town hotel and arrive the night before, I examine and re-arrange the classroom at night if the hotel staff is cooperative. But even if I can't get into the room because set-up will occur the following morning, I remind them that I need to get into the room 2 hours early and always check that any pre-shipped materials have arrived. Most often I've called a day or so before to check on shipments, but I check again upon arrival because it's not unusual for front desk staff to be out of sync with receiving staff. Searching for the pre-shipped boxes will be unnerving if you wait until moments before class begins.

When the presentation screen is in the middle (often electronically lowering from the ceiling) I like to have a small, low, unobtrusive table in front of it. This will hold my projector, laptop and speakers. If the provider has instead set up a long table and can't switch to something smaller, then I turn the table vertically so that I don't build a barrier between the audience and the front of the room. If the table needs to tilt a bit, that's fine too. But I never position the front of the room or myself behind a physical barrier. Even a podium is a problem for me, mainly because I'm short enough to get lost behind it, and also because it can tend to be a crutch or keep me planted in one place. All of this is bad chi! We need to keep the energy flowing for maximum results. The old-time-podium-lecture mode doesn't allow for maximum interaction with your group to stimulate the learning process.

An extra table at upstage stage right (audience left, behind speaker and flip chart and against the back wall) is the place I keep any "show & tell" items, markers, post-its, extra handouts/evals, and props. These easily can be accessed throughout the program without crossing in front of the screen. Plus it's so distracting and nerve-racking to shuffle through luggage or bags to find something during a presentation. Being prepared is just so much better! And this takes time. So give yourself the appropriate set-up time, and you'll be glad you did. This is one factor that separates the rookie from the pro.

Room set-up regarding the layout of the tables in proportion to the size of the group takes some thinking and planning. Let's say, for example, there will be 30 – 40 attendees in a full-day class. If the site offers long tables with one aisle down the middle, I would have 4 chairs per table and an even number of tables. Then, for interactive exercises at their own tables, I can ask a table to work with one partner in groups of two's, or I can ask a table to turn around and work with the table behind them (groups of eight or four if I split the table). Having an even number of tables makes this easier, but if there's one table that stands alone in the rear and you need it, then I ask them to pull back their chairs into a crescent and work together. Moving the actual tables, though, becomes a set-up piece and requires thought as well as time and muscle!

But let's get real. Sometimes, no matter how early you arrive to set up, there will be occasions when the site as well as the provider limits the optimal "stage" you were counting on creating. I've taught in rooms that were too small, too dark, too hot, too cold, or had poles that blocked the view, and I had no way to make changes. And sadly, too many times I've arrived early at a site (the training room of a company or board office) only to wait at a locked door until the provider showed up ten minutes before class was supposed to begin. So there we were - the students and me - trying to be cheerful and nonchalant as we waited outside or in a hallway. Other times I've had the hotel space all set up, and the provider's assistant didn't arrive with the materials and sign-in sheets until a few minutes before class begins. Now we spend another 15-30 minutes handling sign-ins, opening boxes, and sorting and distributing materials. Class begins late, and the mood is less than good.   It's handy to have a super-duper opener to engage and inspire this group!   Or quickly engage the students in an exercise that will be topical and meaningful but keep them occupied for any organizational set-up time you still need. (They will recognize and resent a 'fluff' time-killer exercise, so make this count.)

Interestingly, the most challenging issue I currently face in the classroom set-up is providing enough electrical outlets for students' equipment. I find that most of the early arrivals are coming early only so they may claim a seat near a wall outlet. (The early bird theory!) Providing long extension cords and power strips may be one solution, and asking lap-top/i-Pad users to group themselves at rear tables certainly is another. Having acceptable protocols in place seems to be the key. We're at the 'Wild West' stage at this time, and there's much debate surrounding the issue. I, like so many other trainers, are trying to go with the flow!

So maybe the notion of "going with flow" is a nice way to conclude. Attitude is everything, so no matter how perfect your room set-up, or how fresh the coffee and the muffins, or how timely or legible the handouts, it's the "You" who makes all the difference. You must know your material, be prepared and rehearsed, and always feel genuinely excited and grateful to be there. Granted, it's nicer and easier when all the details are in place, but in this real and sometimes wacky world of training, you gotta love it to prevail!

Curtain Call

"Your Uniqueness Quotient: Differentiating Yourself As a Speaker"

**By Julie Garton-Good, DREI, C-CREC,
National Syndicated Author, Columnist & Speaker**

Julie Garton-Good's real estate career spans more than three decades as a broker, international speaker, book author and syndicated columnist. She addresses thousands of people annually on the topics of real estate trends, consumer-centricity, and fee-for-service consulting. Julie is the sole three-time recipient of the Real Estate Educators' (REEA) international "Real Estate Educator of the Year" award. Author of 10 books and passionate about teaching, according to NAR she is among the most influential people in the real estate industry. You can reach Julie at JulieGarton-Good.com.

Never before has there been such competition among professional speakers. Our maturing profession has hit the loggerheads of fewer live events, shrinking education budgets, not to mention the growth of virtual conventions and webinars. For speakers who want to master the market and grow their business, the answer is simple---specialize.

WHY IT PAYS TO SPECIALIZE

When I first mentioned specialization to my real estate education peers in the mid 1980's, they thought I was daft. Why in the world would I want to limit the topics I taught, choosing instead, to have just a couple of specialties? Nearly three decades later, they all agree that they never really started making any real headway (including increased booking fees) until they decided to specialize. And the positioning created by becoming an SME (subject-matter expert) is even more compelling today.

Here's why. The meeting planner's mission is to hire the best, most capable person available within the budget who will deliver a quality presentation, thus showcasing their skills as a meeting planner by whom they choose. If a speaker's electronic brochure shows them speaking on everything from soup to nuts, he'll be eliminated early on. Contrarily, if a speaker has a national reputation for a topic, has written articles and preferably books on the subject, she'll more than likely be placed on the short list. While it's true, given your specialty topics, you may not win every convention you "pitch", chances are good that you'll be the one chosen when a SME is needed. Subject-matter experts often get the plum assignments of developing a turnkey course, teaching via satellite, and other types of high-exposure, higher revenue opportunities.

HOW TO DETERMINE WHAT TO SPECIALIZE IN?

If you're running yourself ragged teaching myriad topics, it's imperative that you analyze what you want to specialize in, and (equally important) why it's worth your time and effort. Let's cover a five-step process to help you drill down to your three best specialty topics.

STEP #1: Four questions to determine topics. Which Topics...

1. Do I know well?
2. Do I have the most practical experience with?
3. Have I "earned the right" to be an expert in?
4. Do I most enjoy speaking about?

If you have trouble answering any of the previous questions, listen to your gut. Even if your pragmatic mind can't come up with an answer, feeling the excitement that a topic evokes in you can lead you to embrace it as a specialty. Using the topics you uncovered n Step #1, list:

STEP #2: Five Topic Areas Could Be:

1.
2.
3.
4.
5.

STEP #3: Defining Your Most Marketable Topics

In the next step, we'll rate each of the five topics you've chosen in Step #2. The idea here is to determine which of the five topics are the most marketable by answering six individual questions about each topic using a system of 1---low; 5---high. Be sure to record your scores next to the topic so they can be tallied later.

Question 1: Can seminar attendees make or save money with the information, and/or will it keep them out of jail? (This question rates the application of the topic to the real world; can it make money and/or limit loss?);

Question 2: Does the topic have longevity? It should be a "staple" of the industry (or an evolving norm), not merely a short-term trend. (This question rates the longevity or staying power of the topic---why be a SME when the topic is short-lived?);

Question 3: Does the topic require fairly significant updating? (This showcases the timeliness of the topic, the calling card of the subject-matter expert. The more updating a topic requires, the more your services will be needed);

Question 4: Could you present the topic in a unique way in order to personalize it? (This is the uniqueness quotient and it's vital for your long-term success. The more creative you can be in presenting a topic, the more shelf life it's likely to have. And, you're less likely to become bored delivering it!)

Question 5: What do you perceive as the need for the subject in the marketplace, both current and anticipated? (This is the need quotient. Unless there is measurable demand for a topic, you won't have a viable niche);

Question 6: Would it be cost-effective for you to specialize in this topic, and can you pass that cost on to meeting planners/attendees? (This is the all-important cost-effectiveness quotient. If the cost of being a specialist in this topic is high and it can't be recouped from attendees, you'll be going out of business one presentation at a time).

Now tally up your scores for each topic, and enter the top three scoring topics below:

1.
2.
3.

STEP #4: Segmenting Your Topics

Using your top three topics from Step #3, list at least three sub-sections for each. For example, mortgage finance could be segmented into pre-approval, loan application, and troubleshooting the transaction.

1. Topic #1:
     A.
     B.
     C.

                    Best =

2. Topic #2:
     A.
     B.
     C.

                    Best =

3. Topic #3:
     A.
     B.
     C.

                    Best =

Next, prioritize the subsections above using the questions and the rating system (1-5) found in Step #3. Post your findings above for each after the word "best".

STEP #5: Come up with an eye-popping title for the highest priority/best sub-section in Step #4:

_____
_____
_____

Congratulations! You now have specialties, complete with titles, for your three most marketable topic areas! You're well on your way to mining that target market niche as a subject-matter expert.

THE DEFINING TRAITS OF A SPECIALIST

It's one thing to call yourself a subject-matter expert, yet another to deliver the goods. The true specialist has the unique ability to imprint every presentation with three golden extras: personalization, application, and take-away value.

Subject-matter experts pride themselves on using the most up-to-date information, including demography and geography, to personalize the presentation. If there's cutting-edge information regarding his specialty, he knows it and shares it, emphasizing how it impacts the local market and, most importantly, the attendees.

If information doesn't have real-world application, it's doubtful that the specialist will have much need for it. Today's audiences are constantly asking "what's in it for me?" embracing information that can directly benefit their work, their family, and their future. The consummate SME understands the importance of real-world application, and makes sure it's a tangible, solid force in her presentation.

Last, but not least, the specialist makes sure that there's plenty of reinforcing take-away value in the form of real-world exercises, worksheets, and checklists. It's amazing how many times over the past thirty years I've had students contact me post-course to inquire about a checklist or form I offered them as take-away material. That's why it's important to imprint your contact information on every hard or digital copy that attendees' receive. You not only extend the learning and the experience, you are passively marketing your expertise and longevity as a subject-matter expert.

There was a laughable catch-phrase in the speaking industry in the 1980's: "It's easier to change your audience than it is to change your message". It's likely that speakers who heeded this nonsense are either waiting for the phone to ring or are totally out of the business! Today, the road to longevity requires differentiating ourselves from the masses and becoming a focused subject-matter expert…someone who cares enough to personalize each and every presentation and provide outstanding take-away value. That's what it takes to last!

The Art of Getting Started

Teaching is both an art and a science. We suppose that there are naturally born speakers in the world, but most speakers earned their spot through endless preparation and deliveries. Public speaking requires us to surmount our fears about getting up in front of people. After all it was American comedian Jerry Seinfeld who said:

> *"According to most studies, people's number one fear is public speaking. Number two is death. Death is number two. Does that sound right? This means to the average person, if you go to a funeral, you're better off in the casket than doing the eulogy."*

That fear, the one in the pit of your stomach is what paralyzes most speakers. So we have devised a simple rule known as the PALM principle which we apply in the first five minutes of class. PALM stands for:

P – Prepare
A – Actively Engage
L – Leverage an Emotion
M – Make a Point

112

The concept of preparation seems self evident. Which of us would attempt to deliver a presentation without preparation? We think we are prepared, but what does that really mean? Know the first five minutes of your presentation cold. Even after 25,000 hours of live presentations we are certain that people still stare at us when we stop at traffic lights on our way to class, walk down a hallway or pace backstage. That's because to the average passerby we have developed some sort of connection with imaginary beings. We are gesturing, muttering to ourselves and repeating over and over the first five minutes of class.

Have you ever noticed that all of your anxiety seems to disappear once you begin your presentation? That is particularly true if the first few minutes go well. It is the most critical time of your presentation. It is then that the audience sizes you up, assesses your skills and determines whether or not you are worth listening to. So it is in this period that you must not stumble. We rehearse over and over again on our way to class those first five minutes. We know that if they roll smoothly the rest of presentation will fall into place.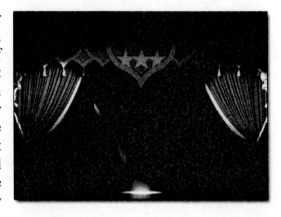

It is also in those first five minutes that we know we must actively engage the class. We must be able to ask a question, touch a point of commonality or establish some type of bond with the audience. Theresa is famous for starting a class by simply asking students, "So, what do you want to talk about? What's on your mind? It's her way of creating engagement within those first five minutes. We do not always need to ask a question but we know that in some fashion we must touch the audience and cause a response from them, even if an emotional one within the first five minutes.

Finally, make a point. There has to be the providing of some valuable informative and practical piece of knowledge in the first few moments of class. That will cause the audience to listen further and draw them in to your presentation.

It is because of the PALM principle that we are such big believers in the use of a great beginning developed and drawn from our theme as we discussed in Act III. A well crafted beginning, will set the stage, accomplish the objective and let the rest of the presentation flow effortlessly.

So here are some Do's and Don'ts for the first five minutes of class to help you put the PALM principle into practice. As we discuss them we will tie them to the GAPE concepts of adult learning so that you realize the validity of their impact.

Do's and Don'ts
The First Five Minutes

✓ **Don't apologize**. Far too many instructors begin a presentation with apologies about the nature of the course, the boring nature of the topic or simply the fact that the students had to come to class. It sometimes sounds like this, 'Well, I know that legal issues is a boring topic, but you have to take this class. You probably already know most of this and I don't want to be here anymore than you, but we are required to do this, so let's get started." We simply can't imagine any poorer tone to set at the beginning of a presentation. No matter what you might think about mandatory education requirements students are not in your room by force. Students today have lots of choices. They chose to take this particular class and probably even chose you as the instructor. (The GAPE concept that adult learners have their own preconceived notions applies heavily here. Can't you just imagine some student muttering in response, "Yep, I knew it!" Now their predisposition and opinion of your presentation has become a fact which you confirmed and you haven't even gotten through the first five minutes.)

✓ **Don't deliver your biography**. Theodore Roosevelt is the one who said, "No one cares about how much you know until they know how much you care." We believe that you should introduce yourself. Maybe even give a tidbit about your background, but your detailed bio and the rest of your credentials will have more impact if you move them from the front of your presentation and intersperse them into the parts of the presentation where they make more sense and actually have relevance to what is being said. (The GAPE concept that adult learners want to learn information that is relevant to them is working against you. Your background isn't relevant until you begin delivering information where that background is important. It is better to sprinkle your credentials throughout the class as you go. If they really want to know they can read it before class. That's why in Act IV we recommended putting it into the first page of the Playbook.)

✓ **Do use "We"** more often than "You" or "I." Chances are you have enough in common with your audience to use the word "We". It is a word conducive to more adherent bonding. After all we are all in this together aren't we? (The GAPE concept that adult learners process information from their point of view can be leveraged here if they understand that you come from common backgrounds and experiences).

Some Opening Strategies

We don't want to dilute what we have already said about the power of a great beginning. We truly do believe that it is the singular most effective and predictive way to begin any presentation. But there are other approaches which can also be effective when executed properly and we have witnessed all of the following utilized effectively by skilled instructors.

1. The State of the Union Message

It seems that most people are interested in the overall state and direction of their industry. It is an easy way to grasp attention early, engage the audience and implement the PALM principle. We leverage everyone's familiarity and awareness of the President's State of the Union message with a script that simply begins, "Before we get started let's take a few minutes to review the State of the Union." We have even used a PowerPoint image of the State of the Union seal as a backdrop. We like this approach because we believe it goes a long way toward establishing your credibility as the expert in the field. It is a particularly effective approach when major events are unfolding in the industry, major changes have occurred or if you have attended a recent conference or event and use the message to deliver your report on what is happening of importance.

2. Starting in the Middle

We have also started a number of presentations in what we would call the "Middle" No introduction. No preface. We just begin with a key point that we want them to take away from the course. We think that the reason this approach has merit, is because it is simply so different from how the students were expecting us to start or what they expected to hear at the beginning of class. It is almost as if we have conditioned them that the first few minutes are just introductory and background material and they don't have to start paying attention to later. When you begin with a key point or just launch into a story it is the unexpected nature of it that holds their attention. Okay, we admit it. We are rebels, but we tend to think like this: If there is a certain way that every presentation begins, then that to us is reason enough not to begin that way. Most successes in life are about differentiation, so our presentations should differentiate us as well. We particularly utilize this approach when using a Great Beginning. We don't start out with anything other than, "Once upon a time…." We immediately launch right into the story around which the Great Beginning is built.

3. Acknowledging the Elephant in the Room

Unfortunately we have had the auspicious obligation of teaching classes on two tragic dates. One was the day of the 9/11 attacks, the other was on the day that Congresswoman Gabriel Giffords was shot at a rally in Tucson, Arizona. You could feel it the moment you walked in the room. You could hear the conversations. For us to have stepped to the microphone and started class would have been a losing battle. Whatever we had to say by default was not the most important thing to the students at the time. If we had started class, we are certain that it would have been one of the worst decisions we have ever made. So instead we simply said, "Do you folks want to talk?" After a few minutes of conversation the issue had been addressed, students were able to express their concerns and class proceeded in a quite normal fashion.

Elephant by Meawpong3405 FreeDigitalPhotos.net

Since those days we have labeled that recognition of over-shadowing events as "Acknowledging the Elephant in the Room". Since those days we have learned that there is almost always an elephant in the room of some type. Adult learners come from their own spaces with their own concerns, experiences and agendas. Sometimes just acknowledging their existence and getting it out in the open is the best way to begin a class.

It is important to realize that the elephant in the room does not always have to be a tragic event; it could be a happy one as well. If you are delivering a presentation the day after a Presidential election or the weekend after your local team won a national championship, don't even think about beginning class without addressing it. You can't ignore elephants in the room and if you try to pretend they don't exist you'll just end up getting trampled by the herd of students who want to talk about the elephants anyhow.

4. The Water Cooler Conversation

Some instructors choose to develop a scaled down version of the elephant in the room approach and can be effective with it nearly every time they teach. We call it the water cooler conversation approach because it sounds a lot like what you might hear hanging around the office water cooler. Yes, we realize we just dated ourselves and none of you are going to the water cooler anymore because you have disposable little plastic bottles that you drink from, but trust us there was a time when people gathered around water coolers for office conversation. It is an unconventional approach, but we believe when executed well it meets the criteria of GAPE and fulfills the PALM principle as well. Essentially the instructor begins with, "What is on your minds today?" or "What would you folks like to talk about?" It certainly does take a few degrees of tension out of the air and immediately engages the students. You didn't really think Socrates or Aristotle walked into those olive groves and launched into a prepared speech did you? It's amazing what we can learn from our students if we just give them the opportunity and invite them to talk. In courses where we have seen this approach utilized the entire class seems to carry through with the open exchange of ideas.

5. Why the "Good Morning" Approach So Often Fails

We believe in quite a few different approaches for the beginning of a class and you will discover even more when we reach the discussion about student interaction that lies ahead in Act VIII. The one approach which we don't believe fulfills the GAPE concepts is the tired, worn and over used "Good Morning" approach. As we recall it often sounds like this:

ter by Dan
FreeDigitalPhotos.net

Instructor "Good Morning"
Students: No Response
Instructor (Louder This Time): "I said,
        "Good Morning!"
Students: (Meek Reply) "Good Morning

Instructor (Now Shouting) "Good Morning!!
        Are you asleep?"
Students: (With Rolling Eyes): "Good Morning!"
Instructor: "Still not great. We will have to work on that!"

So let's see, we've been in the room less than 30 seconds, have vainly tried to establish we are in charge and failed, yelled at the students, insulted them twice and they are not going to say another word if we beg them. We are, however, learning a lot about the application of GAPE in the classroom. Adult learners need to feel secure, need to be encouraged and need to feel appreciated. This approach does little to accomplish any of those objectives.

The Science of Applause Conditioning

A RAND report, *The Performing Arts in a New Era*, by Kevin McCarthy reviewed the trends in live public performances and concluded that the most explosive growth was in the purchase of recorded live performances. Due to a combination of rising ticket prices and the lack of government funding people are more likely to buy a recording than attend a public performance. Add to the RAND report the internet explosion, downloads to mobile phone applications and online videos and the number of people who have live experiences in performing venues shrinks even more.

We believe that this has implications for teaching, instructing and presenting. The audience is not as well trained to participate in live performances as it used to be. Many students are not accustomed to the rules of performing. They simply don't know how a live audience is supposed to react. It is because of these trends and GAPE that we believing in building applause conditioning into our presentations. Adult learners need to feel safe, secure and appreciated and we can do things early on in a class to make them feel this way and also generate some excitement in the classroom.

Cueing the audience for applause early on in the presentation process can help. We have begun many classes by simply telling the students, "Give yourselves a round of applause for showing up." If you accompany it with a gesture such as raising your right hand or raising both your arms then that gesture along with the principles of neurolinguistic programming will make it easier to garner the applause reaction each time you repeat that action in the classroom.

118

In fact we would recommend that every time that we can attribute the applause to someone else in our presentation we should do so. "Thanks that's a great contribution to class, give he or she a round of applause." "Let's give the company a round of applause for supporting education and sponsoring this class" "Let's recognize the following people who worked hard to organize this class a round of applause." We believe that this approach not only begins applause conditioning of the audience, but it also does a lot under GAPE to acknowledge and appreciate others.

On Recognizing Sponsors & Their Introduction

As course developers, keynote speakers and classroom instructors we recognize the necessity and importance of sponsors for courses. However, the rote introduction of sponsors and the yielding of the beginning of a class to a stranger whose speaking ability and approach we are not familiar with flies in the face of everything we have discussed in this Act about starting out a class. So here are a few tips for the better care and feeding of sponsors and your audience.

Practical Ideas for Course Sponsors

✔ Consider moving the sponsorship message to later in the class, either right before or after a break. If the sponsor speaks at the very beginning of a class the audience's ability to approach them personally and ask questions about their product or services is diminished. If done prior to a break new opportunities for the students to interact with the sponsor are created.

✔ Support your sponsor visually. Create a PowerPoint slide as a backdrop for your sponsor. We will discuss some interesting and creative approaches to this process in Act VII. We will also discuss in Act VII the creation of a promotional loop for the sponsor that can be played either prior to class or on break.

✓ At a minimum use the GAPE concepts to increase appreciation and relevancy of the sponsor. It is always a good idea to explain to students that the course is possible because of the sponsors contributions or efforts.

✓ Try to use sponsors that are relevant to the course material being presented. If you can tie the sponsor, any way into the course material, do it. It is not always easy, but it makes the sponsor relevant.

Ten Tips That Will Immediately Improve Your Performance & Evaluations

All of the following tips and techniques should be used throughout your presentation. But they have increased importance in the beginning of your presentation because it is there that we set the stage for all that is to come. Paying particular attention to these issues in the first few minutes of class will pay high dividends as the course progresses.

1. Tell the students what to expect

Formal instruction techniques preach that we should tell the students what we are going to tell them, tell them and then remind them of what we told them. We find it interesting that this process capitalizes on the power of three. We believe that you can carry this concept much further than you realize. The way you characterize the presentation is the way the students will characterize it later on their evaluations. If you say the class is "cutting edge" or "fun" or "exciting" the student will likely remember it that way so long as you actually deliver on your promise.

2. Avoid front row "Asides"

It is very easy at the beginning of a class to get trapped in front row "asides". This occurs when someone in the front of class anxious to interact asks a somewhat informal question of the presenter and we respond only to that person. Remember to always apply the GAPE concepts of repeating the question and thanking the learner for the question. These are principles we will develop further in the section on student interaction. When we get caught up in private conversations with the people in the front of the room the rest of the class is left feeling excluded and unimportant.

3. Teach to the back of the room

We have a natural tendency to teach to those in closest proximity to us. The resulting effect is we are sometimes not heard in the back of the room and we exclude a huge portion of the audience. At the beginning of your presentation don't focus on the people in the front of the room. Teach to the back row. You will find that this technique raises your voice level and is felt by the entire class to be much more of an inclusive process.

4. Invite questions early

Draw the students in early. Invite them to ask questions. Often times even a short moment when you ask, "So what do you think about that?" will encourage your audience to participate and interact. The earlier that you can include this process in your presentation the better. We want to set the stage and ground rules that it is okay to ask questions, that we encourage questions and that nothing bad will happen to you if you raise your hand and interject your comments. Do it early.

5. Smile every chance you get

Smile. Smiling helps to put the audience at ease. I guess it must have been those early school days or some remaining remnants from the Calvinists and Puritans, but most people walk into a classroom thinking that this is going to be formal business, serious business even. That type of atmosphere tends to limit student involvement, impede learning and detract from the overall experience of the learners. Smile. It creates a looser atmosphere, makes the students feel welcome and changes the dynamics in a classroom.

6. Avoid negative pessimism

The denigration of an industry, its members, even the process of teaching happens all too frequently. Now we know that all of you reading this book are smart enough not to walk into a classroom and begin criticizing the audience. But it is our subtle references that the audience really picks up on. When we concur with comments or ideas that the profession is "hard" that other agents are "difficult to work with" that consumers are "stupid" then we give our audience members permission to do the same. A course should be an uplifting, fun and exciting event, don't lose that power in talking negatively about anything. Accentuate the positive, highlight the successes and point the way toward a more optimistic way of looking at things.

7. Get organized

We will share this idea with you, but only if you promise to understand that we too are works in progress trying to master and remember these concepts every day. Has anyone else ever looked absent mindedly around the room looking for where they laid the "clicker?" Did you ever have to stop in the middle of a sentence and say, "Where did I lay my notes?" Stop doing that. We are trying to. If your notes are on the podium, they stay on the podium. If the clicker is lying on the desk of a front row student then it is either in our hand or lying on that desk. Being organized about your props and where they are is something students notice, particularly in the first few minutes of class. If they see you disorganized then they draw the logical conclusion that this is going to be a disorganized presentation.

8. Get excited

Excitement and energy are contagious. If we are upbeat and energetic about our presentation the students will be as well. Walking into a classroom looking like you haven't slept in three days, talking in a monotone, barely audible to the students is a mistake in the first few minutes that is really difficult to overcome later on in class. Allow the students the opportunity to feed off of your energy. It was your dream and choice after all to do this. Look like the person who has achieved their dreams of a lifetime. You have an audience. You are on stage.

9. Play to the strength of your theme

The strength of your opening minutes will be directly proportional to the strength of the theme and the great beginning you choose. If it is a theme that is unique, creates interest and fosters excitement then your class can't avoid being unique, interesting and exciting. Depending on the dramatic nature of your theme, we have seen instructors step to the middle of the room, say nothing, wait for the audience's attention silently and then begin. If you have never tried this we encourage you to do so. It is a powerful technique to immediately take control of a room and it has a much better impact than standing at the front of the room yelling at the students to please be quiet. If you just stand silently in a prominent position, they will be quiet. What is the first impression you would like them to have? Taking control of the room prior to starting your presentation is much more a matter of style and finesses and less of a matter of yelling and shouting.

10. Be yourself

Finally we want to be perfectly clear that it is not our intent anywhere throughout this book to turn you into us. You can't be us. We can't be you; and trying to be the person you are not seldom is pulled off successfully. In training and developing instructors, we once watched a fellow instructor struggle for about two years through classes. Evaluations were mediocre. All of a sudden their evaluations shot through the roof. When we asked them what they thought had changed, their response was simply "I quit trying to be you!" We couldn't have said it better ourselves.

Each of us has our own delivery style and strengths as presenters. Here's hoping that you take the ideas and concepts shared in this book and incorporate them into what works best for you.

Curtain Call

"Why Standards Are Important for Adult Educators"

By Mark Barker, DREI, Past DREI Chairman, Owner of Career Education Systems

Mark Barker is a pioneer in adult education. The company and real estate school that he founded has led both Missouri and Kansas in pass rates for real estate pre-license students for the past 25 years. Students would say that Mark not only helps people pass exams, but the classes are enjoyable and fun. As the past Chairman of the National Association of Real Estate Educators DREI program, Mark crafted guidelines and spent untold hours in order to elevate the level of real estate instruction throughout the United States. You can reach Mark at ceskc.com.

Every industry must strive for continuous improvement or it will fall into decline and be replaced by others. Those of us involved in developing educational standards for the real estate industry have faced numerous issues. Here are the key items and my analysis of each.

Questioning Standards:

It might be simply a carryover from the independent nature of the real estate industry that causes many instructors to believe that standards should not apply to them personally. Those of us involved with the "Distinguished Real Estate Instructor" (DREI) program of the Real Estate Educators Association (REEA) have heard the same retorts from many instructors that were not successful in obtaining the DREI designation, such as:
- "No one has the right to tell me how to teach."
- "But my students love me."

- "My student evaluations are outstanding."
- "I have been teaching this way for many years successfully and I'm not going to change now."

Sound familiar? Every teacher has probably at least "thought" many of the above comments if not actually stated them. Even assuming, however, that all of the items above are true would not mean there is not a need for comprehensive standards that apply to the industry as a whole. Standards require an evaluation. Every teacher is evaluated by someone all the time. It could be your students, your boss, the government, other instructors, or even yourself.

Evaluating Learning

If evaluation is going to take place, isn't it important for some criteria to exist on which the evaluation is based? Let's admit one thing right from the start: students base their evaluations far more on whether they enjoyed your class than on objective criteria. That's not something that is ever likely to change. That's also why student evaluations should be far down the list in considering standards. While we are admitting things, let's admit that our own personal evaluation is likely to be less than objective. This is particularly true for classes that are tested outside the class, such as government testing for licensing or a 3rd party testing service. When the pass/fail results come back from the testing organization and the results are less than optimal, what instructor hasn't defended his or her teaching by referring to a group of students as a "bad class" or a "non-motivated" group? The student evaluations may have been outstanding (meaning they liked you) but apparently the learning did not take place in a way that allowed the students to perform well on the exam. Some instructors even try to blame the test itself with: "It must have been a bad test as my students did very well in class."

Evaluating the Educator

If we can't count on evaluations by our students or ourselves, what can we use? Just like any business when evaluating employees for promotion or raise, there are certain criteria that can be used and some that cannot. Certainly a criterion that is "discriminatory" based on the current cultural mores of our society should not be used. A criterion that is not "measurable" is not something that I would want a government agency or an employer to use when evaluating me as an instructor. I would assert that the final criterion on which an instructor can be evaluated is that the items considered should be ones in which there is "wide, although not necessarily universal, agreement" in the education industry itself. To do otherwise would be to use an opinion of a small percentage of people as a substitute for the accumulated wisdom of an industry. Assuming that we would agree on these three items, it seems that we are then able to accept criteria that are: (1) non-discriminatory, (2) measurable, and (3) widely accepted in the education industry.

Who are the Educators?

The field of real estate education is composed of a diverse group. Certainly some have advanced degrees in education but that is not the majority. Many have little formal training in education but possess great speaking skill. A teaching opportunity opened up and they took it. Over some time they got better and better as a speaker. Speaking, although important, is only one aspect of education. In order for them to improve as an educator, there must be some set of standards that they can use to evaluate their educational performance. If not, they will be left with only their personal knowledge of what works for them as a speaker. Compounding this is that as speaking skills improve, the student evaluations improve and the teacher/speaker might very well mistakenly assume that their education skills have improved proportionately.

Who should Evaluate the Educators?

I believe that it is the members of the education industry itself that must do the evaluation of instructors. We cannot expect the public to have the knowledge and skill to evaluate those in the professional education industry. That doesn't mean that we ignore what the students want or say. It is just that the students will evaluate us based on whether they liked us and that's acceptable from a student's point of view. It's important to consider but it must be recognized that it is only a small part of the education spectrum. Listen to their opinions and certainly consider it in terms of marketing. Just don't mistake student opinions for an objective evaluation.

WHO Should Develop the Criteria?

Development of criteria should be done by a group of people that possess educational experience that cuts across the entire spectrum of the real estate education industry. The criteria must be widely accepted. Although there are several groups of educators, the only national group that meets the criteria above at this time is the Real Estate Educators Association (REEA). REEA has a set of criteria called GAPE (Generally Accepted Principles of Education) that is available for use by all in real estate education. Other groups may accomplish this task in the future and should be considered when they do so.

HOW should the criteria be developed?

This is not something that a few people can put together in an afternoon based on their personal opinions. Much research must be done, not only based upon the opinions of people across the entire industry, but also based on the current educational research on how people learn and effective educational techniques. There are certainly some instructors that teach "outside the normal methods" and still are successful due to factors that no one understands. When developing standards, however, the group must fight the tendency to impose their personal methods, even if successful, on the rest of the industry. That is why standards must be widely accepted across the industry in order to be effective.

WHAT should be in the standards?

Many instructors are outstanding in one category but not particularly good in another. Examples include entertaining and/or motivating "speakers" that people love to hear but for which there is no measureable change in a learner's behavior following the class. The industry needs to develop a better definition for a real estate "educator" than what we currently use. I personally like the word "educator" to be applied to persons that have a high skill level in each area of education. Titles such as "speaker" or "author" should be applied to persons that are highly skilled in certain areas but not necessarily across the board. According to the "Generally Accepted Principles of Education" (GAPE), to be considered a top flight "educator" requires demonstrable skill in 5 areas: (1) knowledge, (2) andragogy (adult education), (3) speech, (4) teaching aids and (5) the learning environment. An "educator" must be skilled in each of the 5 areas. Being outstanding in one area does not compensate for a lack of ability in another. A well-rounded educator with "reasonable" skill in each of these areas is preferred to the person "highly" skilled in only one or two areas. We have all seen instructors with tremendous knowledge that could not communicate it to the learners. Teaching adults with a purely pedagogical learning approach (i.e. child based learning) as opposed to taking advantage of the learners' personal experiences (andragogy) may result in an organized approach to the material but often does not translate to a change in the learners behavior. All educators must possess the ability to communicate to the learners, usually though speech. Speech alone is not enough to constitute education but is usually a vital component of communication. Being able to use instructional aids such as projection systems and modern computer based programs effectively in "addition to" speaking skill is more important today than ever before. Finally, controlling the learning "environment", whether it is in a classroom, on-line or other forms of individual study is an important skill for anyone that desires to be considered an "educator." Each of these 5 areas has multiple sub-categories. A list of the current topics is available at www.REEA.org under "Generally Accepted Principles of Education."

What is the Future?

The education industry is changing at a high rate of speed. Any standards must be in a constant state of revision while maintaining the "constants" that are integral to education. That is why some "organization" must be responsible for maintaining the standards. There will, of course, be disagreements. Each person is at a different level than others as they individually strive for improvement. It is, however, by the working through of these disagreements that an industry matures and pursues the goal of continuous improvement.

Curtain Call

"Why I Enjoy Teaching Pre-licensing Students"

By Dana Rhodes, DREI, President of the North Carolina Real Estate Educators Association

Dana Rhodes, DREI, is the current President of the North Carolina Real Estate Educators Association (NCREEA). NAR® has elevated Dana to the level of a Master Instructor teaching other instructors and the North Carolina Real Estate Commission has presented him with the Billie J. Mercer Excellence in Education Award. In 2009 REEA named Dana national Instructor of the Year. He is a DREI and teaches pre and post licensing in Charlotte, North Carolina for the Mingle School of Real Estate. You can reach Dana by email at Dana@DanaRhodes.com

I'm often asked, "Why do you enjoy teaching pre-licensing students?" Since pre-licensing courses require the most preparation and actual delivery time and pre-licensing students can be the most challenging, instructors of these courses must find a great personal satisfaction and reward in the overall experience.

Help Launch a Useful and Successful Career

I am awed that as a pre-licensing instructor I have the astounding ability to help an individual launch a useful and successful real estate career. To do this, I must first ground the student in their state's license law, their commission's rules and regulations, and the National Association of REALTORS® Code of Ethics. One of the most exciting and enjoyable rewards of teaching is seeing the dawning awareness in the student's eyes as a result of a new technique you learned and used to teach a complicated law or rule.

An effective instructor must also enjoy the real estate business through actual participation in the industry. An old adage states, "Those that cannot do, teach." I firmly believe just the opposite, "You have to be a successful real estate agent in some area in order to convey enthusiasm for the industry and to demonstrate to a student that money can be made in this career." It is my firm belief: "If you cannot do, then please do the students a favor and stop teaching immediately. You are hurting the industry." Just ask this question: "Would you rather have an instructor who is in the top 5% earning bracket and can teach you his/her success techniques or an instructor who just read about the real estate industry?" My enjoyment of the real estate business as a great source of income was the first prerequisite to my enjoying the teaching of proven real estate concepts.

Develop Positive Mental Attitude (PMA)

As a pre-licensing instructor I find it fulfilling to have an opportunity to influence a student with a big dose of positive mental attitude (PMA). PMA will help the student to clear hurdles such as the state test and the many situations encountered with a client or customer in the future. By simply being an instructor, I also have an opportunity to infuse some PMA into each student's personal life and career. One of the best ways of teaching PMA is through role-modeling.

The first thing a student notices is the instructor's attitude towards real estate and real estate sales. One of the greatest rewards I have received from pre-licensing students is the feedback that I'm obviously excited about my career in real estate as evidenced by my positive comments. I start each and every class with a positive thought. Over the years hundreds of students have told me that they remembered a particular thought and have shared how it made a difference in their lives.

One of the most powerful PMA concepts is just saying thank-you. For instance, I always have veterans stand on the first day of class and have the class applaud them for their service. Recently, a Vietnam vet sent an email to my sponsor stating that no one has ever thanked him for serving until he attended my class. He further stated that he will only attend future classes that are offered by my sponsor.

When students tell me that they are "test challenged", I give them the following affirmation written on an index card. I ask them to read it each day before they study the class material: "In the past I was test challenged until I took the real estate course; now, I can pass any test." How exciting to know that this simple act may have contributed to hundreds of students passing their exam on the first try.

Each of these examples helped change the way a student approached his/her real estate career and their life. That is no greater reward in life than to know you've left a lasting influence on another through your simple actions.

Learning and Applying Adult Learning Principles

As a pre-licensing instructor, I find it an exciting challenge to learn and apply the myriad of adult learning principles in our modern world. An instructor who enjoys teaching pre-licensing as I do must have a personal joy of learning and a joy of learning how others learn. Any given class contains a mix of students with many different learning needs such as generational, educational, and experiential.

Example, explain to a class that multiplying by a percent reduces the original amount while dividing by a percent increases the original amount. A "senior generation" student with some college and 25 years experience in the financial market sees your comment differently than a "Y" generation student with a college degree, limited math knowledge based on the new math concepts and no experience in the work force. An "X" generation student who never finished high school and has worked for the past 10 years as a waitress/waiter interprets your statement even differently that the other two students. I get a huge thrill when a couple of good illustrations on the board help all of these students with varying needs and backgrounds understand the mathematical concepts.

I'm also energized by using a variety of teaching aids to excite and stimulate learning. Hand-outs, PowerPoint presentations, overhead projectors, flip charts, smart boards, white boards, chalk boards, and models are some of the various aids that can add interest to the classroom. One of the most memorial presentations I ever witnessed was a presentation of "Church Leadership" through the use of props. The presenter brought in a model train and discussed how each individual in any religious organization was related to a locomotive, a box car, a flat bed car, a passenger car, a dining car, and so on until he got to the caboose. As he talked, he produced from behind the lectern a model of each car in turn and connected it on a stand to the previous car. I remember that presentation in great detail to this day from over five decades ago due to the presenter's effective use of props.

Profitability

I'm very excited when I cash a check earned as compensation for my time, knowledge, and hard work. Realistically, instructors generally teach to earn enough money to offset the expenses of teaching. When that compensation consistently exceeds expenses, then the resulting profit is a great reward, and I enjoy increasing that profit year over year.

To summarize, teaching pre-licensing courses allows me to:

- Help an individual launch a useful and successful real estate career.
- Provide a big dose of positive mental attitude (PMA) to students that will help them handle future hurdles.
- Learn and apply the myriad principles for adult learning in our modern world.
- Earn proper monetary compensation for my knowledge, technique and experience.

My wish is that every pre-licensing instructor could feel the same personal satisfaction, energy and reward that I experience each time I step into the classroom!

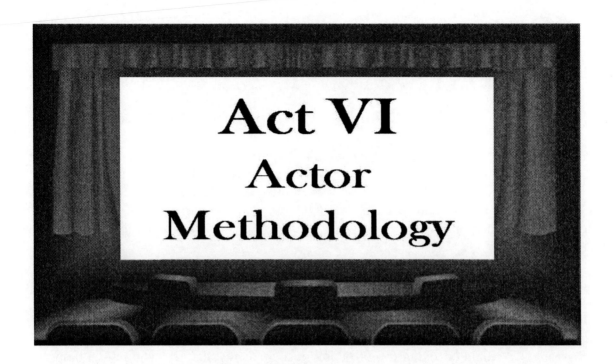

The Art of the Delivery

There are as many ways to teach as there are instructors on the planet. Each of us has our own delivery style and strengths as presenters. Some of us are more lecture type deliverers, others of us excel at interactive exercises. Given the different types of audience members that we discussed in Act II along with learning styles and cycles, we trust that wherever and whoever we are as presenters that we would all benefit from expanding our toolkit of teaching methods and the expansion of our repertoire in the classroom. GAPE tells us that we should use a variety of teaching methods so this Act will help you to understand how some of those differing methods work and how to leverage them for full advantage.

We would hope from all that we have discussed so far in this book that you simply know that the stereotypical image of a speaker standing behind a lectern, reading from their notes to a disinterested audience is the image we would like for you to depart from. There are a variety of ways to accomplish that.

Fundamental principles of public speaking are important to your delivery. GAPE reminds us that of course we need to use gestures and animation, speak loudly enough to be heard by all, identify instructor's viewpoints as our own and teach to the learner's level. How we go about accomplishing these objectives in lecture style delivery is a much more detailed process. It all begins with a basic understanding of stagecraft and positioning.

Tips & Thoughts on Stage Movement

The least powerful position in the classroom from which to make an important point is behind a podium. It acts as a barrier between you and the students, limits your movement and diminishes your gestures and animation. It the reason in the section on classroom set up that we often try to remove these types of barriers. But we could also learn a lot by incorporating some stagecraft concepts into our classroom movement.

All movement in the classroom as on stage should have a purpose. One of the largest problems identified by most speaking coaches is the fact that many trainers and speakers move aimlessly about without purpose. Maybe you would recognize it as the problem of pacing. Movement without purpose and a step here and there is distracting to an audience. So while we agree that you should move to various delivery points in the classroom we would encourage you to think of them as just that: relocation to a point of delivery. In other words, movement followed by positioning and then delivery of the point you are trying to make from a static location.

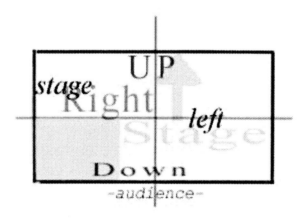

The art and science of stage blocking is taught to every beginning actor yet many instructors operate in disregard of basic stagecraft principles. Think of the starting point of most instructors. It is usually behind a podium and located upstage, stage right. That is the weakest part of the stage. The strongest position is downstage, center. If you remember that the performance begins at the opening of the curtain then you are probably starting your presentation somewhere to the right or left. Try this next time; before you open your mouth to greet the audience simply walk down stage center, pause and wait for the audience's attention, then begin. You will feel a difference in the power of the position and the attention that is being paid.

The second strongest part of the stage is stage left. Do you need verification and an example? Ever wonder why nearly every television host has their desk set stage left? Virtually all television show hosts have used this left stage setup—Steve Allen, Jack Paar, Johnny Carson, David Letterman, Jay Leno, Craig Ferguson, Jimmy Fallon, Jimmy Kimmel, Jon Stewart, Stephen Colbert and Oprah Winfrey. The reason is that in western culture our eyes read from left to right and we tend to watch performances and television that way as well. The net effect is that our eyes end up coming to rest on the stage left position where the host sits.

This means that important points get emphasized by moving downstage toward the audience often in the center or the stage left position. The interesting part is that the principle works in reverse as well. If you are overpowering the audience and in a downstage position they will take a more subservient role and not contribute as much to the class, relinquishing to you their power. By fading upstage, backing away from the audience as you ask them a question they will feel less threatened and more likely to comment or respond.

Team Leader by Renjith Krishnan; FreeDigitalPhotos.Net

If you want the audience to talk among themselves and be more interactive with each other then upstage stage right is a good place for your presence. Do you get it? We started out by saying that many instructors start in that upstage stage right position and then wonder why they have to work so hard to gain audience attention or maintain control. Most of the message they were sending was simply dictated by a lack of understanding of stage blocking.

Since we are on the topic of delivery, let us share with you an important concept that will improve the audience's feeling of involvement in your presentation and also address some fundamental GAPE principles. Have you ever watched an instructor deliver a presentation completely disjointed from the audience? Most of this effect stems from a lack of eye contact. Here's the key. You can look at an audience and never make eye contact. Eye contact is personal and when it occurs it makes each and every audience member feel that you are talking to them.

While is important for an instructor to not appear to be engaged in lengthy one on one conversations with a single audience member in the front of the room, there are two techniques that you can utilize to increase your impact and delivery. First of all, teach to the back of the room. Most of us tend to focus on the people in the front of the room. It results in a lowering of our voices, making it difficult for those throughout the room to hear, but it also makes the other students feel disconnected from the presentation. If you focus instead on the back and sides of the room you can't help but include the people in the front and the middle. When it comes to eye contact try this; when you are speaking focus on a single person in the room and deliver a single sentence to them. Then shift your gaze and deliver the next sentence focusing on a single person. You will feel like you are talking to individuals rather than a group and the amazing thing is that the audience members will feel that way too. Trust us, if you refocus often enough and spread your comments to different sections of the room your entire presentation will be perceived as more personal and memorable.

The one single group of presenters who master this technique are ministers and preachers. Watch them. They don't speak to the entire congregation. They are spreading their focus and attention constantly to individual audience members. If you've ever been in church and walked away thinking, "Wow! The pastor was talking to me," part of that feeling was coming from delivery techniques in action. It makes a difference and your audience members will feel it.

Speech Patterns, Nervous Ticks & Pregnant Pauses

No sound is as powerful as silence. Want to quiet a room? Stop talking. Want to get everyone's focused attention? Stop talking. If there is one common element that most presenters face it is the fact that we don't breathe enough and we don't pause deliberately enough. It's all a matter of pacing. Except this is a different kind of pacing used in a good way.

There are common words and mannerisms we should all avoid which tend to interrupt our delivery and act as a distraction to the learners. Most of them are probably familiar to all of us, but we are certain that you will find additional ones on the following list that you may need to work on.

- Too many "ahhs" and "umms"
- "Ya know"
- "You guys"
- Hands in pockets
- Jingling change

- Forgetting to turn off your own cell phone ringer
- Too many "I" statements
- Leaning on the podium or furniture
- Blocking screen images
- Saying something with your back to the students

We know of no better way to uncover our own annoying mannerisms and speech patterns than to videotape ourselves and watch it. We also solicit candid, honest feedback from those we know and trust in the classroom. Here is another effective way that we have uncovered to help you improve every single time you are in the classroom. Find a speech pattern or mannerism that you would like to break. Explain to the students prior to class that you are trying to improve your presentations and you have noticed that…." Ask them to all raise their hands or yell "Stop" each time you say a particular phrase or display a particular mannerism. We know this sounds brutal, but every time that we have done it, the students see it all as a game and they are far too happy to comply, correct the instructor and have a good time with it. Nothing will break a habit you have faster than getting an immediate student reaction each time it happens. We tell you, one three hour class with this method will cure you. After all, the reason that they have become "habits" is because we are often not even aware they are occurring. Ask your students for help. They will bring it to your attention.

Many notable public speakers have perfected the art of the pregnant pause in presentations to hold audience attention and to increase recollection of the material. The use of these pauses injects a moment of pause in the speech structure and holds back a word or a phrase to allow the audience members mind time to essentially "fill in the blank" before the words are spoken.

The technique has been heavily utilized by trial lawyers in presentations to juries. A great example that demonstrates the use, impact and rational behind this technique would be, "Ladies and gentlemen of the jury, based on all of the evidence that you have heard you cannot help but conclude that this man is….(pause)…guilty." The pause between "is" and "guilty" is held long enough to allow the audience's mind to conclude the sentence before the presenter speaks it. It reinforces

Judges Gavel by Salvatore Vuono
FreeDigitalPhotos.Net

what they are about to hear. Trial lawyers know that their advocacy is best when they lead a jury to a conclusion and let the jurors reach that conclusion first, rather than telling the jurors what their conclusion should be. Done correctly, the jury or audience's mind finishes the sentence before the presenter. It leaves the audience with the impression that they knew the right answer and the presenter is agreeing with them, rather than the other way around. Done too often, it can be a distracting to the audience, but it is a powerful technique that also increases retention of the information. Processed through the brain in this fashion, the information went beyond just being heard by the audience and actually became part of their thought process.

Gestures & Animation

No doubt the most important visual in the classroom is you. One study, done several years ago at the University of Chicago, examined "the spontaneous, ephemeral, made-up-on-the fly" gesturing we do every day. It concluded that at least half of language is imagery and that body language gives form to that imagery more than spoken words. The use of hand gestures and animation must fit the size of the audience. Most people tend to gesture in public speaking in the same manner they do in casual conversation. Gestures that work in one on one situations do not necessarily work for audiences of 20, 200 or 1,000. The bigger the audience, then the larger we must make our gestures.

Business Training by jscreationzs
FreeDigitalPhotos.Net

Some very commonly quoted statistics from a study by Albert Mehrabian suggests that 55% of message impact comes from body language, 38% from tone of voice and only 7% from the use of words. We know this is true from the playful "do as I do" exercise where the speaker asks the students to make a circle with their index finger and thumb of their right hand and place it on their forehead, the instructor does the same. Then the instructor says, "place it on your nose" and the students follow as the instructor does likewise. Finally, "Place the circle on your cheek" and while the instructor demonstrates by placing the circle on the chin, most students follow the action and not the words placing the circle on their chin rather than their cheek. The exercise validates the findings of Mehrabian's work and should remind us that what we say may not be nearly as important as how we say it and how we punctuate it with gestures, animation and body language.

Practical Ideas for Improving the Use of Gestures & Animation

✓**Smile more**. We said, "Smile often," earlier. Here we would like to apply it to a specific application and recognize smiling as a facial gesture. When a student begins to ask a question our natural tendency is to begin to think about our response. In that split second, our faces get more serious, our brows furrow and we look less at ease which puts more tension on the student asking the question. Your facial expressions just "sucked the joy" out of the interaction and exchange. We're frowning and we don't even know it. It happens automatically and it takes practice to break the natural response. Keep smiling.

✓**Move the Gestures Up & Expand Them**. In typical one on one conversation we would very seldom raise our hands above our heads, expand our arms full wide or make broad sweeping movements. In public speaking we do this all of the time. Move the gestures up. Gestures at or just about waist level are invisible to most of your audience members. Chest high gestures and gestures near head level have more of an impact.

✓**Stop Fidgeting**. Whether it is jangling the keys and coins in your pocket, playing with your hair or tugging on your clothing; stop it. All of these are distracting gestures to the audience. Want to know what yours are? Take our advice, videotape yourself and you will be able to identify them instantly. If you want more immediate and less time consuming feedback, find a trusted ally or another instructor and have them sit through your presentation with the sole purpose of helping you identify annoying mannerisms and gestures. They can make a list and the two of you can debrief after the presentation.

✓**Use a Prop Every Chance You Get**. We don't use props enough. It doesn't have to be complicated and we often use our notes or the student handout as a prop. When we are talking in class about contracts and offers for example, the handout becomes the contract or form we are discussing. It gets laid in front of students, we mime signing the agreement, *anything* to add some visual clarity to the words we are saying. Sometimes we are the prop. We mock conversations back and forth with ourselves as if we were the agent talking to a client, playing both roles and moving back and forth and shifting our posture to simulate the conversation between two people. Our students become props, but that is something we explore in Act VIII regarding audience engagement. Think creatively. You have more opportunities for meaningful gestures than you believe.

✓ **Make the Move to Open Hand Gestures**. In a few words, stop pointing. Not only is it overdone, but pointing tends to have a condescending feel to it from the audience's standpoint. It is offensive in some cultures and it is less inviting to student interaction. Open your hand. Open hand gestures are more inviting, calming and tend to put the audience more at ease. It's a direct application of the GAPE criteria that adult learners want to feel safe and non-threatened in the learning environment.

✓ **Gesture from the Shoulders.** Most presenters tend to gesture from the wrists and the lower arms because that is the way we gesture in typical conversation. Open your stance up, spread your arms and make your gestures come from the shoulders rather than the hands. You will be able to feel the difference and your gestures will naturally expand and enlarge for classroom presentations.

We have used some interesting techniques from time to time that we feel capitalize on body language, gestures and expressions. If you want to have a candid open conversation with the audience, then try this; go get a high stool, pull it to downstage center, sit down quietly on it, make eye contact with the room and in a softer voice ask the audience, "Can we just talk for a moment?" Some magical things happen. All of a sudden you will have changed the atmosphere of the classroom. Students will feel less threatened, attention will increase and you will have a more relaxed discussion from the group. Amazing how standing from your seated position and moving the stool back to the side signifies to the entire group that we are done with that discussion and it is time to move on.

Microphones & Student Conversations

Many speakers shy away from microphones when they have the opportunity. Usually it is done simply out of our lack of use of the devices and it is also done under the mistaken impression that the speaker can easily be heard throughout the room. How many times have you heard a speaker say, "Can you all hear me?" and based on the positive response from the audience concluded no microphone was needed. Of course they heard you. You spoke loudly enough to make certain they could, that was the response you were looking for and you adjusted your tone accordingly. Problem is we will rarely deliver the entire presentation in that fashion. Not having a microphone forces you to lose fluctuation in your voice. You can't deliver a quieter line because the audience won't hear it and we get stuck in that shouting mode for the entire presentation.

The lack of a microphone will hurt you severely the moment that someone in the front row asks a question. You will naturally lower your voice and immediately lose the people in the rest of the room. Don't chance it. If your group or audience is more than 20 people you need a microphone. Opt for the lapel or lavalier microphone when you have the opportunity. The hand held micropohone will severely limit your ability to gesture and it will also be much more difficult to maintain a consistent volume.

Even though you have a microphone, remember the students do not. They are speaking to you and in your direction. You will always hear them better than the rest of the audience. That is one of the key reasons, that GAPE urges us to repeat the question that the student asked before we answer it. We also often employ an "across the room technique." It is particularly beneficial when having extended conversations or interactions with a given student. The closer you are to the student the softer they will speak and we have witnessed instructors repeatedly asking the student to speak up. We have also noticed that if the instructor doesn't make such a request, other audience members will. You can greatly limit this by simply backing away from the students. If you back away from the student, moving to the opposite side of the room, the student will automatically increase their volume so that you can hear them. If you are on the opposite side of the room then you will have drawn in the rest of the audience and made it easier for them to hear. Develop the habit of traveling to a further distant point as you talk with a particular audience member.

On Building Bridges & Segues
Schema Theory & Scaffolding

One of the most fundamental principles of GAPE in adult education is that adults build on the foundation that they have already established, in other words, on their existing knowledge and education. It is certainly true with what they bring in to a classroom as we discussed in Act II, but it also true with what happens in the classroom. Learning to build proper segues and bridges in a presentation is key to making the presentation feel like a meaningful whole. It is often in the transition between thoughts, concepts and ideas that bridges and segues get lost.

We have begun creating a list of segues and transitions which we dislike. Here are a few of the ones more commonly used by presenters:

- Okay, for my next point….
- Now, we are going to switch topics…
- On the next page of your material…
- Let's move on to…

All of these are weak transitions between thoughts, ideas or points and don't capitalize on the concept that knowledge and education is strongest when it is built on proper foundations and leverages what the learner already knows. In educational training are discussed the schema theory and scaffolding techniques. Schema theory addresses the organized pattern of thought or behavior. Scaffolding techniques address concepts to progressively build on an idea. Both of these are at work in the classroom and one thought, idea or piece of information should logically build to the next.

When concepts and information are delivered to students and not linked into the overall framework there is a disconnect in the educational process. If you think about, we skipped a major step of the learning cycle and did not conceptualize the information for the students. Learning how to tie concepts together, relate one piece of information to the next and properly transition between the two is important to the learner's grasp and understanding of the information.

People on Bridge by WORRADMU
FreeDigitalPhotos.Net

In your grasping of this concept you probably begin to see why we are such fans of storytelling in the classroom and the art of themeing a course. These strategies lend themselves well to creating meaningful and constructive segues between the chunking of information. If you build your theme as an adventure, a journey or a progressive story then those progressive steps reveal themselves in the segues you create between concepts and ideas. Each successive chunk of information ought to expand or build on the previous. In contrast to the above poorer transition segues we prefer phrases like:

- Now, if we can take the concept we just studied and expand it to…
- Let me explain how what we just learned relates to…

- With a proper understanding of the history and the theory, let's now look at some proper applications.

It is precisely this interconnectedness and the relationship between ideas that separates a great presenter from an ineffective one. Students struggle most with causal relationships and the cross application of ideas. Learn how to tie them together and you will become a more powerful instructor.

Come On, Get Rhythm & About Breaks

Presentations have rhythm to them. Student attention spans have rhythm and there is a constant ebb and flow to the most interesting of presentations. We have seen instructors who never seem to get out of first gear and those who operate at ninety miles an hour so that they effectively wear out an audience. The best instructors change pace, rhythm and speed and know that as a course or presentation progresses, the students are doing likewise.

We spoke in Act III regarding the development of a course into time blocked segments based on the length of your presentation. Now, let's examine just how within one of those time blocked segments we would try and create a rhythm to our structure and presentation of a particular chunk of material. We have tried to graph out the rhythm of presentation segments and have found some remarkable consistency in the rhythms that work. We keep it in our mind with a philosophy we call the two humped camel. Look at the diagram below which is really an energy line that we try to follow in the presentation of a particular segment.

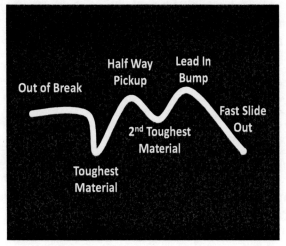

It means that we try to come out of a break with a moderate level of energy. We try to resist the temptation to be extremely high energy coming out of breaks because from that point there is no way to go but down. We want to establish an initial level that we can build on. Because student's attention is strongest following a break we will try and cover the toughest material in that initial period, but it does decrease the energy sometimes in the presentation as it drains the students. We know that needs to be followed by some type of high energy peak. In some presentations that is where we will insert an impactful video or a class discussion or exercise. Then we segue into the 2nd toughest material in the segment and try to end the learning segment upbeat with the highest energy on the second hump of the camel. The high energy bump at the end comes when students are feeling the most inattentive and pushes them into a break with an excitement and energy about coming back. We try to end right at or after that second high energy piece. Otherwise the restlessness in the class grows and the students become less and less attentive to what we are saying.

You have witnessed this effect and the importance of the rhythm every time in a classroom where you ended a segment with high energy and excitement, announced a break and then said, "Before we take the break, one more thing…" We see it happen at the end of a class quite often. Over half the students aren't listening. They already tuned out and it was our rhythm that caused them to do so. Try to hold the additional thought or idea and start there after break. It will have more meaning and you will have more of an impact.

Our particular rhythm pattern, may or may not work for you. However, there is no denying the presence of rhythms in a solid presentation and both the instructor and the material should be conscious of the ebb and flow of energy in a classroom.

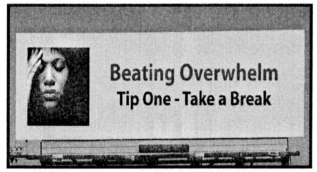

It also leads to a really good question about breaks. We have experimented with just about every style, type and manner of breaks imaginable. We believe that we are only fooling ourselves as instructors on learning segments which are longer than an hour. In our world of shrinking attention spans and 30-60 minute TV segments, the population has become accustomed to material delivered in maximum 60 minute periods. If you are teaching in segments longer than that, you will see a wear in the student's energy as your presentation continues. It's as if they automatically shut off around the one hour mark.

In multi-day presentations such as pre-licensing classes and certification courses, we believe the impact is even more dramatic. The net effect of longer segments and fewer breaks seems to take a cumulative toll on the audience. They will eventually end up in a place where they feel worn out, stressed and tired. So if you are teaching longer segments we would recommend you rethink that strategy toward shorter breaks given more often.

We have also noticed that the same pre-class strategies for increasing energy, such as the playing of music, videos and preview material during the break is a good use of that particular time and tends to preserve the energy that has already built up in the classroom. We look at breaks as another opportunity to entertain and inform the students.

Stickiness, Taglines & Memorability

It should come as no surprise that we have now begun to build your awareness of the fact that presentations are supposed to be memorable for the students. We will discuss the utilization of visual materials and audio which assist that effort in Act VII regarding the integration of multi-media. In fact the heart and soul of this book is all about ingraining your presentations into the mind of your audiences.

Presenters have always used techniques to try and help students retain and recall information. That is particularly true for instructors who teach material in formats that are designed to help students pass standardized tests. It occurs in pre-licensing courses, professional designation and certification courses. There are fundamental presentation skills and educational techniques to add to the memorability of your presentation. It's the reason that rhymes and acronyms are used so often in the classroom. They work.

- In 1492 Columbus sailed the ocean blue…
- Every Good Boy Does Fine (EGBDF, treble notes in music)
- HOMES – Huron, Ontario, Michigan, Erie, Superior (the Five Great Lakes)
- CARLOD – confidentiality, accounting, reasonable care, loyalty, obedience, disclosure (fiduciary obligations in real estate)

Using rhymes, mnemonics and acronyms are all powerful ways to help students remember lists, organized sets of information and to group together certain concepts and ideas. These approaches bring an additional level of sophistication into the teaching arena. Learning to combine different strategies strengthens the teaching environment. Today, thanks to additional research we know much more about the way that students absorb and retain information.

One of the most quoted statistics comes from a landmark study and research done by Chi, Lewis, Reinman and Glasser in 1989. In examining the ways in which students retain material these scholars in "*How Students Study and Use Examples in Learning to Solve Problems*" documented one of the most insightful pieces of research into education and adult learning. The study noted that students retain:

- **10% of what they read**
- **20% of what they see**
- **30% of what they hear**
- **50% of what they see and hear**
- **70% of what they read, see and hear**
- **80% of what they do**

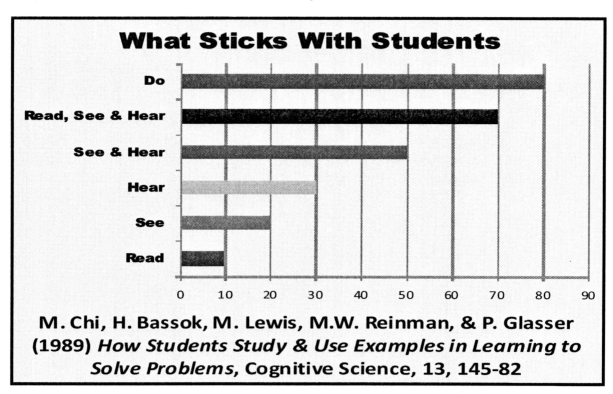

What Sticks With Students

M. Chi, H. Bassok, M. Lewis, M.W. Reinman, & P. Glasser (1989) *How Students Study & Use Examples in Learning to Solve Problems*, **Cognitive Science, 13, 145-82**

This research is pretty good validation of the GAPE concept that adult learners learn best by doing. It is one of the reasons why we have devoted an entire chapter of this book in Act VIII to engaging the student and we will spend more time there analyzing ways to involve the student in the learning process.

Metaphors & Analogies

Because adults rely so heavily on what they already know in assimilating new things that they are learning, the teaching devices of similes, metaphors and analogies are powerful. A metaphor is a figure of speech that uses one thing to mean another and makes a comparison between the two. For example, Shakespeare's line, "All the world's a stage," which we used at the beginning of this book, is a metaphor comparing the whole world to a theater stage. (We just realized that this means that this whole book is a metaphor, so are many of our classes, thanks to the use of themes). Metaphors can be very simple, and they can function as almost any part of speech. "The spy shadowed the woman" is a verb metaphor. The spy doesn't literally cast his shadow on the woman, but he follows her so closely and quietly that he resembles her own shadow.

All of the following are metaphors:

- They are as industrious as ants
- He negotiates like a lion
- This concept is as big as the ocean

Metaphors work because they attempt to take some existing knowledge or perception that the student already possesses and relate it to a new concept or thought that the instructor is trying to convey. When you are struggling with finding images for your presentation, think "metaphor." You'll be able to come up with a great image and a more memorable one for the point you are trying to convey. In other words they attempt to turn the unfamiliar into the familiar.

Analogies are simply extended metaphors. Rather than a word by word or a simple phrase comparison, analogies tend to be more developed examples or stories which relate a principle or concept and move it from something the student currently identifies with so that they can apply it to new areas of learning expansion. Greek literature, the Bible and fairytales are all rich with analogies. An analogy is comparable to metaphor and simile in that it shows how two different things are similar, but it's a bit more complex. Rather than a figure of speech, an analogy is more of a logical argument. The presenter of an analogy will often demonstrate how two things are alike by pointing out shared characteristics, with the goal of showing that if two things are similar in some ways, they are similar in other ways as well.

It is the effectiveness of analogies and metaphors that makes the "themeing" concept we discussed earlier in course development work so well. It is also the driving force behind a technique that we often employ called "The Inside/Outside Approach"

The Inside/Outside Approach

Adult students learn by building on what they know. Just think of our minds as huge file cabinets into which we are constantly stuffing new information. (Hey, that's a metaphor and we're willing to bet you've already conjured up some images in your head). When you give someone a piece of information they are trying to figure out what topic to file it under and which folder it goes into. If we can't relate it to the system that we already have then it goes on the desk in a big stack and never really gets integrated with our existing information.

We have found lots of power in using an analogy or example outside of the new material and then relating it. Let us give you a good example. If we were teaching a marketing class and were dealing with agents who felt that most of their business came from referrals and therefore they didn't need any internet marketing our script would probably sound like this:

> *Okay, let's take it outside of real estate. If we referred you to a great doctor and all we gave you was his name, we'll bet you would Google his name before you scheduled an appointment. The same thing would happen if we gave you the name of a great movie, a great restaurant or a great vacation getaway. That's what it looks like outside of real estate. Now let's bring it back in. If someone gives a consumer the name of a great agent and that's all they give them what do you think the consumer will do before they act on the recommendation?*

As instructors we are constantly searching for things that the audience can relate to and then trying to tie the new material to that existing knowledge. Play with and utilize the inside/outside approach. You will find it helpful because it works to increase students' understanding.

The Effective Use of Humor

Somewhere long ago, a visitor from another planet, in a cruel attempt to ruin public speaking on earth, suggested that presenters begin their speeches with a joke to break the ice. Most people will agree that they enjoy a presentation that has humorous components and they do complete evaluations following such classes with more positive responses. Most would also agree that some instructors are funny and some are not and that the most annoying presentations are from those who attempt to be funny and fail.

Weaver and Cottrell's studies from Bowling Green University found that when asked what motivated them most in a classroom that students ranked humor 3rd out of a list of 17 items. They concluded that humor is much more important to our audiences than instructors think it is. They set about to develop a process by which instructors could develop a more humorous presentation and classroom environment. The result was a systematic 10 step process to empower instructors to bring more humor into the classroom. Their 10 steps were:

1. Smiling

2. Being Spontaneous

3. Fostering an Informal Climate

4. Beginning Class With a Thought for the Day

5. Using Stories and Experiences

6. Relating Things to Students

7. Planning Lectures in Segments With Humor Injected

8. Encouraging a Give-Take climate

9. Asking Students for Humorous Material

10. Telling a Joke or Two

Girl with Bag On Her Head
by Stuart Miles
FreeDigitalPhotos.Net

We believe that Weaver and Cottrell are onto something here. It is rare that we have seen "canned jokes" "opening puns" and other memorized pieces of comedy work effectively in the classroom. Most of the funniest things come about because the instructor was being spontaneous and relating the humor to the classroom material.

That's the best piece of advice we can give you. Search for real stories that are funny. Truth really is stranger than fiction and implement some of the ideas of Weaver and Cottrell.

Curtain Call

"The Power of Our Words On the Stage"

By Terry Wilson, DREI, GRI, CRS

Terry Wilson is the owner of Wilson Realty in Charlotte, North Carolina. He is a Distinguished Real Estate Instructor with the Real Estate Educators Association and is a past member of the DREI Committee. Terry teaches pre-licensing and continuing education classes for Superior School of Real Estate. He is the author of "Hiking the Real Estate Trail: Your Study Guide for Passing the NC Real Estate Pre-licensing Exam." You can reach Terry at WilsonRealtyNC.com.

Fear and panic were my only emotions… "Keep talking" was my only thought…this is what I experienced when I said to a young African American woman after a day of calling me "sir" that she could call me "master." Am I a racist? Of course not! Did I simply not think? Of course!

We learn best from our mistakes, and hopefully we learn well from other's mistakes too; so please take heed my fellow thespians.

We are all committed to the greater good of teaching. From the moment class began this young, bright and engaged African American woman started each question with "Sir I have a question…" with only a few minutes to go in the class and hearing her start a question like this for at least the tenth time, I thought I could have fun and wind up the day. I interrupted her (mistake number one) and was going to say something like… "You don't have to call me 'Sir', you can call me 'your royal highness'…" had you been there you would have seen how it was in context and how it would have made the room laugh. What came out though was "You don't have to call me 'sir' you can call me 'maste…'"

I never did finish the word; I realized my mistake and panic set in. I'm serious when I tell you that the only two words I could think of were "keep talking". Break was coming up in another ten minutes but it seemed to last for hours. I was on auto-pilot for those final few minutes as my mind raced furiously through the maze of issues and potential law suits I had just created with that one quick, fly-by-the-seat-of-your-pants desire for humor. That moment happened over 20 years ago and as I share this with you, the horrid feelings I felt are as raw today as they were then. I believe there's a bit of a thespian in every teacher. That we come alive when the clock ticks nine AM and class begins. Some of us gain energy, some of us are drained but all of us, if we're passionate, give it our all to provide the best possible experience the adult learner can have.

When we're on that stage there are moments when things are going beautifully and the flow of the class is easy. There are also times when we drag, what seem like, "dead elephants" through the day. In either case we CAN NEVER CROSS THE LINE. Adult learners come from different paradigms, different experiences, different cultures and different problems. As instructors we want to be engaging and drive points home. We want not only the material, but our presentations (and yes, we must admit, ourselves) to be memorable; "Bravo" is what we long for from the students.

With that being said though we must always be mindful of our words, our mannerisms and gestures…but mostly our words. You know the old saying "Sticks and stones may break my bones but (finish it for me)…" do you believe that? I don't. Words do hurt. Words destroy friendships and can even make nations crumble. ("Mr. Gorbachev, tear down this wall!" said President Ronald Regan and with that East Germany was no more).

Your choice of words in the classroom can make a student's experience exhilarating and enlightening or uncomfortable and disappointing. I urge you to think about the canned lines you use in class… you know, the ones that always get a laugh. Take a fresh look at them from the student's perspective. Is it possible that what you've been saying is offensive to your students but they simply haven't shared their concern with you? Are there times when they've laughed but only because it made them uncomfortable, not because your words were genuinely funny? What is your paradigm? How do you view societal relationships? I know of an older instructor that calls every woman in his class "honey" and "sweetheart". In all the years I've known him I've never once heard him call a woman by her name. He doesn't mean anything by it but I know that some of his student's have found it offensive because they've told me and some who have told me were men.

Even if you're not getting the negative feedback that would clearly tell you that your words are offending, is it possible that they are? Videotape yourself over the course of a few days and watch what comes out. Be mindful of the "throw-away" lines and the "off-the-cuff" remarks... when we go "off script" this is when we often slip.

Be mindful too of when you're getting tired and you begin to go on auto-pilot. Gently remind students that you need breaks too (especially if they are dominating your breaks with questions). Find a quiet place for your break and reflect on the previous hour. Was there something you said or did that could be considered offensive? There is a bonus to having this moment of quiet reflection... we often teach the same material over and over to the point where we can (and sometimes do) teach it in our sleep. The problem is we can skip a point or misstate some important concept without even noticing it.

I urge you to always remember that what you say on that "stage" is gospel to those students. 2 + 2 = 5 if you say it does. Like a **good** play, they hang on your every word. Like a bad play, though, they may applaud out of politeness but it doesn't mean they liked what you had to say. I now have (courtesy of my wonderful wife) a drawing stuck to my laptop of a stick figure putting his toe over the line and a big circle with a line through it. It is my visual cue to NEVER CROSS THE LINE. What is your cue?

By the way, the young African American woman I mentioned at the beginning of this story gave me one of the best evaluations I've ever received. To this day I wonder if she even heard what I said or made the connection to that horrible part of our country's history. I don't know and I don't know if I want to know.

In the words of my grandfather and probably yours too... "Mind your words!"

Curtain Call

"Say Something Funny!"

By Karel Murray, DREI, CSP, Author of Multiple Books and Business Trainer

Karel Murray, Certified Speaking Professional, is an author, humorist and business trainer who speaks nationally and internationally. She is the author of "Hitting Our Stride: Women, Work and What Matters", "Straight Talk – Getting Off the Curb", co-author of "Extreme Excellence" and publishes a monthly online newsletter, "Think Forward® which has thousands of subscribers and numerous articles in local, regional, and national publications. You can listen to exciting interviews at JustForAMomentPodcast.Com. Karel can be reached at karel@karel.com or call 866-817-2986 or access her web site at karel.com.

"Say something funny!" an unidentified caller excitedly exclaimed recently. He announced that he had visited my web site and felt I should be able to liven up the conversation since I am a motivational humorist. He also informed me that fifteen people from the company were listening in over the conference room speaker phone. Oh, the hazard of humor.

Many people believe that my "funny bone" should be continually active and creative. What if I just don't feel jovial? Perhaps I'm dealing with a headache, a laborious expense account, or a cat who is coughing up hairballs at a faster rate than I can clean them up? The challenge to be entertaining in the classroom is even greater these days when trainers and presenters have to maintain audience interest when classroom participants are used to the pace and visual drama of Top Cops!

So, let's evaluate how trainers and presenters can use humor during presentations by exploring four vital questions:

1. Where does humor come from?

2. Are there different kinds of humor as well as delivery systems?
3. How do we know when something is funny?
4. When is the appropriate time to use humor?

I was raised to believe that living was a serious business--contribute to society or be condemned. As I shouldered my way through the world, I watched other people skip through their lives smiling. They chose to exist with their arms outstretched to greet the new day rather than holding heads down as they watched their shuffling feet. For these people, life is pure joy and the good humor naturally bubbles forth. However, there are others who have learned to view challenges in an irreverent manner which helps them survive life's painful episodes by laughing at them. A turn of phrase or a cocked eyebrow lets everyone around them in on the joke. They will thrive in spite of the challenges.

Humor comes from observing life as an active participant. Recently during REEA's annual conference opening keynote address, a historian spoke passionately for an hour updating the audience on Texas history beginning with the early 1600's. As he progressed throughout the centuries, his earnestness regarding the subject matter increased. He had just finished a lengthy segment on cannibals found by the Spanish in Texas early in its history. He gazed at the audience and then asked the rhetorical question – "Can you imagine what the cannibals thought when they saw the Spanish for the first time?" He then surged forward to discuss other turn of the century events. I, however, had to whisper something to my tablemate as soon as I heard his question. I visualized the pork industry media campaign and blurted out, "Oh--the other white meat!" It was gratifying to watch my REEA colleague spit out her morning coffee and bend over at the waist to try and stifle her laughter. Humor--just follow where the brain goes.

Humor also takes its origins from current events or previous speakers. For example, REEA member Chuck Jacobus, attorney-at-law, renowned for his impish humor, took the stage at the national conference later to introduce a gentleman who was receiving an award. He began his introduction with "I'd like to begin telling you about Mr. Smith. Let's begin at the year 1812…" From that point forward, the running joke was on.

Humor is normally introduced through the telling of jokes or stories. Jokes embody a short, to-the-point commentary with a one-line punch line. They are delivered quickly, efficiently, geared to generate as much laughter as possible in a short period of time. This is the realm of the consummate comedian. Comedic styles range from innocent stares and monotone delivery (Rita Rudner) to manic energy rebounding off the stage (Robin Williams).

Humorists also utilize anecdotes which are stories or parables of life that have humor interjected into the story. Ultimately the story must offer a moral or life lesson. Bill Class used to describe Cosby as a master humorist who delivers his stories with a twinkling calm, bringing the audience in on the joke with his "I'm one of you" technique. Frequently, his shows have him sitting on stage for the entire performance, simply having a chat with his closest friends.

The level of energy used by the speaker to elicit a laugh from the audience depends on the desired response:

Chuckle – includes a small smile and a head nodding in agreement

Speakers will typically get this type of response if they have mentioned a truism looked at from a different point of view or a made a general observation stated for the world to see on life's idiosyncrasies. The audience acknowledges the simple truths in your words. It might begin with a simple observation like; "Why is there only one type of camouflage uniform for the military? All those green, black and brown swatches of color on their garments. A camouflage dressed solider stood at attention in front of a bright red door, holding it open for me and my husband as we entered into a countryside café. I leaned forward and asked, "You do know I can still see you…right?" I saw his puzzled look and then pointed to his uniform and then the door. His grin was dazzling as he retorted, "I'm still new at this."

Broad grin and short laugh

Chuck Jacobus' introduction of his colleague elicited this type of response. The humor is usually quickly delivered in an unexpected way or time. The object is to catch the audience by surprise by revealing what everyone was already thinking, usually accompanied with a quirky expression to enhance the statement.

Recently, during my keynote presentation at an awards banquet, I spoke to a packed room standing in front of a bar area which actually was a sunken pit. The bartender's head would appear behind me periodically at a level even with my hip. She continued to work quietly behind me while I spoke. At one point during a particularly active section of my talk, her walkie talkie squealed loudly. The bartender squelched the device quickly and left the bar area. I spun around, looked down, then peered out at the crowd with a confused look and asked "Did that noise just come from my rear?" It brought the house down. Working with the unexpected and acknowledging it made the situation positive rather than embarrassing.

Sustained laughter

Stories are a perfect avenue for generating this type of participant reaction. If a presenter takes on the persona (acts out various parts), the audience becomes mesmerized by the performance. In fact, they often begin to live the experience as you enact it for them. By including all of the small details, making the situation alive and specific, the anecdote develops a richness audiences appreciate. Facial expressions and gestures, told with complete sincerity and zeal will be rewarded by a very positive participant response.

The "running joke" also enters into this category. I had the perfect opportunity to do this at a Chamber of Commerce retreat for community business leaders. The event, held in a new convention building, was still undergoing final touch-ups to its paint and mortar. When I assumed my position at the podium (which was placed grandly in front of the floor-to-ceiling windows that overlooked the spacious veranda), a strikingly handsome heavily muscled young man strolled across the veranda behind me, removing his shirt as he neared the column he needed to paint. Gasps of appreciation arose from the female contingency and necks craned to keep the young man in sight. I looked at the construction worker over my shoulder, and then returned my gaze to the audience. I commented, "If that young man checks out my rear end, would you let me know? At age 49, I'd like to thank him if he does!" With a roar of approval, we were able to continue with the session. However, throughout the introductions, several females commented on the outside view as being distracting. An older, overweight, balding man stood up to introduce himself, and stated, "I'm what that young man will look like in 40 years!" Going with the flow can create some truly hilarious moments.

What It All Means

Speakers may not know when something is funny until they have said it or acted it out in front of an audience. Whether something is funny or not boils down to timing and appropriateness. I've heard speakers share off-color jokes which resulted in audience members feeling uncomfortable. It's very important to know your audience and adjust your material accordingly. At a speaker training session I attended, accomplished humorist, Tim Gard from Montana, declared with a twinkle in his eye "95% of all facts are made up!" Appreciative chuckles greeted Tim for his use of a subtle joke. I tried using the line in front of County Engineers. Such a wrong choice! They took the comment literally and began to discuss vehemently how facts and numbers can or can not be manipulated to reveal whatever the reporter wishes to report. Oh, boy.

You can use the same stories and jokes from one keynote address to another but relate them to the world your audience knows. Attorneys, surgeons, or administrative assistants are all human and face the same issues every day. By keeping your jokes and stories inoffensive and true, you will not only win respect, but be rewarded with genuine laughter and audience involvement. It's a matter of caring enough to make it special for each group.

It's appropriate for speakers to use humor when it's relevant, when it moves their talk or program forward, or is needed to bring audience attention back up to an alert status. I've often used toys to accomplish this...most recently a magic wand that projects a cheery "brrriiiinnnngggg" sound when waved vigorously in the air. Discussing the topic of handling difficult people, I announced that it would be wonderful if we could wave our wand and make difficult situations disappear! With a flourish, I reveal the wand and brandish it with skill and flair. Locating a volunteer who wishes to assume the role of "official" problem solver, I then hand the wand to them for safe keeping. This simple toy always takes on new meaning and becomes a focal point for the remainder of the talk.

Often, spontaneous remarks from an audience will give speakers excellent fodder in which to develop genuinely funny responses. Some speakers are not fast on their feet mentally, so they stick to the practiced, well-placed stories and comments in their material. Speakers who are not comfortable venturing outside of the established "script" should not even try.

Ultimately, humor comes from our genuine selves which often provides entertaining physical and witty opportunities to make others laugh: The rueful look, screwed-up eyes, or pouting mouth all project our feelings and thoughts in a manner which audience members can easily understand.

Humor doesn't always work, but when it does--start clutching your sides.

Act VII
Lights, Camera,
Action

Integration of Multi-Media Tools

Legendary movie director Steven Spielberg was once asked during an interview what was his favorite part of making a movie. Everyone waited for the answer. Some expected him to say the great set locations that he traveled to, working with top actors or even the thrill of reading a script the first time. His answer was the audio production booth. Yeah, that was pretty much everyone else's reaction too. Then he explained the reason. It was because when the camera clips had been edited together and you started to insert the sound effects and the music in the background that the movie seemed to come alive. We identify with that.

It is hard to be a presenter, trainer, teacher today and not use multi-media effects to bring presentations alive. If we are not doing so, then compared to all of the other stimuli and experiences that our audiences enjoy, we by contrast can look like we have totally lost touch with present day society and consequentially our students. That doesn't mean that the addition of multi-media is always for the best.

Entertainment by digitalart
Freedigitalphotos.net

The Art & Science of PowerPoint

"Death by PowerPoint" is now an entry in Wikipedia. Noted comedian, Don McMillan, has created an entire stand up routine on Death by PowerPoint and you can find some of his routines on YouTube. They have over a million views. We don't know which is sadder: the fact that a comedian has found enough bad material about PowerPoint to do a stand up routine, or that misuse of PowerPoint has become so familiar to the public that audiences identify with what he is saying and that he can make a living poking fun it. Either way, we have read enough scathing comments about the use of PowerPoint that we think from the outset we ought to clarify something. It's not the tool that's the problem, it's the way it is frequently used that justifies most criticism.

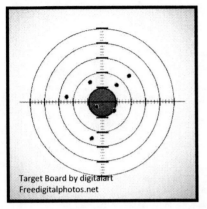

Target Board by digitalart
Freedigitalphotos.net

Bullet points: (n) the marks left on a speaker from the audience firing rounds into them after the 23rd slide of detailed material.

We don't intend to make this a primer about the technical function of PowerPoint, although we will address some common questions which often get asked about that topic such as the insertion of videos. Microsoft publishes manuals for the technical use of PowerPoint which are several chapters long. There is also the likelihood that each of us are using different versions and there are several books available written by independent authors. If we were to turn this book into a PowerPoint manual you would be reading for the next 500 pages or so and we would be teaching that subject in the worst format of all, a book. So instead we intend to share some concepts about the use and misuse of PowerPoint, interweave some of our philosophy and relate the technology to GAPE.

Top 10 PowerPoint Mistakes

1. Failing to Square or Center the Screen.

This is one of those details we were supposed to be paying attention to when we set up the learning environment in Act IV. It's hard to think of anything which poses such a long term distraction to the students as displayed images which are lopsided, not properly framed on the screen or out of focus. Once you have a PowerPoint image up on the screen, select the most detailed slide you have, display it and then make a trip around the classroom from all angles to ensure that it is visible to the students from all angles. The image should fill the entire projection screen and remember what we said about projected images in Act IV, the bigger the better. When the venue permits, we often try to avoid a screen and display the image directly on a light colored wall so that we can make the image much larger. It also will lessen your space requirements that are taken up by the presence of a screen and the distance consumed by trying to project on it.

2. Inattention to Lighting

This issue also should have been addressed when you were applying the principles of Act IV. The screen has to go in the darkest part of the room. The precise location will depend on the lighting in the room, particularly the location of the windows. Are there shades? Can you close them? Do you need to? Don't be among the instructors who are displaying visual material that is so washed out by the available lighting that the images are difficult for the students to see.

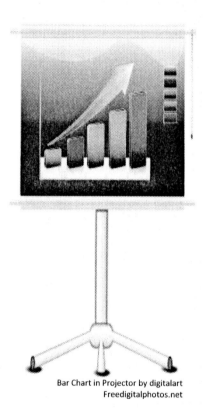

Bar Chart in Projector by digitalart
Freedigitalphotos.net

3. Reading the Slides

We happen to believe that reading from the screen is worse than reading from notes. The reason is because at least when we were reading notes we were still facing the students, facing the screen turns our back to the audience. We can easily correct the tendency to do this in a number of ways. First of all, we should know our slides. We should be able to recite the content on any given slide without looking at it and we should know what the next slide is before we even display it on the screen.

Here's our trick. Sometimes we put information on the preceding slide that cues us as to what is coming up next. If you've ever seen our presentations, you probably didn't even notice, but in the lower corner of the slide we typed in small letters "Video." That reminds us that the next slide coming up is a video and it allows us to segue into it properly. (Yes, Virginia, it's true. We cheat and use every trick we can think of for the benefit of a better presentation for our students). So if you were wondering how we remember every slide, we don't. We just use techniques to help us remember what is coming next). Most of us are running the PowerPoint presentation from a laptop. The laptop ought to be in front of us displayed below the eyesight of the audience. We can then glance at the slide if we need to and always know what is displayed on the screen behind us by using our laptop as a monitor.

4. Too Much Information on the Screen

The natural tendency is to try and put too much information on a slide. It doesn't take very long for the information to become invisible or confusing. We operate on a principle that no slide should have more than 10-15 words on it. Usually four or five words are the slide title at the top and then a maximum of 3 lines, 3 words per line. The PowerPoint becomes less effective the more information and detail it contains. There are instructors who would argue that our 10-15 word guideline is too liberal. We have seen some amazing powerpoints created with a single word on the slide, or no words at all, using an image instead. Just remember with PowerPoint less is definitely more.

5. Too Many Bullet Points

We've been bullet pointed to death in PowerPoint presentations and so have our students. There is no excitement or interest created by throwing ten bullet points up on a screen. If they are important topics then they each deserve their own slide. Better yet, why not just teach to major concepts and forget the bullet points.

6. Poor Font Choice

This error shows up in choices of both font type and font size. Fancy fonts might look cool, but they are difficult to read. Arial Black works well. Arial bolded works well. Mixing fonts of different sizes, shapes and varieties tends to give the presentation a makeshift unprofessional feel. Unless there is a compelling reason to have a different font, uniformity wins. The other issue has to do with font size. Anything less than 24 point can probably not be seen in a classroom of twenty or more students. Keep the font sizes large. Fill the screen with the words. Don't make the students struggle to read the slides. Have you ever watched a foreign "subtitled" movie? Did you just give up on the reading part way through? So will your students. If you are reading this and thinking I won't even watch a subtitled movie…well then…what does that mean for all the text on your PowerPoint slides? Just sayin….

7. Poor Color Choice

Some colors work well together and some don't. The basic concept is that you have to keep the contrast strong between the font color and the background color. Using two different shades of the same color makes reading the slide tough. Trust us, the color contrasts look different displayed on a classroom screen than they do displayed on your computer monitor. When you add to this the fact that as a projector bulb ages, the sharpness and distinction of colors starts to fade, we are always better off picking two striking contrasting colors such as white on black or black on white. By the way, it is easier for people to discern black letters on a white background than white letters on a black background. Need some proof? How is the eye chart that your optometrist uses configured? The lighter color is always the background and the darker color is the text.

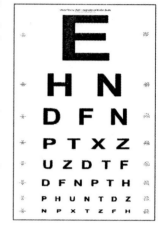

8. Spelling & Grammatical Errors

It's bad enough when we improperly mispronounce a word or misspeak in class, the good news is that the impact only lasts a second. Put those misspelled words on a PowerPoint and you burn them into the brain of your audience. They will find them. They will point them out. When that occurs we are left with no choice as instructors except to say, "Thank you. How did I miss that?" or "I'm sorry, I should have caught that." There sit our students wondering what else did we as the instructor "miss," what else should we have "caught".

9. Detachment From Student Materials

If we provided the students with written material then we should remember that they are trying to follow the PowerPoint presentation in those materials. If we want to see looks of confusion all we have to do is title the slide differently from the way the information is titled in the student materials. Be parallel in the language used on the slides and in the materials.

10. Distracting Animations

Animations used effectively in PowerPoint slides are powerful. Movements without purpose are just pointless animations. If you are going to use bullet points at all, then animation is your friend. They should be revealed sequentially as you deliver the material so that you can focus and direct the attention of the students. Don't display them all at once.

A Picture is Worth a Thousand Words

PASSION
Expand Your Mind & Soul. Live Your Dreams.

The year was 1921 and Frederick R. Barnard published a piece in Printer's Inc, commending the effectiveness of graphics in advertising. In his article he wrote "One look is worth a thousand words." That's right the guy who popularized the phrase that later was transformed into "A Picture is Worth a Thousand Words" wasn't using a picture at all, he was writing a magazine article with words. (Kinda like some silly authors trying to convey how to teach from a book). Nonetheless we agree. Images are more powerful than words, so if you can find an image to get your point across then you are probably conveying meaning better than with words alone. Remember the statistics from Act VI:

- **10% of what they read**
- **20% of what they see**
- **30% of what they hear**
- **50% of what they see and hear**
- **70% of what they read, see and hear**
- **80% of what they do**

So if we are combining images with what we say then we are increasing retention from 10% to 50% and we'll take those odds as instructors hands down. Even more so if the image we are using is a reflection of the "concept" we are teaching. We could share with you all day the fiduciary duties that professionals carry in agency relationships, try to explain to you that they are heavy burdens, but if we pair them up with a photo of an overloaded donkey, students remember the point. In fact they will remember the picture of the overloaded donkey and associate it with the burden of fiduciary duties better than they will remember anything we said.

Mule in High Atlas by m-bartosch Freedigitalphotos.net

PowerPoint is a great tool for conveying images and we believe that you have great leeway in the photos you use and where they come from. We realize that such a statement probably raises some eyebrows and we will explain more fully in the material we have researched and summarized regarding copyright and intellectual property in Act XII. For now, the point is, if you can replace your words with images do so.

The other point that we would like to make about the use of images surrounds the use of screen shots or the displaying of documents on the screen in a PowerPoint presentation. The best advice we can share is that we should all go to the back of the room and see if we can really read the document or the screenshot (usually of a website). If we did, our answer would almost always be "No" and we would all stop displaying whole websites or documents in our PowerPoint presentations. It is too easy today to crop the part of the document or the part of the website that you really want to address and put only that on the screen. Sometimes we will even display the entire document on the screen as background and then zoom into the particular portion or clause we want to focus on by inserting it as an image and animating it.

We should be more cognizant of how visible the image is and how ineffective it is to display too much information on the screen.

Upgrading Your Powerpoint Presentation

There are lots of resources out there for instructors to upgrade their PowerPoint presentations to give them a more multi-media feel and create a more enriching experience for the student. Crystal Graphics has some innovative plug-ins that can take your PowerPoint to the next level. If nothing else, trying googling PowerPoint presentations and you will find some very interesting and novel approaches to the use of this tool in the classroom. There are several good examples of these hanging at WorkAwesome.com as "Innovative PowerPoints."

The Time Warping Effect
& Other Advanced Techniques of Powerpoint

We have heard it said that PowerPoint distracts from the instructor. It can, it has, but it doesn't need to be a distraction and it shouldn't be. It should facilitate classroom learning. Think of PowerPoint as the exclamation point for your sentences and not the sentences themselves. It's not supposed to be the presentation, we are the presentation and the images and technology we use should elevate us, not diminish us. Understanding that concept will lead you into applying a whole new timing philosophy to the use of

PowerPoint in the classroom. It is much more effective to say the point or make the statement then show the image than it is to show the image and then make your point. Point first, image second is almost always a better sequence. As we said, use the PowerPoint as the exclamations at the end of your sentences. It means to use PowerPoint effectively, we have to get better at the timing in our presentations.

In fact the structure and nature of your PowerPoint slides can warp time for your students. It's this simple. If you have a slide with ten bullet points and you spend ten minutes on it, the students tend to feel that the time in the classroom is dragging or that it is a slow paced course. If by contrast you used one slide per point and went through ten slides in ten minutes the students would feel that time in the class went by much more quickly. They will even make comments such as "This class flew by..." Their sense of time is affected by the movement of the images on the screen. The more images, the more movement, the more attentive, the faster paced the

Clock Background by digitalart
Freedigitalphotos.net

course seems to them. We have the ability to make the coverage of dull material seem to move faster by simply spreading the material across multiple slides. Part of this effect is also due to the fact that when a slide with multiple bullet points is displayed the students will read the entire slide, then they will turn their attention back to us and to them it feels like they are waiting on us to finish in order to move forward. Our fault. We should have used separate slides for each point or at a minimum, animated the bullet points.

The reason that some instructors feel that PowerPoint distracts from them is well based. The projected image is a point of student focus in the classroom. Here is a little exercise for you to try in the classroom. Get a remote that allows you to black out the screen. Then tell the students that you are going to turn the screen on but you don't want them to look at it. Turn it on. All their heads will turn instinctively to the screen no matter what you say. Now with the screen displayed tell them you want them to continue to stare at it. Turn it off and start talking. They will all turn their attention immediately back to you.

Seasoned instructors practice what we call the Art of Direction. Understand that we have the power to direct the students' attention in the classroom. When we want their attention on the slides, turn it on. When you want the attention back to you so that you can make a critical point, just turn it off. You will immediately have their attention and you don't have to utter a word.

The GAPE concepts and some of the DREI criteria urge us to not let screen images remain on the screen when we are not referencing them in our presentation. Now you know why. They are distracting. They are powerful commanders of attention. We shouldn't fight that and we shouldn't abandon the tools because of it. We should be leveraging that power to direct the students where we want them to be looking at any given time.

If you don't have a remote to advance your PowerPoint slides you can find them inexpensively at any office supply store. Make certain you get one that allows you to black out the screen. If you use it regularly and you practice the Art of Direction you will have made one of the best investments in your teaching ever and we promise you that your students, may not know exactly why they enjoyed class more, but they will thank you for it. Being able to black out the screen also enables us as instructors to fulfill the criteria of GAPE not to block displayed images. It looks bad, it's distracting and it's not professional. Black out the screen before you walk in front of it.

The Power of Videos in the Classroom

If a picture is worth a thousand words then we have no idea how many words a video might be worth. We know the answer is a lot. In a world where students are sitting in a classroom prior to the start of a course watching YouTube videos on their $79 cell phone, it's a little difficult to justify why with a large screen, projector, laptop and $5,000 worth of equipment in the classroom we can't play a video. The application in the classroom is huge and the technology that surrounds us today makes the use of videos easy and seamless.

The consumption of video material and the statistics surrounding it are absolutely astronomical. While there are hundreds of video sites on the internet today, the king of video is very clearly YouTube.Com. Just how popular is YouTube?

- **You Tube has over 100 million users visiting their site every month**

- **The YouTube audience is double the prime time audience for all three major U.S. television networks combined**

- **More material is uploaded to YouTube in 60 days than all three of the major television networks created in 60 years**

We don't have to be a movie producer in order to be able to show movies in our theater. We don't have to be some great film director to show movies in our classroom either. We just have to be able to utilize the videos and tools that are available and integrate the multi-media with what we are already doing.

It is amazing what videos can be found on YouTube. No matter what topic you are teaching we are willing to bet that there is a video hanging on YouTube regarding it. In fact a recent study performed at the University of Minnesota found that 38% of all online video usage was for educational purposes. This doesn't mean online distance learning, it means knowledge about all kinds of topics and issues. All of the videos on YouTube are available to us an instructors. Today's technology has made it easy for us to play and use the videos on YouTube in the classroom. We can bring a video of an expert into the classroom, find videos as examples of whatever we are teaching, inspire students with motivational messages. The choices are all up to us, but as instructors we can't ignore the power that video tools have for enhancing our presentations and the learning environments for our students. We have created some simple steps you can do right now to enhance your classes using those videos.

Instant Guide to
Using More Videos

✓ Open a YouTube.Com. account. They are free. Once you have an account you can even create our your own InstructorTV Channel in your name. It gives you one uniform place that you and your students can go to access these videos.

✓ Identify and locate videos that are important to your students. With an established YouTube account you can save your favorites and organize them into play lists that you can use in class.

✓ Download the FREE software upgrade from Microsoft called "YouTube Add In for Powerpoint." It will install an additional option onto your PowerPoint toolbar that simply says, "Insert YouTube video" That will allow you to play the YouTube videos directly from your PowerPoint when you want to use them in class and you will not need to leave your PowerPoint presentation, open a browser bar and go searching for your videos.

✓ Download the FREE software program called "YouTubeDownloader." This program will allow to save videos from YouTube and download them into the video file on your computer. Remember that PowerPoint is a windows media product so the videos files will need to be an AVI or WMV format in order to insert them into a PowerPoint presentation. The good news is that the YouTube downloader program also allows you convert the files if you need to. It is simple and it is easy to use. The benefit to the instructor is that by downloading the videos onto your computer you can play them in a class free from buffering (the obnoxious interruptions caused while trying to play the videos) because they can be played without any internet connection and without limitation of either the speed of the internet connection or your computer's processing ability.

What Can't You Do With a Simple Camera & YouTube?

We guarantee that once you start using other people's videos from YouTube in the classroom, it won't be very long until you are wondering how to make them yourself. As instructors we are only beginning to leverage the power of videos in education. Making them today is as simple as acquiring a handheld video camera such as The Flip, from Cisco or the Kodak Zi8. Both of them are simple, hold lots of video and retail for less than $150. Microsoft's programs of WindowsLive or Windows Moviemaker are powerful FREE editing tools and if you are a Mac

Video Presentation by renjith krishnan Freedigitalphotos.net

user then iMovie has amazing capabilities.

If you think of the multi-media ability that this provides for us in the classroom there are some fundamental things from previous models of teaching that you probably won't see us doing anymore.

- ✓ We won't just talk to you about what a tax adviser, a mortgage consultant or an appraiser might say on a given issue. We will simply video them and play the short clip in the classroom. Now there is no expert we can't take into the classroom with us.

- ✓ We won't guess what it would be like to try and buy a home for a person with disabilities, we will simply go interview them and intersperse their insights throughout a fair housing course.

- ✓ We won't try to describe what a particular neighborhood, subdivision or area looks like, we will just show you a video of the area.

- ✓ We won't try and describe what goes on during a home inspection, we will just videotape the home inspector walking us through what they do and develop an entire class around those comments and activities.

- ✓ We won't try to describe the various ways that people are marketing and advertising, we will just bring in examples that you can see.

- ✓ We won't just talk our way to inspiration, we will use images and music in the background to make you feel and experience that excitement.

Social Media In the Classroom

In the 1980's and 1990's advertising dominated the television and radio stations from car manufacturers and food vendors with commercials that began "A hundred thousand people can't be wrong." McDonald's had in front of their restaurants for years signs that read "X million people served". The point of this advertising was to convince consumers that if that many people thought it was a good idea, we should embrace it. The number of registered facebook users has surpassed a half a billion people. The number of our students now using social media as their primary communication tool outside of the classroom is staggering. We are ready to adopt the messages of those former advertisers. That many people can't get it wrong. Said differently, as instructors today we cannot ignore the power of social media and the impact it has on teaching and the classroom.

We teach all of the time in both Instructor Development Workshops and to our other clients that social media is a lot less about which button to push than it is about understanding the societal shifts and changes that social media has caused. This is true in the classroom as well. When we analyze the impact that social media and technology has had on the classroom we find that it has affected our students in five distinct ways:.

1. **Accelerated student demands for speed**
2. **Increased student demands for access to technology**
3. **Increased needs to share opinions and ideas**
4. **Heightened willingness to collaborate and share**
5. **Magnified expectations of multi-media**

The accelerated student demands for speed show up in the classroom in strange and unusual ways. We have known for some time now that today's students and consumers want what they want, when they want it and that when is usually now. In today's classroom the dialogue would probably go something like this:

Student #1: "Is there a website where we can find more information on this topic?"

Instructor: "Yes. I will find that for you after class."

Student #2: "Can't we just go there now?"

Social network by jscreationzs
Freedigitalphotos.net

Instructor: "We really don't have time."

Student #3 now shouts over to Student #1: "Here it is. MoreInfo.Com. I just googled it on my phone. What's your email I will shoot you the link."

We know what some of you are thinking. It's all our fault that we lost control of the classroom in the first place. We accept that responsibility as instructors, but understand that the end result of us making a rule at the beginning of the class that the students could not use the technology, only resulted in us delaying the delivery of useful information that the students wanted to get at that point in time. The question from Student #2…"Why can't we just go there right now!" was our real opportunity to teach the students and convey to them information that they wanted. Instead, because the instructor had a preconceived outline of what the instructor wanted to say we ignored what the students wanted to hear. Maybe the real lesson for us in the age of TIVO, jetting past commercial messages and the decline of newspapers and network TV news audiences is that the consumer will find ways to ignore information you think is important in exchange for information that they think is important. Rather than competing with the technology we would be on firmer ground if we simply uncovered ways to bring it into the classroom.

Innovative Use Of Social Media in the Classroom

✓ **LIVE Internet Searches.** There really is no reason we shouldn't be connected to the internet and able to go live to the internet as the needs of the class and the continuing class discussions dictate. If we don't have a good internet connection today in a classroom, we need one. We understand not every area or classroom venue is not set up for internet connections, but every mobile phone provider has an internet connection for your laptop that today are reliable and fast. Saying as an instructor that you can't access the internet sounds a little strange to our students. After all, they are connected with the cell phone in their pocket, but we won't let them take it out and use it. If we are concerned about the students leading us into an area or sites we are unfamiliar with and unprepared to visit, then we should just let our old friend Socrates do the walking. It would probably look like this:

Student: "Is there a good place on the internet where we can go to find additional information."

Instructor: "Probably, how would you find such a site?"

Student: "I would just go to Google."

Instructor: "Let's do that. Now that I am on Google, what would you like me to search for?"

In an instant we are turning a classroom question into a true teachable moment. They are learning not only where to find information, but how to find it. We would argue that in today's world you may be teaching them the most important lesson of the day.

✓ **The LIVE Twitter Feed.** There has long been a teaching tool in the classroom called a "Parking Lot". The parking lot traditionally was an area on the wall where students could stick a post-it note with a question they might have. It was also a place where instructors could create a post-it note for themselves as a reminder when they said in class, "We are going to cover that topic later." The parking lot concept worked well in successive series of classes (such as pre-licensing) when students could post up questions before class, over lunch or even on a break as those questions occurred to them. At the end of the class it was the goal of the instructor to clear the parking lot of all unanswered questions.

Today, we can take a page from the CNN or MSNBC playbook. Part of the reason for the current success of these networks is their ability to reach out and create active dialogue with the audience. Most of the news anchors now are watching live twitter feeds and comments from the audience as they broadcast. They are continually adjusting the broadcast and addressing direct audience input and feedback in real time. There is no reason why the screen in a classroom cannot become our live twitter feed and combine what we have learned from today's broadcast journalists with what we already knew about the traditional "parking lots."

Twitter is an easy tool to use. Just as with most social media sites we can create a free account and with the use of a hash tag set up a back channel for the classroom discussion. We would see student comments and feedback instantly. Who knows we might even find that the quiet shy person in the back of the room who rarely raised their hand and offered little was all of a sudden a major contributor on the twitter feed. It isn't magic. What does it all have to do with GAPE? Well, make students feel comfortable and at ease (some of them today will be more at ease asking their questions on a Twitter feed than they will raising their hand. GAPE implores, answer all student questions fully. It's hard to answer them if we don't know what they are so we should be constantly on the alert to uncover their questions, thoughts and ideas. Social media is a great tool to enable us to do that.

✓ **The Classroom Facebook Page**. By now we believe that all of us as instructors ought to be using facebook. We will make a believer out of you when you talk about course promotion in later chapters. If you don't have a facebook account go create one. They are FREE at facebook.com. Once you have a personal page created on facebook you can create supplemental business pages. The link is on the bottom of the sign in screen at the bottom of the log in page. There is no limit to the number of facebook business pages that you can create. It means that you could create a general page for teaching or you could create a separate page for each class you teach. Understanding how we might use a live twitter feed in class makes the understanding of the facebook page easy. Students would simply be able to add their comments and ask their questions as the class progresses. It's not a supplement for dealing with the live questions, but it is a way for us as instructors to accomplish our objectives using tools and technology that our students are using every day outside the classroom.

✓ **The Concept of Collective Blogging**. Do you remember when we used to make a list on the board and then have the students copy it down? Do you remember when we graduated to being able to write the list on an acetate overhead and then take it to the photocopier and make a copy of the list for the students so they could take the information with them. Today, the power of blogging allows us to do all of that effortlessly and leaves the material in a format that can be utilized in a variety of ways.

Some of us may be thinking, "I don't do blogging." While that may be true we are here to say that all the tools of creating a blog were honed a long time ago and that each of us possess those skills. Just think of a blog as a word document or an article that can be posted to the internet. Just open your blog and type the responses into the blog up on the screen during a collective exercise with the students. At the end of the exercise simply post the blog and show the students how to find it or send them a link after class.

If you don't have a blog you can accomplish the same goal through writing a note on facebook. If you want to start your own blog then the best place to start is WordPress.com. Their site will allow you to create a blog for FREE.

In Act VIII we will look at these tools as a way of engaging students outside the classroom and creating classrooms without walls. More than anything else we hope that this section inspires you to do more with technology in the classroom. Hopefully we have helped to awaken that little creative genius inside of you to start using some tools that have been right there at our fingertips all along.

Curtain Call

"Don't Discount the Low-Tech Approach"

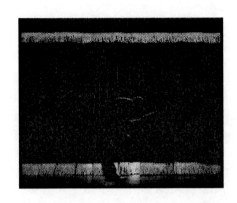

By Cindy Chandler, DREI, CCIM

Cindy Chandler is a member of the North Carolina Real Estate Commission. She specializes in commercial real estate training and consulting. Cindy was the 2006 North Carolina Associtaion of REALTOR® President, the 2003 REALTOR® of the year for the Charlotte Regional Commercial Board of REALTORS® and received the 2003 Presidents Award from the Charlotte Regional REALTOR® Association. A respected trainer and teacher, Cindy is a DREI instructor with REEA. You can rach Cindy at Cindy@CindyChandler.com.

When I started teaching pre-licensing many years ago, I used acetate sheets (transparencies) and an overhead projector. When I learned to make my transparencies on the computer using the original version of PowerPoint, then colored them in with Vis-à-vis markers, I thought I was HOT STUFF! I even had a remote that turned the overhead projector off and on…… (so I would not be walking through the light!)

Then I graduated to a suitcase sized LCD projector and a laptop. I was really rolling then. I'd spend hours on one slide to make sure it was perfect! However, it became apparent that my students weren't as enamored with my works of art as I was. (Well, WHAT did THEY know?) I received pretty good evaluations as an instructor and when graded on "visuals", I got good to excellent scores. I got higher scores in other categories, though. I continued to stew over my PowerPoint presentations, spending far too much time on unimportant details. (We've all done this at some point!)

A few years ago, I was teaching a new REALTOR® Code of Ethics course to a large group of commercial practitioners - "Ethics for the Commercial Agent". We started the class by breaking into groups. Each group was charged with describing an assigned article and coming up with actual examples to illustrate their Article in the practice of commercial real estate. Since commercial folks typically do not embrace group work, my instructions were met with groans, rending of garments and rolling of the eyes. But like good soldiers, they did as asked and … really got into it. The questions this exercise generated blew me away. I got caught up in the number of hands in the air (this is unusual for commercial folks unless you are taking drink orders). Then I was so distracted by all of the relevant questions that I forgot to keep up with my PowerPoint slides. I finally had to turn the projector off. I got outstanding evaluations even though I badly fumbled my slides. Next time I taught this class, I vowed to keep up with my visuals and thought I was doing a smooth job when someone called out – "Hey, that stuff on the screen is distracting. Do we really need it?" I turned the projector off. At the end of the course, no one bolted for the door, instead the questions kept coming. Hmmm….. What's THAT all about?

I worked harder on my slides for the next time. Those slides were really special with sound and animation. Boy, this will knock their sox off, I thought! It didn't. What they wanted in the class was simple …They wanted to know how to do things right. They wanted to know how others might do it and they wanted me to weigh in on their ideas. In other words, "Is this OK?" This was real different from pre-licensing. (In pre-licensing I mostly heard, "Is that on the exam?")

My slides weren't working because they restrained the group from going where it wanted to go. To compare my course to a trip - I created the basic map, a timetable and an arrival destination, but my class wanted to choose the sidetrips, where to eat and how fast to drive. My slides dictated the sidetrips, where to eat and the pace, so I ditched my slides and have never looked back. I use a variety of visuals for other courses, but on the "how to" courses, especially those for my commercial folks, too much tech can smother the thought process because it provides too much structure.

When a class sees there is no projector they realize pretty quickly that there's no sleeping in the car. Everybody has to take their turn driving or reading the map. I tell them that THEY are the visual aids and by golly, they always rise to the occasion and usually exceed my expectations. How cool is THAT? Doing a class like this is tough. The instructor has to be on constant alert, track their time, and make sure they get to certain places by certain times.

Another lesson learned is that sometimes I have to tell folks quickly and in no uncertain terms that what they are saying is not a good idea because it is ILLEGAL. Generally, if I field the question skillfully, someone else in the room will say it first. If not, then I have an obligation to deal with it. I know not to sugarcoat things with my commercial folks because they will lose all respect for me if I do. "Call it as you see it" "Play it as it lies" "It is what it is" "Play the cards you are dealt" are all common mantras.

I make it clear in my classes that I goof up too, and try to respond in a non judgmental way. I just wish I could keep my eyes from rolling up in my head, sometimes….. But hey, they give as good as they get, so we stay even. This is an important part of the culture when dealing with the commercial folks.

Coming to a class is NOT just some social gathering for commercial agents. They will network and joke around, but it is clear that this is a business event, they conduct themselves accordingly and they are always "on". I must exhibit the same behavior to be credible. No silliness, no fluff. No non-relevant side trips. Funny is appreciated if it is clever, relevant and not canned. Disingenuous behavior fails every time. They are not there to be entertained, they want information they can use today and they want the bottom line. ("Don't waste my time!")

I treat everyone with respect, but if anyone is out of line, I have to call them on it. They usually are OK with it and everyone in the class appreciates it. Blowing smoke in class means their time is being wasted, which is unacceptable. Because of this "townhall/case study/open forum" style, returning students come to class ready to ask questions and expecting to be asked questions. I now have a better idea of what they don't know…..because they ask! I get to learn new stuff from them every class. What a gift!

Now, when I write a course or plan to teach one already written by someone else – like the Real Estate Commission – I first decide what I want the take-aways to be. (Learning Objectives) Then I decide on the best method(s) to make that happen. Sometimes it is a full blown PowerPoint presentation, sometimes it is video, sometimes it is low tech as described earlier, sometimes it is a quiz and sometimes it is a combination. People learn in different ways, but everyone sitting in a class has to see *what's in it for them" to be truly engaged.

Curtain Call

"Twitter in the Classroom: What Every Instructor Should Know About Tweets"

By Amy Chorew, National Technology Trainer, Author & Creator of Tech-Bytes

Amy Chorew is a national trainer who is highly experienced at helping managers and agents maximize the opportunities that technology offers. Her work on the e-Pro Course for REBAC earned a "Course of the Year" award from REEA. She also participates in CE, GRI and skill development courses across America and Canada. You may know her as the author and creator of Tech-Bytes or as the author of three social media books. Amy is dedicated to education that is designed to inspire, train and implement. You can reach Amy at Amy Chorew.com

Twitter is a micro-blogging service created to answer the question, "What are you doing?" It is much more than just answering the question. It is a way of establishing relationships which enable us to exchange links, share ideas, expand a topic and interact during class. This is done with 140 character messages and sent to those who "follow you" or to the public with a "Hashtag" (words with # attached) that interested parties can search.

How and why would you use this service in the classroom?

First of all, the ability to interact real time with students makes this tool the new way to answer questions and pass notes in class. We are always expecting our students to share their experiences with us and Twitter can be another tool which helps you facilitate this in the classroom. Those of us who are using it have seen our students looking forward to these short periods of time in which they can "speak, tell, invite, greet, etc."

Twitter in the Classroom

Twitter can replace the class listserv. If you have used groups or listservs (also called a mailing list or discussion list) to extend your discussions beyond the classroom. Students will first of all need to set up an account and choose to follow the Twitter username of their instructor. The instructor can then follow them in return if it is to be used solely for educational purposes.

By putting "d username" and then inputting the (maximium 140 character) message, the details will be sent to the intended recipient instead of being sent so that everyone can see via the public timeline. Depending on the notifications the recipient has set up (instant messaging online, SMS, email) they will be alerted that they have a new message. They can then respond to this in similar fashion.

The best way to learn things like this is through practice - try setting up your own account and sending a message beginning d amychorew. (to me!)   Twitter allows you to create "lists" to see particular sets of people all in one stream. They are very easy to setup.

Hashtags

Use a Hashtag to organize comments, questions and feedback posted by students to Twitter during class. What are Hashtags?

Definition: The # symbol, called a Hashtag, is used to mark keywords or topics in a Tweet. It was created organically by Twitter users as a way to categorize messages. Hashtags help users find interesting tweets. People use the Hashtag symbol # before relevant keywords in their tweet to categorize those tweets to show more easily in a Twitter Search. Clicking on a Hashtagged word in any message shows you all other tweets in that category. Hashtags can occur anywhere in the tweet. Hashtagged words that become very popular are often "Trending Topics."

Students will either post tweets by SMS or via a twitter app on their smartphone or tablet. When possible you can project the live tweet stream in the front of the class for discussion and interaction. You may find students will participate in the discussions more than previously.

Using your Hashtag you can select a time to meet after class on line and continue the discussion. Some call this a "Micro Meet." You can also hold discussions involving all the subscribing students. As long as everyone is following the whole group, no one should miss out on the Twitter stream.

| **Timeline** | @Mentions | Retweets ▾ | Searches ▾ | Lists ▾ |

amychorew Amy Chorew
I am writing an article on using twitter in the classroom and want to demonstrate the use of hashtags #twitterinclassroom

Use a product to manage the ongoing conversation. TweetGrid is a powerful Twitter search dashboard that allows you to search for up to 9 different topics, events, conversations, hashtags, phrases, people, groups, etc. in real-time. As new tweets are created, they are automatically updated in the grid. No need to refresh the page.

Play-By-Play
Ask some of your students to tweet a play-by-play from their smartphones during class. Other members of the class, as well as those following the "Hashtag" and stream will find the Twitter feed and then post their own tweets. The conversations continues even after the event because of connections made.

Pass Notes During Class
Once students warm to the idea that they were encouraged to "chat" during class, they may begin floating ideas or posting links to related materials. In some cases, a shy student may type an observation or question on Twitter, and the instructor could then see the link or comment posted by a student and stop class to discuss it.

Announcements
Twitter can be a place to send links to videos, blog posts, articles about things learned in class. Now everyone can view and share. First, a guide to Twitter shorthand. You will see examples of these in the sample tweets that follow:

- @username: creates a link to that user in your post
- RT:Retweet: to copy some else's post in a new update. Give them credit by adding their @username
- #: hashtag helps to organize your tweets into categories for easier searching
- DM: direct message, send a tweeter a private message instead of an update that all your followers can read

Other Uses for Twitter in the Classroom

- Ask students and other trainers for recommended books, lesson ideas or teaching tools.
  Sample tweet: Can anyone share their successful ideas on buyer agency?
  Sample tweet: What are some good books for setting up teams in real estate? We are considering doing more of this.

- Write a book list one tweet at a time or link to a book list on the web.
  Sample tweet: #resocialmediareads The Long Tail by Chris Anderson
  Sample tweet: #bizbooks updated list of re business books. Thanks for all your rec's.

- Tweet about a useful web resource, a particular blog post, video, website book or porduct or service that students would find useful.
  Sample tweet: Great blog find tips for integrating technology into the classroom. www.iLearntechnology.com

- Provid a daily tip like a word of the day, book of the day, random trivia, useful fact or helpful resource.
  Sample tweet: If you are looking for twitterapps, try: http://oneforty.com/i/toolkits

- Celebrate timely events. Recocognize famous birthdays, and other events happening in your community.
  Sample tweet: September 28 - Apple Harvest Begins! http://Southnews.com/apple

- Tweet about your schools website, blog or podcast. Add a new tweet to let your followers know when you make updates.
  Sample tweet: A link to our Fall CE and skill training is now available http://bit.ly/14DHwX

- Invite followers to an event (online or offline). Events can include programs, events at local boards, extracurricular activities, meetings, your online book club, webchat, etc.
  Sample tweet: ePro® to be held at local board. Be one of the first to sign up and receive SocMed books http://bit.ly/eproclass

There are always great apps to make your twitter experience easier. Visit oneforty.com/i/toolkits for all sorts of apps. Here are a few to get you started:

Use a social media platform to read your tweets. Try www.Hootsuite.com. You can use Hootsuite for free for three streams which can include multiple twitter accounts and facebook. You can monitor and post to multiple social networks, including Facebook and Twitter using the Hootsuite dashboard. You can follow Hashtag streams very easily as well as monitor specific people and their tweets.

www.wuoteurl.com helps you group different Twitter updates from different people into a single page that has a permanent URL. So you can put it on your blog or sent interesting conversations to friends.

www.tweetree.com puts your Twitter stream in a tree so you can see the posts people are replying to in contet. It also pulls in lots of external content like twitpic photos, youtubevideos and more, so that you can see them right in your stream without having to click through every link your friends post.

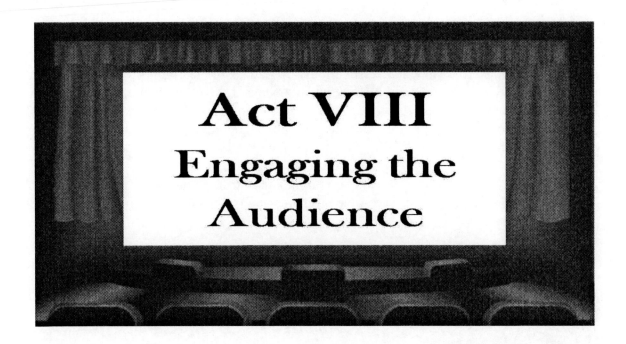

Understanding Engagement & Interaction

Students seek to be engaged. We do not have to look much further than GAPE to understand how important the relationship is between instructor and student. Look at how many of the GAPE principles focus on the connection between the presenter and the audience:

- Answer all questions logically and concisely
- Present new ideas by relating them to pre-existing knowledge
- Teach at the learner's level
- Show in a specific way how new material will benefit learners
- Encourage questions and motivate involvement
- Call learners by name
- Involve learners in the learning process through planned activities
- Teach to all participants, not just to those who show interest
- Speak loudly enough to be heard by all
- Restate an individual learner's question to the group as a whole prior to attempting to answer the question
- Refrain from ridiculing either the learners or others
- Use physical movement during the presentation to minimize the physical distance between the instructor and learners and try to involve all learners equally
- Build learners self esteem and thank them for their questions

Our interaction with learners is judged and based on some basic things that we can all do to make the students feel like they are part of the learning process. It is also based on how we respond to and interact with students in the classroom. Certainly, all of the things that we have discussed earlier have an impact on student involvement and interaction, from the structure of the course itself to the environment that is set up in which the students learn.

Rudyard Kipling used a set of questions to help trigger ideas and solve problems and immortalized them in the poem:

I have six honest serving men
They taught me all I knew
I call them What and Where and When
And How and Why and Who

These questions can be used in a classroom setting as stimuli to get thinking and discussion going in many situations. The simple approach is to take one of the questions, either at random or with a more particular purpose in mind and ask it of the situation. You will find that having these questions at your fingertips will allow you to create interaction in any classroom setting. You will also find that the extended use of these questions can draw the students in further and accelerate the level of discussion.

For example, if we were teaching a class on professional standards a student might say, "I don't think a lot of people in government or big business adhere to high professional standards." Rather than allow the classroom discussion to take this negative turn we can use this comment as a springboard to encourage more classroom interaction and discussion and create from the statement a teachable moment. It is matter of applying Kipling's short poem. How much do you think the learning environment surrounding that statement would change into a more engaging one if we were to reply:

What would be a good example of this lack of standards?

Where do these lapses occur in business and government?

When do you think we should voice our opinion or comment on such activities?

How do you think these situations impact the business world?

Why should we care what someone else does?

Who do you think ought to be creating and enforcing such standards?

Over the years we have learned a few principles that will increase your connectivity to the students and help you break down the traditional barriers between instructor and student. In our coaching, training and development of instructors we have found that if you really want to increase your course evaluations it has more to with attention to audience engagement and connectivity than it does with your polished presentation as a speaker. (Wow! Imagine that…pay more attention to your audience than yourself). So we have come up with some simple things that you can do right now that will change your teaching and instruction forever.

Ten Audience Connectivity Tools You Can Use Right Now

- ✔ **Call The Learners By Name**. We know of nothing more powerful than using students names. It is one of the items we discussed in classroom set up regarding the use of placards. There are times in more keynote type presentations when we don't have the opportunity to have student name tags or placards. In those situations we simply ask for the student's name when they pose the question, and give them permission to ask it by saying, "Joe, what is your question?"

- ✔ **Repeat the Question**. It is amazing how often other students in the class do not hear the question that is asked. Get in the habit of responding to every question by repeating it or restating it. Sometimes we have to add clarity to the question in the presentation. It's easy to do by simply starting out with, "Okay, Joe wants to know..."

✓ **Thank The Learner for the Question**. Always thank the learner for the question. It helps build the student's self esteem and encourages others to participate. The problem with implementation of this process in the classroom is that done incorrectly it can get repetitive and insincere, so vary your responses. There are a multitude of ways to recognize the importance of a student's input than simply saying, "Thank you for the question." Here are some of the responses we have heard used effectively:

- I appreciate you asking that…
- That's a great point…
- Wow! You were paying attention…
- That question is important because it helps us understand…
- What an excellent question…
- You have asked a very insightful question..
- You're making an important contribution to this class…

✓ **Applaud the Learner**. We use this approach often. We think that it recognizes the importance of the student and thanks them for the question. It works simply by saying to the rest of the class, "Let's give Joe a round of applause for that." The reason that we like this approach is because it also leverages neurolinguistic programming and begins conditioning the audience to applaud as we discussed earlier.

✓ **Gather Collaboration**. As instructors we are not expected to know everything. You will build a lot more interaction and engagement if you simply admit that in the classroom. Often when a student asks a particular question, rather than answer it we will let the students respond. The easiest transition to do this is when a student asks, "So what do you think about…" It is then that we see the opportunity to engage other students in the discussion and instead of answering the question we simply ask the class what they think.

✓ **Don't Denigrate Anybody or Anything**. Most presenters we would hope are far past ever calling a student "stupid" or labeling a particular question as a stupid one, but the denigration we often see in a classroom happens with much more subtlety. When we respond with phrases such as "I thought you would know that…" or "Isn't it obvious that…..." or "Most other people know…" we are denigrating the student and the question as much as if we had simply said, "That's a stupid thing to ask." It also happens when we make derogatory references that we think are to things outside the classroom, but are actually

186

within it. Saying to a group of real estate students that "Most real estate professionals are lazy…" or that "The problem with most business people is…" damages our ability to teach and destroys our ability to involve the interactivity of the students. Aren't they real estate professionals? Aren't they business people? Even if the students can't directly relate the comment to them, derogatory comments about anything leave students wondering "What will this instructor say about me?" Because GAPE addresses the need of adult students to feel safe in a learning environment we will find ourselves challenged in trying to involve the group who may already fear what we might say.

✓ **Develop a "We" Mindset**. The "We" mindset can also carry you a long way in the classroom. Try replacing every single "I" with "We" and try replacing every single "You" with "Us". Such language has a much more inclusive sound. It reinforces that we are all in this thing called teaching together. Using such language and making that subtle shift will change the way that we are perceived by students. Let's presume that we are talking about a contract and some change that needs to be made in the way we handle the agreement. Can you feel the different impact between the following two responses:

- What I think you should do is…
- What would benefit us as a profession is if we….

✓ **Admit Your Shortcomings & Struggles**. Only we expect ourselves to be perfect. Your students don't seek perfection; they seek honesty, candidness and sincerity. It's okay to admit you don't know. It's even better to say, "I don't know, but I know where we can find out." We get asked all of the time to address situations we haven't thought about or to explain things beyond our experience. Admit it. Don't forget that there is a lot of experience in the classroom. How would they answer the question?

✓ **Stress Their Expertise, Not Yours**. In the opening chapters of this book we referenced a statement by Frank McCourt that said, "They thought I was teaching. I thought I was teaching. I was learning." Excellent instructors often say that they learned more in the class than their students did. Think about that for a moment. That process cannot happen without engaging and interacting with the audience. We should leverage that every chance we get. Not only we do start out a lot of classes recognizing that some members of the class may know more than we do about particular topics, but we also invite them to bring that expertise into the classroom and share it. Here is short script we sometimes use at the beginning of class to set a more collaborative and sharing tone.

> *Okay, how many of you have been in business for more than 5 years? More than ten? More than 20? Great. Then let's just admit there is a lot more experience on that side of the classroom than there is on this side. This is your class and you can all learn as much from each other as you can from anything we have to say, so we hope you will contribute and share based on your experience so that we can raise the value of the class for everyone.*

✓ **Practice Breathing**. We witnessed a great presentation one day by Andrew Wooten. Andrew does a lot of classes across the country on personal safety and security issues. In addressing self-defense, Andrew made the point that we simply forget to breathe. A victim getting attacked tends to draw in a deep breath and then hold it. With that action they lose the physical power and concentration to respond. Andrew's message, "Breathe. Then act." Classrooms might be perfectly normal and routine places for you to be. They are not normal and routine places for our student to be. Some days you can cut the tension with a knife. In a tense atmosphere there is no contribution, sharing or collaboration. Stop. Ask everyone to just take a deep breath. In fact it's so important we sometimes start class with the deep breath exercise. It relaxes people. It puts them at ease. If they are relaxed and at ease you will find it easier to solicit their responses and contributions.

Dealing With Common Classroom Situations

If we teach for any period of time we are likely to encounter a number of recurring issues in the classroom that if not handled properly will impede our ability to engage the students with collaborative contribution. Gerald Amada, holds a Ph.D. in social and clinical psychology at the Wright Institute in Berkeley, California. He has published eleven books and over 100 articles and reviews on the subjects of mental health, psychotherapy and disruptive students. Two of his leading works, *"Coping With the Disruptive College Student: A Practical Guide Model* and *Coping with Misconduct in the College Classroom* are both worth reading.

Recognizing disruptive behavior and knowing how best to deal with the situation are important to our success as instructors. All of the following are common classroom situations that we should be alert to and have fundamental strategies to diffuse their impact in the classroom when they occur.

Six Common
Classroom Situations &
How to Deal With Them

✓ **The Smart Aleck**. We recognize them. They are the ones who interject smart aleck comments to just about every other sentence the instructor utters. Often times it is more disruptive because the comments are not heard by everyone and half of the class is left wondering what was said. The rest are chuckling and whispering. This person usually does not make comments that are very helpful or educational to the class, they are just seeking to create attention and their behavior often challenges the authority of the instructor. Just don't confuse a spontaneous student response that is non-disruptive with this type of behavior. If students are responding spontaneously and their responses are appropriate, encourage more of them. You are succeeding in encouraging engagement. It's not always pretty, but it does mean that the students are motivated and engaged in what you are teaching.

Best Approach: Suggested approaches involve reminding the class that because it's better if you involve everyone they should simply raise their hand when they would like to add to the discussion. Because most of the smart aleck comments really are not helpful or educational to the class, this approach usually ends this type of conduct. Another tactic is to simply pretend that you didn't hear the comment and then say to the student, "I am sorry, I didn't hear that. Would you please repeat your question?" We prefer the first approach because we believe it is less demeaning and confrontational, but if the conduct continues the second approach may be necessary.

Worst Approach: The worst approach usually involves the instructor asking the student not to interrupt or please hold their comments. It has a chilling effect which will dampen and lessen the input from other students. Because the motivation of the smart aleck student was to gain attention, we are probably reinforcing more of the same conduct.

✓ **The Know It All Challenger**. This role belongs to the student who feels it is necessary to contradict or challenge whatever the instructor is presenting. Sometimes it is a flagrant confrontation and sometimes it is a debate about the accuracy or position that the instructor is professing. It's one of the reasons why GAPE advises us to clearly delineate between factual matters and the opinions offered by the instructor. Clearly delineating the difference between these two types of information will create better options for the instructor when such challenges arise.

Best Approach: Use the opportunity as a teaching engagement moment and explore in more depth what the student is really saying. Asking them why they believe in their position or what causes them to take a different viewpoint is a

Business Man with Boxing Gloves by Ambro
Freedigitalphotos.net

good start. If the student truly does have better or more current factual information, accept it. Tell them that you always appreciate additional information and that you are looking forward to doing some additional research on the subject. When the confrontation focuses on two different viewpoints acknowledge that different viewpoints are a good thing. Tell the student you understand that they believe differently about the issue than you do and comment that it is always good to respect other people's opinions that may be different. It all adds to education you know. If all else fails we can always engage the rest of the class and use them as our allies to facilitate the discussion by simply asking them what they think.

Worst Approach: We know when we have taken the worst approach because we end up in a confrontation head-butting contest with the student. Just remember this: the instructor loses all battles between who is right and who is wrong the moment the battle begins. Some students have pre-existing ideas or philosophies. We would all do better to remember that in the classroom we are not evangelical zealots trying to win the student over to our side. It was never our job to convince a student of anything. The foremost job of the instructor is to present information in an accurate and engaging way and provide students with information so that they can form their own conclusions and decisions about what to do with the material that is presented.

✓ **The Whisperer**. Some students just have soft voices. They are hard to hear, sometimes shy and when they sit near the front of the room and speak softly, no one can hear them. As instructors it is really easy to get engaged in one on one conversations with the people in the front of the room and immediately sever the rest of the class from what has now become a private conversation.

Best Approach: Always repeat the question. When this first occurs try to enlist the support of the other students. When we think a student has spoken so softly that the rest of the students did not hear we will ask the other students if they heard the question. When we do this we hope the student who spoke softly will get the message that they didn't speak loudly enough. When a student begins speaking softly we will sometimes just back slowly away from the student. You will often notice that the further you back away from them the louder they will speak. You might also try the approach of pretending that you didn't hear the question and ask the student to repeat it.

Worst Approach: Things start to go downhill really fast if you ever ask a student to repeat their comment more than once. We can literally feel the anxiety and impatience rising in the room. Remember every student deserves your respect if for no other reason than the fact that they chose to walk into your classroom. "I'm sorry, could you please repeat the question, I didn't hear you," is always preferable to "Ask it again." We should all realize that the first response lets the student know that we are engaged and that we care. The second response leaves them wondering whether we were ever listening in the first place.

✓**The Late & the Tardy**. Interruptions once class has begun are disruptive to other students and in instances where adult education credit hours are being given we are sometimes limited as the instructor as to whether students can even be admitted to class late. All kinds of situations can make students late for a class, so we might as well have some strategies to deal with the issue because it is a

Nine O'Clock by graur razvan ionut
Freedigitalphotos.net

191

circumstance we know will happen at some point.

Best Approach: The best approach is to make certain that the ground rules were clearly communicated prior to the class in promotional and registration material. Where administrative and regulatory agencies have strict rules we have seen instructors close the door at the start of class and post a sign on the outside door that says, "Per administrative or department rules no admittance or credit for this class after _____." They put the time in the notice on the door.

Worst Approach: Don't let the late arriving student be a distraction. We have seen instructors ridicule, comment or point out a late arriving student. We believe that approach goes against everything GAPE advocates. We have even watched instructors stop class and say to the student, "You know you're not getting credit for this." Everyone would have been better off had we just let the student take their seat and then addressed the issue with the student personally at break.

✓ **The Disconnected**. You may have given them another name. Donald Levi in *How To Teach Adults* called them the "Recently Relocated". We don't know if a professional licensing course has ever been taught without at least one of them in the audience. They used to live in another state, area or country and would like to offer their view of how things were done there or they question why things are different in a new location.

Best Approach: Thank them for their input initially and then explain that different areas and different states have different laws and standards of practice. Let them know that sometimes understanding contrasting different approaches is helpful and now that they have let you know they have that expertise you will let turn to them when such a contrast would be helpful. If the information from other areas continues, we have turned to students and said, "Sometimes there are students who want to know about other areas. How many of you are planning on moving to…." Because the answer is not very many of the students, we will then simply ask the student if they mind if we concentrate on the things that will be important to most students.

Worst Approach: We have heard instructors openly say," Let's not discuss that, it will just confuse the other students." We don't know how you would perceive that comment, but to us it sounds condescending and demeaning to the other students. We might as well just have said, "These other students aren't smart enough to keep the information straight." If you feel you need to eventually take that kind of approach with the student then do it quietly and outside the hearing of the rest of the audience.

The Non-Participatory Class

Sleeping Young
Businesswoman by Ambro Freedigitalphotos.net

We have all been here as instructors. We walk into a room and begin a class. We are upbeat and excited and shortly into the class we are wondering if we are teaching in a cemetery. No feedback. No responses. When questions are asked no one will answer. It is a frightening moment for any instructor as we try to figure out what is going on and get the group engaged. Certainly the use of some of the devices we talked about in previous chapters such as playing music before class, talking to the students before class and using great beginnings and openings help minimize the risk, but at some point we are going to have to confront this issue. Having some quick and ready tools in your arsenal helps. What we know doesn't help is yelling at the students, telling them to get excited or asking them why they are so dead. Asking such questions highlights the obvious and places the instructor in an even more precarious situation especially when those additional questions and comments also fail to generate a response. We have developed a couple of tactics we use to get a group to engage in the class.

1. **Ask the students what they would like to talk about**. Even if it takes you off topic for a few minutes, it does get the group engaged. We have known to even ask such questions as "What did you do over the weekend?" "What's the best movie currently playing?" "What's the best book someone has read."

2. **Always have a "hot topic" in your head.** Controversy draws commentary. For each class there is probably some controversial issue that would get the group talking. Let's say for example that we were teaching a class on lending that started out more slowly than we would like in terms of student participation. We might ask, " Do you think appraisers are getting the values of the homes correct?" "Do you think that automated valuation systems like Zillow are accurate?" Anything to get them talking and the more controversial the subject, the more willing students are to get involved.

3. **Jump to a group activity.** We should always be equipped to do a group activity at the beginning of any class we teach. A group activity will force the students to interact with each other and from that platform we can foster interaction with the instructor and the rest of the students by simply gathering feedback from the group exercise.

Making Group Play Effective

We have to tell you that we originally titled this section "Making Group Exercises Work." (That just struck as something we didn't want to do.) Guess that would have been the traditional approach. We're not big fans of the words "exercise" or "work" when it comes to classroom activities. Remember we are the ones who keep saying that classes should be fun and exciting and we just can't get into that mindset by telling the students that they have to do the following "exercise" or that it's time to do some "work." Earlier we mentioned that student learn best by doing. Students who work in collaborative groups also appear more satisfied with their classes. Beckman, 1990; Chickering and Gamson, 1991; Collier, 1980; Cooper and Associates, 1990; Goodsell, Maher, Tinto, and Associates, 1992; Johnson and Johnson, 1989; Johnson, Johnson, and Smith, 1991; Kohn, 1986; McKeachie, Pintrich, Lin, and Smith, 1986; Slavin, 1980, 1983; Whitman, 1988).

Boy Playing With Blocks by iStock Freedigitalphotos.net

Group activity can be extremely successful or a miserable waste of time depending on the skills and ability of the instructor to leverage and conduct the group activity. Most of the time, the failure of a group activity occurs because it was poorly orchestrated or not set up properly. Here are some things to keep in mind in setting up group activities:

1. Plan Out How the Groups Will Be Formed

In general, groups of four or five work best. Groups larger than that tend to let certain students hide in the anonymity of the group activity. While some instructors simply allow people to form groups according to their own desires, we believe that the activities are stronger when groups are randomly formed. The advantages are two-fold. The groups tend to stay more on task when they are not self-selected and it also serves to enhance the networking function of groups.

The easiest way to get people into groups is to simply have people count off. Put the 1-5's together, put the 6-10's together, the 11-15's together and so forth. Here are a few other ways to get people into groups quickly and easily. For ease of understanding in all of the methods shown below we are forming groups of four.

- **Candy Favors.** Get four different kinds of candy and hand them out to students as they enter or already have them randomly on the desks. Tell students they have to form groups that include each of the four different types of candy.

- **Playing Cards.** Arrange a stack of playing cards with all the aces together, the kings, the queens, the jacks and so forth. As students enter the room hand each of them a playing card. At the time of the group exercise the jacks simply need to pair up, the kings, the queens and so forth.

- **Grouping Cards or Name Tags**. Use four different colors and simply stick a colored dot on the index card, the student materials or the name tags. When it comes time to break into groups simply tell the students they need one of each color in their group.

There are lots of creative ways to form groups, the important part is that the instructor give some thought to the method before-hand so that in the classroom the formation of the groups can be fast and efficient.

2. Clarify the Rules and Goals of the Group Activity

A lot of time and energy can get wasted when students do not clearly understand the objectives and the purpose of the group activity. Keep the concept simple and short. The clarity or lack thereof in our group activities is critical. If the task is kept short, concise and pointed it will be more successful. We have found it helpful to put the rules, objective and goals into writing and provide it to the students either in the student course materials, on cards or on a sheet that is handed out separately.

We told them to get into groups and make a list of the important elements of success. There goes ten minutes as they are trying to figure out what group they want to be in, where they are going to gather and how big their group is going to be. It's simply ten minutes of class time we could have used more effectively if we had planned it out like professional presenters. We thought the instruction was simple, "Make a list…" However, as soon as they got into groups the questions began:

"Are we supposed to make one list or is each of us going to make a list?"

"How long is our list supposed to be?"

"Are we supposed to write our list down?"

"What if some of us don't agree, does it still go on the list?"

"Are the lists supposed to be one word or a list of sentences?"

At this point we are thinking, "Geez, people, we just wanted you to make a list." We thought it was a simple instruction. They didn't. In hindsight we should have said, "Each group should make one written list of single words that the entire group agrees are important to success." Clarity in the formation and the task of the group is harder than we think. That's why it's easier to give them written instructions and the precise format of the response you expect them to produce.

In fact the separate instruction sheet can be designed to capture the work of the students during the group exercise. Consider creating a focus worksheet to facilitate what you want from the group.

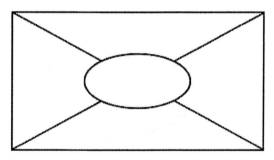

Here is a good example used for a group of four. We like this approach because it requires involvement and input from all of the group members and then captures the overall result of the group. The instructions below go with the diagram drawn to the left.

1. Have each group member determine one item that they would like to learn from this class.
2. Write each of the four group member's responses in the spaces on the outside of the diagram.
3. Debate which one of the four concepts is most important and write that one in the center.

We could have just as easily had the students write down four elements of a contract, four provisions of the Code of Ethics or four things that every salesperson should know and had them put the most important one in the center. The diagram will assist the students in discussion after the activity and the instructor has fertile ground to

196

explore in asking them what they discussed and how they determined the refinement down to the most important idea.

Some instructors make excellent use of a group reporting tool referred to as a PMI card. A PMI card simply has each group participant complete a card that shows:

P – Pluses – What they like about what was said in the group
M – Minuses – What they didn't like about what was said in the group
I – Intriguing – What they thought was most interesting.

Here is what a sample PMI card might look like:

What I liked *Pluses (+)*	
What I didn't like *Minuses (-)*	
What I thought was intriguing *Questions or thoughts*	

3. Create Groups That Require Interdependence

One of the important aspects of group actvities is that they need to be structured to involve everyone in the group. They should feel that each member is responsible and that they all need to contribute to the group activity. That is why we like the above group tools so much because they force every member of the group to take some role in participation.

Another way of facilitating the inclusive nature of the group is to assign roles. In the teaching of real estate for example if we were going to say "Get into a group and discuss how you get clients to hire you." We could improve the activity by saying, "In your groups of four, all of the 1's are going to play the role of a homeowner. All of the 2's are going to play the role of a listing agent. All of the 3's are going to take notes of what is said in the group and all of the 4's are going to report on the group activity. The task within the group would be for the listing agent to give the homeowner their best reason why they should hire a real estate professional.

4. Always Create "Take-Aways" From the Group Activity

We believe that if you are going to do a group activity then the instructor ought to allocate time to be able to debrief the groups, create more student interaction following the group activity, summarize the results or points regarding the activity and give the students some meaningful information to take away from the activity. We have seen instructors break an audience into groups, have them engage in an activity and at the end of the activity return to teaching as if the group portion had never occurred. We think that such a process diminishes the power of the activity and fails to leverage all of the teachable moments that could have occurred.

Team Leader by jscreationszs
Freedigitalphotos.net

Some Cool Ways
to Utilize Groups

We hope that you are realizing that groups can be powerful teaching tools and that they engage and activate the audience. Here are some different and unique ways to structure and form group activities.

- ✓ **Best & Brightest.** Have the student groups identify and highlight their best and brightest ideas. The focus worksheet we discussed earlier works well for this type of group activity. It could built around the best study tip, the best marketing idea, the best customer service ideas or any such issue.

- ✓ **Judge & Jury.** Give each group a fact pattern and have them act as the judge and jury in determining what result they would reach. This type of activity works well for legal issue or compliance classes.

- ✓ **Solve the Problem.** Give each group a problem to solve and have them come up with the best solution. This works well in any kind of class that is built around problem solving and can be used to bring in math and science issues as well.

✓ **Be The Manager.** Provide the students with a business issue and have them act as the advisory or management committee appointed to solve the problem of the employee. The primary goal will be to have them issue a recommendation as to how to approach a given situation.

✓ **List It.** This type of approach works best when trying to get groups to brainstorm a particular list of topics. The instructions might require each group to list all of the reasons that they can think of why someone would sell their home, or list all of the ways in which you can market a particular property or product. In classes where instructors are trying to get students to network they are asked to simply list all of the possible entities and types of people that they would want to have in their business database.

The Power of Roundtables and Panels

We have said it multiple times throughout this book. You don't have to be an expert on every subject. However, as a professional presenter you should be able to moderate any subject. That is the powerful application of roundtables and panels. Students want to know that they are listening to experts on any particular topic. We know some very successful instructors who have utilized panel discussions and such classes can generate powerful interest and attendance.

In the real estate industry it makes sense to create panels of experts on subjects such as contracts, short sales and lending. The list is really endless. It is an easy way to bring a high level of expertise into the classroom and lower the preparation and research that might otherwise be needed on some technical and complex topics.

The success of roundtables and panels is directly proportionate to the organizing skill and moderator skill of the presenter. So here are a few things to keep in mind when conducting roundtables and panel discussions:

- Make certain to confirm, re-confirm and then confirm one more time the location, time and expectations of the panel members

- Consider putting their lengthy bios into the course material and while we believe that they should all be introduced at the beginning of the class, you can save a lot of time by simply putting the detailed backgrounds into the hands of the students rather than in rambling expositions by the panel members which takes up valuable class time

- Find out who's attending as audience members early on and solicit questions from them that can be used during the class. That way you will generate pre-class excitement and you also will assure that you are addressing issues that are important to the audience

- Guard against monopolization. It can occur from both a single audience member or someone on the panel. Make certain to spread the dialogue around

- Consider dual microphones. The panel members will need one and there will need to be one available for the audience members as well. This is going to be a highly interactive session, but only if people can hear and participate in the discussions that are occurring

The Art of Role Playing & Utilizing Case Studies

Somewhere along the line role playing got a bad rap. Want to make certain no one shows up for your class, promote it as one which utilizes role playing. Want to make certain that students don't sit in a certain section of the classroom, just place placards there that say "Reserved for Role Playing Section". We find this sort of sad. Role playing can be a very effective way to learn and the only explanation that we have for students' aversion to the name is that they are afraid that they will have to participate. Remember the number one fear of people is public speaking. (Thanks, Jerry Seinfeld, we'll never forget that they would rather be in the casket than delivering the eulogy).

Nonetheless we think role playing is often construed in much too narrow of a light. We role play all of the time. It just might not look like what you first expected. Sometimes the role playing is just with one or two students, other times it is just with us. We think of role playing as not much different from acting. It can be a great way to bring more excitement, realism and practicality into the classroom. By the way, when we are employing this concept we never ask a student if they want to role play, instead we simply ask, "Can we play for a moment," or "Want to play?"

We use it particularly when students ask how we would say something to someone else. It's easier to see in an actual context, so let's presume a student asks in class how we would explain the Code of Ethics to a client. We would use the student in a role play. We would simply act out the role of the agent and have the student pretend that they were a seller or buyer. We also use it when we are talking about things like the offer and acceptance of a contract. It's difficult sometimes for students to hold multiple parties in their heads as to who is who. So, we would pick one student in the class and ask them if they would mind playing the seller. We would begin the role play by saying "How much do you want to list your house for?" Then we would choose another student and say, "Would you mind playing the buyer. How much would you be willing to offer Joe?"

If you do this be attentive to everything you already know. Get some papers in your hand and use them as a prop (the contract) to carry back and forth between the two students. Pay attention to using the students' names. Pause occasionally and ask the rest of the class what you should do next, that will foster interaction.

We strongly encourage you to turn what traditionally would have been straight lecture material into this highly interactive and an engaging type of theater. We promise you that your students will remember it better, will enjoy it more and will thank you for elevating the level of the presentation. The reason that it will be so well received is because you have turned the entire process into a game. That leads us to a whole other way to increase student interaction and engagement in the classroom.

Order in the Court

One of the best and most well liked (notice how we realize those are two different concepts) courses that we ever taught was a mock trial. We created a fact scenario based on the procuring cause of a real estate client and a subsequent arbitration that occurred because someone else claimed it was their client first. We had fun with the fact pattern. It was a funny fact pattern to read and it's all that the students had when we started class. As select students came in the door we handed them was looked like a subpoena and we asked them if they would help us in class by memorizing a few key facts we wrote inside the subpoena.

At the beginning of class we explained that those holding the subpoena were witnesses and that the rest of the class would act as the arbitration panel. Then we conducted the class as if it were an actual arbitration, calling each of the witnesses to the stand and asking them questions. It was easy for them. Their answers were inside the subpoena.

After each witness, we would engage in a discussion with the class about the testimony. We asked them what are the key issues, what else would they like to know and who they thought was winning. At the end of the class the students voted on who they thought won the arbitration and they had to defend their position as to why. It was a great way to liven up a class on the Code of Ethics and the students went away with a much better understanding of the concepts than we ever could have conveyed through a straight lecture. What's more important is that they had fun along the way.

The Games People Play

Domino Pyramid by posterize
Freedigitalphotos.net

Games have enormous power in the classroom and we have seen them utilized in a variety of ways. Games can simply be ice breakers for a keynote or feature presentation. They get can be utilized as a bonding exercise to get students to know each other better. They can also be used to interactively involve all of the students in a review course or a test preparation scenario. One thing is certain. If the game is well designed, well orchestrated and lively, it is rare that the students don't participate. If we tried to make a list here of all of the games that presenters have utilized you would be reading for the next couple of days on this topic alone. So our point here is to simply try to get your creative juices flowing and try a few new things that you may not have explored fully with your audiences.

Let's start with the ice-breakers. Ice-breakers usually are not content driven. That's simply not their purpose. Their purpose is to get the audience involved and interacting as soon as possible. Their secondary purpose is to get the audience to know each other better. Did you ever go to class and have the instructor go around the room and have each student introduce themselves and provide some information about themselves. If the group was any larger than 15-20 people you might not remember it, because shortly after the process started you lapsed into a coma. So did everyone else.

Want to give it a different twist? Then here are a few ice-breaker, get to know you games that can help bond students. Can you imagine using any of these at the start or in the middle of a pre-licensing course or a keynote presentation:

✓ **SuperPowers.** Say a few words about how great it would be to have superpowers and then go around the room and ask students if they could be any superhero who would it be and what superpowers would they like to possess.

202

✔ **The Lottery.** Everyone thinks that winning the lottery would solve all of their problems, so if you won…what exactly would you do and where would you live?

✔ **The Fortune Cookie.** Give the audience a chance to write their own fortune cookie. You will be amazed at how much you will learn about them. You will know instantly who the comedians are, who the serious people are and which ones have a flair for the dramatic, the practical and the creative.

✔ **Beach Ball Buzz.** Take a plastic beach ball and in each of the different colored sections write a question. Toss the ball to a student and tell them they have to read and answer one of the questions on the ball. Then they get to toss it to another student who must do the same. If you are a pre-licensing instructor, then write different topics on the ball, such as contracts, agency, legal issues, deeds and transfers, when a student catches the ball they pick a category and you get to ask them a question in that category. It's just a way of providing a little more fun and excitement into a typical question and answer review session.

✔ **A Few of My Favorite Things.** Have each student simply state their name and say two or three of their favorite things. The students will get to know each other better and you'll get to know them better as well. Some of these are great things to do throughout a pre-licensing course. It will add to the bond between you and the students and it will cause the entire group to be more interactive.

✔ **Who Am I?** We particularly like this game in any class where the instructor is trying to get the students to network, such as a professional development or designation class. The instructor makes up names of recognized characters; they can be movie stars, cartoon figures, prominent political or social figures, alive or dead. The names are written on name tags and stuck on the backs of the students. Their job is to figure out who they are by interacting with other students. They can only ask questions which provoke a yes or no response. By the way, asking "Who Am I?" is not a yes or no question.

Games can also be used to convey content, particularly in a review session or a test preparation type class. In fact, we think that is the most underutilized of all of the venues for classroom games. Think about playing scrabble with acronyms, jeopardy with definitions and bingo with correct responses.

One of the best games we have seen lately was so intriguing because it sought to develop skill levels. It was called *The Dating Game*. The instructor chooses three students and has them sit on stools in the front of the room. He called these students the bachelors. Then he took a 4th student and let her be the bachelorette on the opposite side of the room. The bachelorette was asked to pretend she was a seller and that the bachelor agents were trying to get her listing. She got to ask them whatever questions she wanted and at the end had to choose which one of them she would date. Among the questions the bachelorette asked were:

- Bachelor #1 – Would you reduce your commission?
- Bachelor #2 – What's so different about you and why should I hire you?
- Bachelor #3 – Tell me what type of marketing you will do for me?

In today's teaching world there are lots of games you can buy for specific use in the classroom and they allow you to customize the questions that are contained within the game. Jeopardy makes a version for the classroom you can display through your computer on the classroom screen. Another great product is Game Show Presenter. Just google "Games for the Classroom" and you will find more games than you could use in a lifetime.

Interactive Student Polling

The ability to have students interact with technology today in the classroom has created many options. The advent of SRS (Student Response Systems) allows students with a handheld clicker to remotely interact with the material on the screen. Obviously the larger drawback to these systems is the initial investment in the student hardware of the clicker devices. There are several systems on the market and as instructors we should be investigating these types of systems to determine which one will work best given the circumstances and venues in which we teach.

There are two options which will allow us to bring interactive polling to the classroom without purchasing any additional hardware or equipment. Microsoft has launched an additional add-in for PowerPoint called "Interactive Classroom". It allows students to take polls and otherwise interact with PowerPoint so long as they have a program called One Note on their computer. One Note is a computer program for free form information gathering and multi-user collaboration. It can gather an instructor's notes (handwritten or typed) and share them with students over the internet.

Another option is an internet site called, PollEverywhere.Com. It is a FREE program that allows the students to participate in a live classroom poll and displays the results on screen. You can create all forms of questions and the students simply text their choice of answers using their cell. The results are displayed in real time on the screen. The big advantage is that you don't have to buy any additional hardware or software. All the students need to participate in the interactive "on screen" poll is their cell phone.

Creating a Classroom Without Walls

We think that one of the most exciting things about today's technology is that with a little creativity you can engage and involve your students in the learning process  like never before. It means that the classroom discussions no longer have to start and end at the classroom door. When we teach business professionals we have been telling them that their clients and consumers today expect service and information 24/7. The same is true for our students. How many of us would have liked the opportunity to chat with, prep or talk with our students before they walked in the room? How many times has something come up in class that was a great opportunity for discussion, but the class time was too limited to go into that topic with much detail? How many of us would benefit from a preclass survey to find out what our students want to know before they walk in the door? How many times has something come up in class and we had to get some additional information and provide it to the student after class? How many of our students have asked if they could have a class roster so that they could stay in touch and continue to share information once class was over?

Education of our students should not start and stop at the edge of a classroom door. It never really did, although as instructors we acted as if this were true. So we sat down and we brainstormed and agreed to share our top ways of creating classrooms without walls. We think you will find these not only incredibly beneficial to your time in the classroom, but executed properly, they will create bonds between you and your students that will last forever.

Reaching Out With Classrooms Beyond Walls

✓ **Preclass Surveys.** Many of us have some contact information prior to class about our students. Today emails are common. We could easily use any of the tools previously discussed in this book to do a little preclass surverying of our students. We know a lot of instructors who use post class surveys to ask students what they thought of the class. We don't very many who use sites like facebook or even simple email to ask the students a few questions prior to class about what they expect.

Can you imagine how much better we could serve the needs and demands of our students if prior to class we created a facebook business page just for that class? We could post up some questions such as, "Why did you sign up for this class?" What are you hoping to learn in this class?" "If you could be guaranteed to take just one piece of knowledge out of this course, what would you like it to be?" All it takes is to simply send the student an email with directions on how to find the facebook page and ask them if they would mind answering a few questions prior to coming to class.

What's the worst that can happen? We suppose that some other prospective student could see the discussion and also want to sign up for the class. Wow! That's a consequence we can live with.

✓ **Preclass Biographical Exhanges.** We believe that a big benefit of students coming to live classes is to give them an opportunity to network with each other. This is particularly true in pre-licensing and professional designation courses. We have been in professional designation courses of as many as 40 people where the entire first hour of the class was spent going around the room and having people introduce themselves. It is a valuable process and that's why we have done it for so many years.

Today we could have much more efficiently set up a facebook page for the class and asked each student to please go there and share a bit of information about who they are. They could have written a short post about how long they have been in the business, their area of specialty and why they were taking the class. We could have recovered an hour of class time. Even more importantly, in addition to more efficiently sharing their biographical information, we would have given the students a way to connect if they decided to network with each other.

✓ **Orientation Procedures.** Some courses, such as prelicensing often begin with an hour or more orientation for the students. There are important things prelicensing students need to know about the qualifications for a license, the testing procedure and school policies. We're just not sure if it is worth spending valuable class time discussing such things when we could have preserved them on line and allowed the students to digest that information at their own pace prior to class.

It could have been done prior to class with a video that we provided and uploaded to YouTube. It could have been contained in a blog linked to a facebook page or even on our website. For those of us who have the ability to create online presentations or articulate presentations such instructions could have been provided in both of those formats prior to class. Doing this has the additional benefit of preserving the material so that the students can come back and review all or any part of it in the future as their needs dictate.

✓ **Slidesharing & Blogging Student Content.** We all have the ability to open a free account on Slideshare and provide our PowerPoint slides to our students. Powerpoint slides can even be saved as a comprehensive PDF file that the students can open and review at their leisure outside of class.

We have used blogs to expand the nature and scope of our presentations. There have been many times when we wanted to reference an article or cover ancillary material in a course, but did not have time to do so. Blogging is the answer. We can create a blog on the ancillary material and simply provide the link to that additional information, site or even a video in class. Employing this method is a great way to drive students to your websites or blogs long after the class has ended.

There are some of us who still believe that polling students prior to contacting them, inviting them to our facebook pages and drawing them to our blogs is just getting too personal with the students. They might after all find out other things about us, read extraneous comments or heaven forbid, "Google Us". (p.s. They are already doing that).

We believe that the more we reveal about ourselves, the more our students will reveal about them and through that process we will be better able to reach them in a classroom.

The Art of Revelation

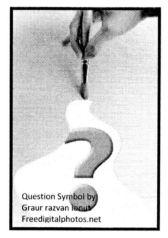

Question Symbol by Graur razvan Ionut Freedigitalphotos.net

If you want students to open up and share with you, then you have to practice the art of sharing with them. We tell real estate professionals all of the time that people do business with people that they know, like and trust. We think that students go to classes taught by instructors that they know, like and trust as well. Up until this point most of us have been building that reputation in a passive, reactionary way. We count on the fact that if students just get to experience who we are in the classroom that they will eventually develop that bond and connection with us. As proactive instructors we shouldn't simply be waiting for that bond to occur, we should be making it occur.

Think about practicing the art of revelation. Have you created a PowerPoint that let's students know a little bit about who you are as a person as well as an instructor? We're not talking about the dull and dry credential stuff, though we think you should include that, how about including your favorite quotes, hobbies and photographs that convey who you are and what is important to you. If you put it into a PowerPoint loop you could play it in that time prior to class or have it playing in that "dead space" known as breaks.

Engagement and interactivity is a two way street. The more open and revealing we are, the more open and revealing our students will be as well. Now, just what was it that you wanted them to know about who you really are?

Sound Like Too Much Work?

At this point in this book many of us are reevaluating our decisions to teach. Guess it's not just a matter of knowing the subject and standing in the front of a room. Those of us who are veteran instructors already knew this. What we are suggesting in this book requires dedication, commitment and excellence.

One of the fortunate side benefits of our speaking, traveling and teaching has been all of the people we have met. During a speaking engagement at the National Association of Realtors Expo & Convention we had the opportunity to meet and talk with legendary boxer, Sugar Ray Leonard, holder of World Titles across five weight divisions and the first boxer to win more than a $100 million in purses. If you have never heard this amazing man speak, we would encourage you to do so. He is not what you might expect. He stands 5'10" tall and weighs about 160 pounds. He is articulate, gentle, brilliant and cordial. As he steps to the microphone and looks out over the crowd he says, "I know what you are thinking, we can take him!"

"More than average" boxer Sugar Ray Leonard With Course Creators at NAR Convention 2009

Of course the crowd laughs and then he explains how good a question that was and how they should be asking themselves, how does someone who is only average become something more than that? How does someone not built for boxing or fighting become a legendary champion? Sugar Ray Leonard explains that the lesson came for him in his fight against Roberto Duran. In case you don't remember, Duran was the hands on favorite. At the time, professional boxers were fighting 3 minute rounds and Sugar Ray's camp brought word back that Duran was training in 4 minute rounds. Sugar Ray said the answer seemed obvious to him. He needed to be training at 5 minute rounds. Sugar Ray won that fight and no one was more surprised than him.

It taught him a lesson he still carries with him today. If you want to be extraordinary, if you want to be more than average then you just have to find one thing that your opponent is not willing to do and do it every day. For Sugar Ray that was an extra minute in the ring. That's unimportant. The important question is: What is that for you? Thank you Sugar Ray!

We tend to think of it this way:

**If you don't want to be average,
You have to be better than average
And you have to be willing to do
What the average instructor is not....**

Curtain Call

"Engaging the Learner… And a Few Other Keys for Success"

**By Rhonda Hamilton,
Professional Speaker & Trainer**

Rhonda Hamilton has made a name for herself as a professional speaker & trainer specializing in life success, business building, and people smart communication skills. She offers keynotes and training for businesses and organizations and is an expert at raising morale, facilitating team building and creating forward momentum. She also offers Instructor Development Workshops and Train-the-Trainer seminars nationally. Rhonda energizes people and organizations to shift their thinking and implement success strategies creating bottom-line results impacting growth opportunities, productivity, and ultimately profitability. She is a member of National Speakers Association and can be reached at www.RhondaHamilton.com.

As a professional speaker, trainer, and seminar facilitator, I recognize the value of engaging the learner. I also recognize the challenges. In today's learning environment, we not only deal with behavior style differences, we deal with generational differences, gender differences, cultural differences and more. Making that crucial connection is based on so many varied and sundry preferences! Engaging students is definitely easier said than done. Yet, it IS a very important key to success in any learning environment. Not only does engagement increase student learning, it brings enjoyment and reward to the facilitator as well.

As I have moved along in my speaking career, I have learned so many things! I have fallen down, I've bumped my head. I've experienced presentations where I've felt down in the dumps when I completely "blew it," and I've felt the exhilaration of being on top of the world when I "knocked it out of the park!." Striving for a level of excellence is definitely a journey. My first gig as a local instructor was downright scary! I kept putting the participants in groups to discuss a question so that I could get a sip of water to calm my nerves! My first seminar for a state association was almost as scary. I wish I could say that I wasn't fearful when I did my first national convention seminar, but I'd be lying. And now, besides seminars, I'm also offering and providing keynote speeches. Each new level, each new environment contains challenges, ups and downs, and yes, YIKES...FEAR! For me, the destination is worth the journey that consists of study, planning, fear, falling down, getting up, more study and preparation. But, prepare as I may, experience continues to be the best teacher. I have learned both from my mistakes and successes. As I examine the learning environment, observe other instructors and reflect on my own experiences, here are a few things I think you (uh hum... WE) need to know and remember:

- **Don't take yourself too seriously** – When I do something stupid, it seems it is REALLY stupid! During a seminar I was presenting on communication skills, I called a man by the wrong name several times during the first hour. Unfortunately, I misunderstood his name (I guess the hearing is going), and although I thought it was odd that his name was "Bark," who was I to judge...right? So, I continued calling him "Bark" until, with a sheepish look on his face, he said, "I need to tell you something... My name is Mark." The room was completely silent, but only for a couple of seconds because I busted out laughing at my own mistake and everyone else followed. Mark actually seemed relieved that it was okay to laugh...at me! I told him I had been wondering why in the world parents would name a child "Bark" -- and with a first name like that, what might his last name be... Bow Wow or maybe Bowser? Everyone, including me, had a great laugh at my expense.

- **Sometimes you have to be willing to let go of one thing to have another** – If you want a learning environment that is rich with participant activity and discussion, it will not be an environment that is completely quiet and structured. This really bothers some instructors. They feel that they are losing CONTROL! However, control should mean that the instructor guides the process, NOT that there is complete quiet and structure. I call it "controlled chaos" and I strive to have it! It brings about more learning and retention in a fun and relevant way.

- **Give back control, let them choose** – Adults love to have choices, so give them choices. For example, rather than assigning case studies, let them choose the one they want. Rather than giving them review questions to study, put them in small groups and let each group write review questions for another small group.

- **Topic questions, if used appropriately and in this order, will speak to each behavior style:** Why? (Drivers), What for? (Analyticals), How? (Peacemakers), What if? (Expressives)

- **Strive to strike a balance** – Using teaching techniques that engage the whole person is best. Move back and forth between lecture and participation to improve learning and retention, and to provide comfort for each individual's preferences.

- **Keep it moving!** – Some instructors make the mistake of using PowerPoint slides incorrectly. They put up a slide with tons of information on it. They leave the slide up and stay on that slide for what seems like an eternity. This will drive certain behavior styles to insanity! Instead, put less information on a slide and use visuals. Use the slide for illustration and/or for key points.

- **For maximum retention, information must be tied to emotion** – Some say that for learning to occur, the learner must have an "Aha" moment. There is some truth to that. Aha moments are moments of emotion, so learning occurs. Stories well told can also strike an emotional chord and if the story is one of relevance, learning and retention increase.

- **A great activity for participation: Review & Report -** (Bonus: helps with time) This is a great activity for interaction and participation, but it also is helpful when you need to make up some time with the material. Divide the class into groups. Assign each group a section of material to be covered. Each group reads and discusses the material and then writes down the key points. A person from each group reports the findings to the entire class.

- **Learning is tied to motivation and motivation is tied to relevance** – Learners need to know the answer to WII-FM – what's in it for me. What is the pay-off for attending the session? How is the information going to benefit them? What is the practicality for their day-to-day business? Is it relevant to their life? If they see the relevance, it peaks their interest and there is perceived value in participating. You must do the work to know your audience – their issues, interests, and concerns. By providing a connection to life experience, real life scenarios, topics regarding issues or interests, you bring about for the learner an ability to relate, which in turn is motivating. You, as the instructor or facilitator, get their buy-in, which is vitally important.

- **Think and plan for interest** – Take the time to prepare your session for participation. Go through the materials and slides in advance. Add visuals, activities, and questions that direct discussion and encourage critical thinking. A great presentation doesn't just happen. It takes a great deal of thought, time and preparation.

- **Enjoy yourself** – A number of years ago I sang on stage (a little known fact: I was on the Nashville show, You Can Be A Star). One thing I learned early on about performing: If you are having fun, the audience is having fun. If you are comfortable, the audience is comfortable. If you are uncomfortable, the audience is uncomfortable.

- **Read body language and adapt** – For the last year and a half, I've been doing a Train-the-Trainer session for REBAC® -- training real estate instructors on instructional training techniques. There is a lot of knowledge in that room! For that reason, I have to gauge my timing and presentation based on feedback and body language. Body language speaks the truth! If we will only listen, it can be a great tool. We have to have an arsenal of tools in our speaker toolkit and stand ready to shift gears and adapt to the needs of our students.

- **Be real** – There is nothing like being real, being authentic, true to who you are. Don't be afraid to show your vulnerability. Being vulnerable is actually a trait that makes you more likeable. When you don't know the answer, don't be afraid to say, "I don't know." People who are able to admit their mistakes and people who are able to admit that they don't know everything are seen as more likeable. Most of us can relate to those characteristics, which reinforces the fact that you are real, authentic and trustworthy.

- **Evaluate yourself** – After each session ask yourself these questions: What did I do right? What could I have done better? Then, focus on the positive. In your mind, make the needed corrections and literally see yourself doing all the right things over and over again. This will positively reinforce the behaviors that you want to keep.

- **Have a positive mental attitude** – Your feelings come from your thoughts. So, if you want to change your feelings, change your thoughts. Decide to honestly like and care for people. When you do that, others cannot help feeling connected to you.

I hope you will benefit from my experiences and observations, and that you will use one or more of the above suggestions to change your business today.

Here's wishing you "top of the world" success!

Curtain Call

"Meeting Students on Their Ground"

By Beverly McCormick, Professor of Real Estate at Morehead State University

Beverly McCormick is a Professor of Real Estate at Morehead State University and a member of the National Real Estate Educators Association. She obtained her B.A. from the University of Kentucky and her J.P. Law Degree from the University of Louisville. Her research and teaching interests cover real estate education, service learning and civic engagement and business law. You can reach Beverly at bmccormick@moreheadstate.edu.

I have to state unequivocally that I love to teach! I love working with students! And I love the process that is involved to make a successful classroom experience. The focus is on learning. I first decide what knowledge, skills or attitude the student needs to do well in this course. I love the process that comes next: the "how", the creation of an activity, assignment, lecture, quiz, or test to assist the student in learning. Usually it is a combination of several strategies to create the kind of learning experience that has the highest probability of being successful. But even before a teacher gets to this point, the environment in the classroom must be established in a way that will forment learning.

The first hour of a class is very important in creating the learning environment that encourages students to be engaged and learn. I start the class by introducing who I am. In a long course, I do this by bringing items that tell my story. I bring my favorite book and something new I have quilted. I bring a teapot from my collection or a wooden doll that I brought with me when I came to the U.S. from Germany as a child. I tell them a little of my professional and personal story. This helps the students to see me as a complete individual with family and hobbies that I love. Then I ask each one to share basic information and to answer a question such as "If you could own any piece of real estate in the world, what would it be?" Students need to talk the very first hour of class if they are going to contribute during the rest of the class. That is why I follow the introductions with a small group activity. If students start talking in a small group, they feel more comfortable in the class and are more likely to answer or ask questions. The environment must be one of acceptance and appreciation of the value of each member of the class.

The classroom I like to create is very interactive. I love the question, "What are we going to do next?" Students look forward to being involved in their learning, which is the only way it can ever happen. That means I like to do a minimum amount of lecture and a maximum amount of interaction. I usually cover some material in a short amount of time and then give them an activity to apply this information, usually in some real world application. This will create a classroom that is noisy with students talking with each other while involved in the assignment. It is through this application of information that students really internalize and learn the material. This is also where they build the skills of the profession. Students need to do in the classroom as much as possible of what they would do in the profession. The practical makes the theoretical make sense.

As I have mentioned, I love preparing assignments. It allows me to be creative and put myself in the shoes of my students. I ask myself, "What can I do to make this information easier to learn and how can I do it in an enjoyable way." Making the classroom effective and enjoyable is my goal. I try to do both by making my classes very interactive. Also, I do it by not taking myself too seriously. Let's face it, I make mistakes. I say something unintentionally funny on occasion. So, I laugh. The students laugh. And we all relax! They know if they make a mistake or say something funny, it isn't the end of the world. I want my students to contribute without retribution. This does not mean that my classes are not rigorous; it just means we have fun in the process. I ask myself on a regular basis, "How can I make it interesting and fun?"

I enjoy the challenge and I enjoy the step-by-step process of creating the assignment to give to the students. I use my PowerPoint more as a way to discuss the information. I ask students questions, solicit comments, give examples, and explain significance. Often, I do a few slides, stop, and students do an activity using the information. Students need the information and they need to use that information.

Students need to use their creativity. I frequently ask students if they are creative. It never fails that only a few ever raise their hand. I tell them that each one of them is creative. We are all creative in our own way. To prove that, I immediately give them an activity to do that requires creativity. They are always able to do the activity. We then discuss that it took creativity to do it. I then ask them again if they are creative, and usually most everyone will raise their hand. Sometimes, they just need to be encouraged to recognize and use all the skills that they have. Students need to be empowered.

One of the best ways for students to utilize their own knowledge and abilities is in small group activities. In some classes, they are in many different small groups during the course and in others they stay in the same group throughout the course. I do many activities with these groups so that they get a sense of the strengths of each member. This is useful in processing a task and when division of labor is necessary. Small groups place the learning on the students. They must complete the task and communicate with each other. It is much easier for students to talk in a small group. Quiet, shy students are much more likely to contribute.

Another way that I foster student learning is by occasionally sharing the teaching responsibility. Small groups present a section of the content to the class. In their presentation, they must create some discussion questions or an activity for the class using that information. It enables them take the extra step to engage their classmates. Teaching is the best way to learn information.

I do sometimes ask my students why we just did a particular activity. They often find more reasons than I had thought of when creating the activity. It also causes them to give it more importance and to connect it to their learning. I want my students fully informed as we travel down the learning path.

If the course has exams, I always conduct a review. If I merely told them what would be on the test, they would nod because they would have heard the words before. They would not know whether they really know those facts, terms, or concepts. Review needs to be active. So, many years ago, I bought a college bowl buzzer system. I divide the class into groups. I ask questions and the teams score points. Every five correct answers, the team gets candy. The candy keeps them motivated throughout the game. The students learn to study for the review if they want to do well. They also, most importantly, learn what they know and what they still need to study. The students love the review game and they say it really helps them get ready for the test. I also have created a version of Trivial Pursuit, that I call "Essential Pursuit". I use it in my Real Estate Law class to review for the exam over the real estate license law. I have created categories and cards with license law questions to be played with the game board. This is a very effective way to make what can be a challenging and boring subject fun!

Exams can be made more interesting as well. I use funny names, interesting scenarios, and humor to lessen the tension and make the exam more enjoyable. Sometimes, the whole test will have a theme or story. Use of the students' names in the questions makes the test more interesting. I also will have a lot of application on the tests.

This could be creating an ad for a Marketing class or completing a contract for a law class. Many classes, have both knowledge and skill components to be tested.

Although learning can be fun and interactive, that does not mean that it is not challenging. A good way to build skills is by using continuous improvement methods. For example, the student writes an advertisement and then another student critiques it. The student then rewrites the ad. The same thing would happen when the student turns it in to me. Students get into the habit of improving what they do until it is the best it can be. When students are in an environment where they know they can make a mistake and then correct it, they are less stressed and they ultimately create a better product.

Imagine that fun, lively and learning-filled classroom. Meet the students on their ground and create some learning fun!

Measuring Progress & Taking Stock

Just like the players on Broadway we live for the reviews. The quality of our days is often defined by our review of what the critics think about our performance. Sometimes that is measured in the pass/fail rate on standardized tests and quizzes which students complete either during or following class and sometimes it is based on what we read in the student evaluations following the presentation. No matter what, the basis of our assessment and our self-worth often lies in the hands of the students that we instruct. We will discuss those types of assessments in this Act and we agree that probably the most important measure of what we did is always in the mind of the audience.

We would challenge all of us as instructors though to think critically about how we can self-assess ourselves. Let's face it, we are the experts in teaching and education and we ought to spend more time trying to improve our craft through some objective self-evaluation of our performance. We will discuss those tools and that process as well.

Who amongst us has never read through a whole handful of evaluations that were glowing only to dwell on the one that is not? We seem to get stuck there as instructors, beating ourselves up, wondering what we could have done better. We hope this chapter helps you deal with that phenomenon a little bit as well. We all strive for 100 percent of excellence and we should have the tools and knowledge to deal with the situations where we may have fallen short. Knowing how to turn those occurrences into constructive educational opportunities for ourselves fosters our own progress as instructors. After all, we hope you haven't forgotten, we are students too!

When It's All About the Test

We admit it is different teaching classes to students where the students at the end must pass a standardized test than it is teaching classes where no mandatory testing is attached. We certainly don't believe that one is in a higher hierarchal level than another, that one deserves more time and attention than another, or that GAPE and all we have discussed in this book don't apply equally to both. But there are differences.

Real estate, as a profession, has a very low bar of entry. The education and the testing requirements are higher for a two year degree. In a lot of states we can acquire a real estate license more easily and cheaply than becoming a dental assistant, a paralegal, a nail tech, a bartender, a cosmetologist or a hair salon employee. It is also a profession where there are relatively very small start-up costs. We don't have to lease space, buy office equipment and obtain additional state and local business licenses. It's not like we are trying to open a restaurant or a hotel. The point is not that real estate is easy. It is not. However, as instructors this basic structure creates a phenomenon that encroaches on our classroom.

We want you to imagine that you are a single mother who was just laid off, or a guy who after 25 years with the company in a particular industry was just downsized. We want you to imagine you were a stay at home person whose spouse just died and now you have to go back to work. We want you to imagine that your child has been diagnosed with a disease and you are looking for additional part time income to cover the medical costs you know are coming. Now, quick…what are your career change options? Most of those options would cost thousands of dollars and months to complete. Many don't have the luxury of those options. Hey, how about we get a real estate license?

If we could figure out how to do it in a politically correct way it would be interesting to poll the life transitions of people in a real estate pre-licensing course. Imagine asking, "How many of you are recently divorced, relocated, downsized, had a family tragedy strike you, or have family members with major medical issues?" Would you rather think of a pre-licensing class as a halfway house for wayward souls or the Statue of Liberty standing in the harbor attracting new immigrants who want to start fresh in a new world? Both scenarios highlight feelings of fear, self-doubt, concern or panic and yet people come to these places and to pre-licensing with the hope that things can change and be better and with the belief that it is all going to be okay. As instructors we have the ability to nurture that hope or crush it.

The importance of this is that it brings an additional element into the classroom. Go back and reread the passage from Frank McCourt that we put into Act III. "In the classroom we are…*a shoulder to cry on…a counselor…a mother…a father…a priest…a psychologist..the last straw.*" All of it means that if you were to ask us what are the most important traits of a pre-licensing instructor we would tell you that they have to have compassion, concern for others and a pretty big heart. Okay, maybe that's a good prerequisite for all instructors, but the need is heightened and accelerated for those who teach in any environment leading up to a standardized test in a classroom where people are in major life transitions.

We remember teaching pre-licensing and having people, well to use their language, "freak out" about passing a test. Sometimes the fear, the drama, the pressure that they exhibited was irrational. Here are two different perspectives on what is going on with the student curled into a fetal position crying about an upcoming exam:

> **Staff Member to Instructor:** "What is wrong with that person? Gee, it's just a test. If you don't pass it, you can take it over again. Tell them to stop worrying about the test and could you ask them to please quit crying and stressing out over everything."

> **Student to Instructor:** (Said in Between Sobs): "You don't understand. My husband recently passed away and now I have to get to work. I have enough reserves for a few months, but if I don't pass this test I can't get a job. I have two little children. Oh my God! What I am going to do? This is a lot of material. I don't understand it. What if I don't pass the test?"

Such is the life of a pre-licensing instructor taking novice students toward an exam that will help them through a life transition. You see, all of a sudden teaching isn't about the exam at all. It isn't even about the class. It's about how as instructors we can deal with a crippling emotional entity called "FEAR". It exists in the classroom and it can run rampant in courses involving standardized tests. Teaching effectively, especially in pre-licensing requires empathy with your students. Don't confuse empathy with sympathy. Sympathy to us means feeling sorry for someone. Empathy means we understand and identify with the feelings that another possesses.

Fear of Failure

Due to a number of personal and professional changes that we were going through, we turned to a good friend who is also a motivational speaker and said, "We have come to the conclusion that fear is the worst of all emotions." He started to laugh. Then he said "Do you know why that is?" We admitted that we didn't, but urged him to share his insights because we knew that this was information we could use in a classroom. He responded that fear is the only emotion that you cannot channel in a positive direction. Think about it. If we have other emotions, such as pain, hurt, loss…those can all be funneled toward some positive direction. Let's take the worst case scenario. Someone who has a loved one killed in a car accident with a drunk driver can turn their attention to helping others through efforts with Mothers Against Drunk Driving. What do you do with fear? Fear can't be channeled, it has to be overcome.

The most identifiable fear of our students is fear of failure: fear of not passing the test, fear of not being successful, fear of failing at the profession with which they are involved. There are methods and techniques for us as instructors to help our students move beyond their fear.

Moving Beyond Fear Classroom Techniques For Prelicensing

✓ **Instructor Demeanor.** In pre-license classes there is a lot of doubt, uncertainty and apprehension. More than any other setting the students wander into the classroom looking for a friendly face and a welcome. Be that presence. Get there ahead of the students. Smile as often as possible. Be warm, friendly and congenial. The more friendly, open and receptive you appear in the time before and immediately after the start of class will help ease the fear and apprehension that many students were facing when they first came into the room.

✓ **Instill Confidence.** Pre-license classes are about building people up. (Maybe all classes should). We need to make the students feel that they are going to get through this. We have to increase their confidence and self-esteem. GAPE reminds us that the need to build an adult learners' self-esteem is important in any teaching setting, but the skills are demanded heavily when teaching pre-licensing. Everything we have learned about thanking the students for their questions and using their names contribute to instilling this confidence. As often as possible we should be reminding them of how much they have learned, how far they have come, how smart they are and how proud we are of them. Building the students up is an art form tied heavily to the language and comments we use. Find the encouraging ones which work best for you and deliver them every chance you get.

✓ **Shrink the Downside.** In most states and in most schools, passing the real estate exam can sometimes be a matter of persistence. If you don't pass it; take it again. We know that a determined student will get a real estate license. They don't. The students fear that the test or qualifications may somehow bar them from their dreams. We have to assure them this is not the case. If they study, are determined and pay attention then the passing of the test becomes no big deal. Don't make the test bigger than it is. If we tell them the test is really hard, that people fail it, that some people never pass then that is the expectation and mindset we create. We are not urging you to hide or diminish the truth, just put the facts in proper perspective for the students and the truth is most people will not struggle with the test. Most people pass it the first time and everyone who is determined will get through it.

✓ **Create Additional Tools.** Think about the questions students ask themselves that adds to the fear. What if I don't understand the material? What if there is a concept I can't get? What if my math skills are not good enough? All of these doubts and fears come from a student believing that they will not have a resource available should this occur. It's why we all should encourage study groups, test preparation exercises and exam prep courses. Most of us tend to evaluate the effectiveness of these tools based on how many students are utilizing them. They have an importance and an impact on the instruction regardless of how many students sign up for the review class. The importance is that all of the students had more confidence, trusted us and relied on us simply because the tools existed. These tools send the message loud and clear that we will do anything to help them achieve their goals and they will always have resources should they struggle in any way.

✓ **Share the Fear.** Here comes that word, empathy again. Seems everyone thinks that they are somehow unique in the fears they face. We all share fears from time to time, but breaking the taboo of sharing them makes students feel connected and less isolated. Every support group you have ever heard of is based on this principal and so is a lot of therapeutic counseling. In some regards our classroom is a group therapy session if we can use similar principles to get the students to share and expose their fears. Sometimes we do this by simply sharing the fears we had when we sat in their seats. Sometimes we do it by simply asking, "How many of you are afraid of…." When that question fails to get a response we follow it up with "Okay, how many of you are unwilling to admit you are afraid of…." The second comment is almost always followed by laughter, then participation and then a frank discussion of what they are afraid of. Here is what we know: fear confronted and exposed is fear defeated.

✓ **Inspire & Uplift.** Don't underestimate the role we play in inspiring and uplifting students. Remember our ancient heroes from Act I. It was Aristotle who said, "The goal of all education ought to be to remind us of what we do not know and inspire us to learn more." Go find those inspirational videos on YouTube we talked about in earlier Acts. Find your favorite inspirational stories. We use them often. Interspersed throughout a prelicensing course they will elevate and encourage the entire class..

One of our favorite stories is the true life saga of Alexandra Scott. In the middle of a pre-licensing class or close to the examination it unfolds like this in the classroom and we tell this tale complete with accompanying PowerPoint slides and music to leverage the emotion. It has been a source of inspiration for many of our students. We hope it is a source of inspiration for you as well and we encourage you to create your own telling of this tale and share when the circumstances in your classroom dictate. It is a true story.

Lessons from a Lemonade Stand

We know that some of you may be feeling a little overwhelmed at this point. You may even be wondering if you can do this or get through it. So we thought we would find you a mascot to get you through the test and her name is Alexandra Scott.

In 2000, Alexandra Scott was about as sick as a four year old child can get. She contracted childhood neuroblastoma, which is one of the most deadly and incurable forms of childhood cancer. The disease, the chemo and the surgeries had ravaged her little body so much that she could barely speak, but she could think. One day while laying in a hospital bed she turned to her mother and said, "When I get out of here, I want to open a lemonade stand." 'Right' thought her mother. Then Alexandra shared the rest of her dream. She said, "But I don't want to keep any of the money. There are a lot of little kids with cancer and some of them can't afford the treatments, so I thought if my brother and I sold our toys and made and sold lemonade we could give the money to them."

The way that some children are persistent about candy and Christmas presents, four-year-old Alexandra was unrelenting about the lemonade stand. So her father eventually constructed a makeshift lemonade stand, her mother opened a savings account and four year old Alexandra was about to go into business. One of her relatives, however, leaked word of the lemonade stand to the local press and the first cars started showing up the night before. They brought toys for her to sell, lemonade mix and gallons of water. The next morning the line reached down the block and by the end of her first day, Alexandra had collected over $1,500.00.

Her parents chalked it up to a one time event, an isolated experience, but the next morning when they got out of bed, Alexandra was back out at her lemonade stand. She continued to grow her little business and her parents eventually relocated just outside the city of Philadelphia where so that they could be closer to the children's hospital where Alexandra had to go regularly for treatment. When they relocated, her mother called the local chief of police and explained that her daughter operated a lemonade stand and that he might want to send over some cruisers to control traffic. "Right," said the chief of police. But the officers did show up later that day when traffic within a two mile radius of Alexandra's lemonade stand came to a complete and total standstill.

On that particular day, Alexandra had long since abandoned her little Styrofoam cup that said "Lemonade 25 Cents" and had procured a large bucket on the side of which she painted "Stuff in What You Can Afford". The general manager of the Philadephia 76's was in line that day and paid $500 for his glass of lemonade. More press coverage and customers followed and at the end of that particular day, Alexandra's lemonade stand had taken in $15,000.

At the end of 2003 she was interviewed on the Oprah Winfrey show. When Oprah commended her for raising several thousand dollars for childhood cancer and asked seven year old Alexandra what her goals were for the future, she replied "In 2004 I am going to raise a million dollars." We wish you could have seen her parents turn green on national television.

Alexandra found out she couldn't do it herself. So on her frequent trips to the hospital she began to recruit other kids and trained them how to operate lemonade stands. Six months later Alexandra was supervising 300 lemonade stands from Maine to Los Angeles and her little savings account which had been converted to a non-profit charity contained over a million dollars. Shortly after Alexandra achieved that goal she succumbed to cancer and died on August 1, 2004. Her parents today still oversee and operate the lemonade stands and they have turned them into a multi-million dollar non-profit cancer benefitting charity.

Here's the point for you today as you approach an exam. Your head is saying, "I can't do this." "This is a lot of material." "What if I fail?" That's where Alexandra comes in as your mascot. If a little girl between the ages of 4 and 8 can build a million dollar business with 300 franchisees across the United States, all of the time fighting a childhood disease from which she cannot escape, what part of taking this exam do you think is hard? What part is it that you think you cannot do? What makes you think you can't accomplish your goal?

If the use of this type of emotion seems a little sappy to you or if you've been in one of our courses when we were telling such a story and wondered why we made you cry, here it is in a nutshell. One day walking toward a classroom, a staff person said, "There they go, off to make the students cry." Another instructor, overhearing the comment, questioned the staff member trying to figure out if we were being cruel to the students or threatening them in some way. The staff member replied, "No, they just go in there and tell stories and the students come out with tissues in hand." It was then that the other instructor said something that we didn't realize fully until that day, but has stuck in our heads for a long time now. He said, "They are not going into the classroom to make the students cry, they are going in to the classroom to make the students feel."

All of that has led us to the conclusion of why emotion and empathy are important in the classroom setting. We would like to share with you the biggest thought we have on the use of emotion in the classroom.

You can't get people to change until they want to act
You can't get people to act until they care
You can't get people to care until they feel

So there it is and we admit it. We are going to try and make you feel. If you feel, you'll care, and if you care you'll act, and if you're willing to act then we can teach you anything. Why is that important to us? Why are we writing this book and sharing all of this with you? It's simple – We Care. It comes from the way we feel about you and teaching.

Is That On the Exam?

Unfortuantely, No. There will not be questions on the test about Alexandra and her lemonade stand on the final exam. We know that we can't afford as pre-license instructors to ever forget job #1 of prelicense education and that is to get students through a final exam with flying colors. We don't think that diminishes our role as instructors, we think it elevates it. Anyone who has taught pre-licensing or any course tied to a standardized test has heard that question at least a million times. There are some important do's and don't s for responding to that common question of students.

Techniques for Dealing With "Is That On the Test?"

✓ **Set The Expectations Early.** It is worth our time and effort to deal with this issue early in the course. We know it is going to come up so why not preempt some of the concern. We should emphasize to the students that we understand that job number one is to empower them to pass the exam. We should also tell them that we have a secondary objective and that is to help make them successful after the exam. From time to time in a class we may address certain practice techniques that are important to your success, though the tests typically don't ask practice skill type questions.

✓ **Don't Diminish the Importance of the Students Question.** One of the things that we instructors can do to damage GAPE is to simply say to a student, "We are not going to cover that. It is not on the test." That simple response just told the student that their questions wasn't important enough to address. When that occurs the impact will be an immediate chilling effect on the student asking other questions or contributing to the class. That is the last thing we want to occur as instructors. If the student has a question they deserve an answer. We can avoid this by setting the stage early and telling students that from time to time issues may come up in the classroom that are not on the test. Explain that in order to achieve the number one objective we as instructors from time to time may limit the scope of discussions. Always inform the students that when that happens we will provide them with an alternative way of getting their question answered, even if we don't involve the whole class in that discussion.

✓ **Provide Alternative Sources for the Answer.** The easiest way to do this is to simply tell the student that the information they are asking about may not be important to other students, but that we would be happy to discuss it with them on break or after class. What we have learned is that there are some common "off the test" questions which get asked all of the time. This is a great opportunity to employ the Classroom Without Walls concepts discussed in Act VII and have an existing blog post or article that addresses those concerns. It enables us in class to simply say, "We are so glad you asked that. It gets asked often and you can find our answer to it at….."

✓ **Figure Out How to Refocus the Question.** It is rare that students ask questions that have no bearing whatsoever on test content. They may not have framed it right, they may not be asking the right question, but a skillful instructor will figure out how to take what they are asking and turn it into a beneficial question for everyone in the room by refocusing it to something that is on the test. The dialogue begins with, "Let me answer that in a way which is beneficial to everyone and in a manner that can be applied to some test content you will encounter." If you choose this approach we encourage you that when you rephrase a student's question, it is always a good idea to ask them at the end of the response if your answer was helpful and if it addressed their concern.

Writing Course Objectives

If we desire (and we believe we all should) to measure our progress and take stock as instructors, then we should have meaningful and objective ways to measure our effectiveness. In order to do that, each course ought to have some well defined learning objectives. In fact, most regulatory agencies approving classes for credit require course developers to submit learning objectives for the course.

The major problem with most learning objectives written by instructors is that they are neither objective nor measurable. They tend to be written from the viewpoint of the instructor and not the progress of the student. A good example would be a course objective which reads, "I will teach the students the concepts of agency." The question becomes; What will this enable the student to do and how will we measure whether or not we have "taught" it? A better objective would be "At the conclusion of this section students will be able to recite the six key fiduciary duties." There is a big difference to these two objectives and in this section we will explore how to craft learning objectives that work.

The Purpose & Components of Course Objectives

The best course objectives describe an intended instructional result. One way of getting our head around course objectives is to realize that they are not the same thing as goals. Goals are broad and objectives are narrow. Goals are general intentions and objectives are precise. Goals are intangible and objectives are tangible. Goals cannot be evaluated and objectives are measurable. Objectives are not for the instructor, they are for the student, yet many learning objectives are written without the student in mind.

Most of the material that has been collected concerning learning objectives refers to the ABCD's of learning objectives and they include four characteristics that help an objective communicate the *intent* of the education:

> **A**udience – Who will be dong the behavior?
>
> **B**ehavior – What should the learner be able to do?
>
> **C**ondition – Under what conditions do you want the learner to be able to do the task?
>
> **D**egree – How well must it be done and how will the instructor measure or assess that ability?

There are some fundamental things that we should recognize about these ABCD's. First of all the action is directed at the learners. Second the objectives must be made tangible, in other words they aim to help the learner achieve to do something that can be seen or heard. Third, they set parameters for what the student may use or not use as resources in obtaining the objective and finally the instructor must be able to complete an objective assessment as to the achievement of the learning objective. The assessment could be based on speed, accuracy or quality.

A fundamental key in constructing valid learning objectives is to use measurable verbs. Students can be expected to: define, memorize, list, recall, discuss, relate, repeat, name and identity. Yet we commonly see learning objectives that say "At the end of this section students will "understand" "appreciate" or "learn". Really? Exactly how are you going to measure that? It's impossible for instructors to insure that a student learned or understood. Even though we strive for those "goals" they are not valid, objectively measurable learning objectives.

Another component of course and learning objectives involves the application of Bloom's Taxonomy. The Taxonomy is important to course development, learning objectives and the crafting of test and quiz questions. It's background and application is something that should be known by all educators.

Bloom's Taxonomy & Cognitive Levels

Benjamin Bloom (1913-1999) was an American educational psychologist who contributed greatly to the classification of educational objectives. He also directed a research team which conducted investigation into the development of exceptional talent and categorized the thought processes and analysis skills of individuals. His framework led to the creation of *Bloom's Taxonomy*. It remains one of the most familiar educational books of all time and it is estimated that it has been translated into at least 21 different languages.

In the *Taxonomy*, Bloom organized six categories of learning: knowledge, comprehension, application, analysis, synthesis and evaluation. He put them into an order based on the level of learning they required. In other words the levels of learning are built on each other and reflect the cognitive domains in which students operate at different levels. We get a better understanding of *Bloom'sTaxonomy* by expanding what is meant at each level.

1. **Knowledge (Recall)** - the recollection of data, expresses the natural urge to recall previously learned material. So knowledge or remembering can be a foundation for learning. It provides a basis for higher levels of thinking, but is rote in nature. Insight rides on top of it. Just think of it as recollection.

2. **Comprehension (Grasp)** - the ability to grasp meaning, explain or restate ideas, means understanding the basic information and translating, interpreting, and extrapolating it.

3. **Application (Apply)** - the use of learned material in new situations, involves applying information, ideas, and skills to solve problems, then selecting and employing them appropriately.

4. **Analysis (Analyze)** - suggests separating items, or separate material into component parts and showing relationships between parts. It also means breaking apart information and ideas into their component parts. It also involves evaluating the accuracy or applicability of the knowledge.

5. **Synthesis (Synthesize)** - suggests the ability to put together separate ideas to form new wholes of a fabric, or establish new relationships. Synthesis involves putting together ideas and knowledge in a new and unique form. This is where innovations truly take place.

6. **Evaluation (Judge)** - is the highest level in this arrangement. Here the ability to judge the worth of material against stated criteria is explored. Evaluation involves reviewing and asserting evidence, facts, and ideas, then making appropriate statements and judgments.

We can get even a better grasp of Bloom's concepts if we translate then into what is actually expected of students and we see them as stepping stones in the proper hierarchal order of learning.

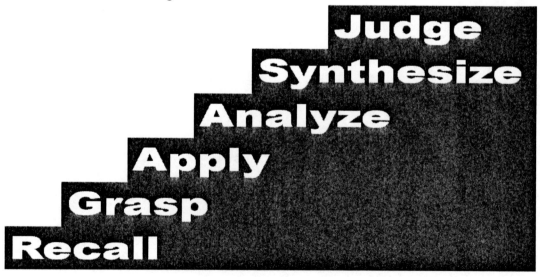

Relating Bloom to Real Estate Education

The applications and implications of Bloom's work is everywhere in real estate education, but it goes largely unnoticed by the majority of instructors, schools and even regulatory agencies.

If you think about it, most pre-licensing courses never move beyond the mere recollection of material. It is all together fitting and appropriate that introductory courses to the industry should start there. The cognitive levels were arranged in a basic order for a reason. You can't apply material you can't recall and you can't judge material you don't know how to apply. However, we believe that one of the objectives of pre-licensing and introductory courses should be to advance the learner through *Bloom's Taxonomy* levels. How many times have we heard that pre-licensing is just for the test? That's because we don't typically try to teach students how to apply or analyze pre-licensing material.

In an attempt to elevate the usefulness and value of pre-license education we might choose to focus on how it can be positioned higher in *Bloom's Taxonomy*. In the defense of regulatory agencies and standardized testing services we should recognize that the higher you progress in *Bloom's Taxonomy* the more difficult it becomes to objectively measure and assess the progress and mastery of the learner. It is easy to grade a test where the answer is black and white and based on pure recollection of material. It is time consuming and more difficult to read essays the learner may have written in critical analysis of something they have learned.

Not all professional licensing ignores Bloom's heirarachy. Bar exams for the legal profession often tend to be divided into three parts. One part is a series of multiple choice questions which require the learner to recall or grasp the material. The second part is a series of fact patterns with multiple choice answers, but they require the law student to apply and analyze the information. Finally there is usually a series of essays which require the ability to synthesize or judge the knowledge. The point is that there are standardized ways to test objectively at Bloom's higher levels, but they require more attention, time and effort.

We also believe that *Bloom's Taxonomy* has an impact on the engagement and interest of the student. We believe that when properly executed, the higher one goes in the taxonomy the more interesting and engaging the course becomes to the student. We don't know of very many students who get truly excited or engaged with having to memorize a list or a principle; though some excellent pre-licensing instructors have even managed to make the memorizing of terminology fun and engaging. We have, however, had many lively debates in our classrooms when we moved to the areas of analysis and judging. If you want to elevate the level of your course, then elevate the content in *Bloom's Taxonomy.*

Writing Effective Exam & Quiz Questions

Most people underestimate the skill and knowledge required to write effective test and quiz questions. In order to write effective questions it is necessary to have three key skills: full command of the subject matter; an understanding of *Bloom's Taxonomy* and the cognitive levels of learning; and finally an understanding of testing methodology.

Test questions can be a large and varied sort. There are selected response type questions where the learner is provided with a set number of potential choices and asked to select the appropriate answer. Multiple choice questions would be a good example. There are also constructed response type questions where the learner is expected to provide their own answer. Fill in the blank questions are a good example of this. Most standardized tests tend to be multiple choice type arrangements. We believe that is not because they are the most effective type of testing, but they are easier to administer, easier to evaluate and more objective in their approach.

Because most of the standardized tests are based on multiple choice frameworks we will focus on that aspect of testing. However, following our 10 step guide for writing effective test questions we will examine expanded testing options and discuss some creative ways to examine and test student progress in the classroom.

10 Steps For Writing Effective Test & Quiz Questions

1. **Select An Appropriate Topic.** Most standardized testing, including that in the real estate field, spreads the testing out over a variety of subjects in a very straight forward and methodical way. For example, 15% of the questions will be in the area of contract principles and 10% will in the area of fair housing. Depending on the jurisdictions in which you are teaching and the testing company

which is utilized, this information will change slightly, but is usually made readily available to us as instructors. Questions therefore should be created to fit a particular topic or area. The questions should fall cleanly into that category and should not incorporate information from other categories. (Yes. We understand that is part of the reason why students don't learn to cross apply principles or relate one body of knowledge to the other in many courses. While we are not ready to carry the banner to restructure the educational paradigm for state regulatory agencies, we think that a fertile area for future course development is along the lines of this cross application. Think: "How Agency Law Applies to Social Media", or "Fair Housing vs. Disclosure" as a single class.)

2. **Determine the Cognitive Level of the Question.** Make a decision of what you want the student to be able to do in order to answer the question correctly. In making this choice, refer to Bloom's Taxonomy. Do you want the student to simply recall a particular piece of information? Do you want them to be able to apply it? Questions that are written to the lower end of Bloom's Taxonomy tend to be easier. Questions written toward the upper end are more difficult. For the purpose of writing test questions, some people prefer to simplify Bloom's Taxonomy into three categories:

> **Recollection Questions (Recall & Grasp**
> **Application Questions (Apply & Analyze)**
> **Assessment Questions (Synthesize & Judge)**

For example, just because a student can recite the definition of an encroachment doesn't mean that they can provide examples of when an encroachment exists and it doesn't mean that they can assess what to do when an encroachment exists. These are three different levels of knowledge. Here are the three different level of questions in ascending order of difficulty:

> Which of the following is the proper definition of an encroachment?
> Which of the following is a good example of an encroachment?
> Which of the following would be the best solution for resolving an
>   encroachment?

3. **Structure The Question Properly.** Questions should be short and concise. They should also be written using action verbs. A good question avoids open ended statements so as not to mislead the student. They should also be written in complete sentences in question format. Here's a hint, if it is inappropriate to put a question mark at the end of the sentence, it's not a question:

Here are some good examples of acceptable and unacceptable question structure:

> A listing agreement is: (Unacceptable)
> A listing agreement is what type of contract? (Acceptable)
> An agent who is hiring a client would have the client sign: (Unacceptable)
> What is the name of an employment agreement signed by the seller?
> (Acceptable)

4. **Review the Question for Alignment & Focus.** Examining a question for alignment and focus means that we should ask questions which the learner really should know. The question should align with the test's purposes and test practical working knowledge. The most common failures in this regard is when test questions require the student to recall benign, non-important knowledge simply for the sake of regurgitation. It is hard to defend the purpose of a test question which asks a student, "What year was a particular law passed?" That question really does not address what we hoped the learner would fundamentally take from the information taught, nor is it anything that the student will benefit by if they remember it after the exam.

Here is another example of a poorly aligned and focused question:

What does OSHA stand for?
   a. Organization for Security of Homeland affairs
   b. Occupational Safety and Health Administration *
   c. Office for the Study of Horticultural Activities
   d. Overseas Service for Human Advancement

Was the purpose of the instruction really to get students to memorize what the letters OSHA stand for, or was the purpose of the material to get students to be able to properly identify the function of various federal agencies. If the latter, then the following is a more properly aligned and focused question:

What federal agency conducts workplace safety inspections?
   a. FEMA
   b. USGS
   c. DEA
   d. OSHA *

5. **Check the Question Mechanics**. Misspelled words and punctuation will drive your students crazy. The testing phase of instruction is the last place that instructors want that to occur. Make certain the question is clear and concise, free

of jargon and slang and contains proper punctuation and spelling. While we are at it we might as well get rid of all the unnecessary modifiers we throw into normal sentences, especially the absolute words like always and never. There are exceptions to every rule (see what we mean, you are already trying to think of a rule without an exception.) Remove the words "always" "never' and "every" in test questions. Reviewing them before hand will keep your students from complaining about them and arguing with you later.

6. **Remove Bias and Prejudice From the Question**. We all know to avoid questions that reference specific races, nationalities, color and religions, but we are less watchful about questions which contain gender specific pronouns. Avoid personal or place names and remove the vague. Change the "him" or "her" to person or people or them. Remove the vague pronouns. When words like "it" "they" and "them" appear in your questions reword them to avoid these references.

7. **Craft the Correct Answer.** Once the question is drafted the first thing we should do is draft the correct answer applying the same rules we have just discussed. The answer can be a sentence, a single word or a phrase. It doesn't matter which form the answer takes so long as the detractors that we create later are done in parallel fashion.

8. **Write the Distractor Responses.** We happen to think writing the distracters is the most difficult part of question writing. At least that is where a lot of people struggle with a well crafted question. We can make the original question much more difficult or very easy based on the distracters that are chosen. Every distractor should be a plausible alternative. Avoid the temptation to write silly or nonsencial distracters which everyone knows cannot be the correct answer. If we write distracters which are "throw-aways" then we probably should do just that with them and save the students the time and the trouble of reading them since they add nothing to the testing process, evaluation of the students or our feedback from them.

9. **Make Certain Everything is Parallel.** The correct answer and the responses should be in parallel form. If each answer begins with the same phrase or word then consider moving that phrase into the question to eliminate the redundancy. Parallelism also means that the correct answer and the distracters should be written with the same verb tense. Here are two examples. In the first one the detractors are not parallel. In the second example this issue has been resolved:

Which of the following clauses in a mortgage allows the lender to demand repayment if a borrower sells the property?
　　a. Defeasance clause
　　b. Prepayment clauses demand this
　　c. Acceleration
　　d. Alienation clauses included in the note

Which of the following clauses in a mortgage allows the lender to demand repayment if a borrower sells the property?
　　a. Defeasance
　　b. Prepayment
　　c. Acceleration
　　d. Alienation

10. **Avoid the Deadly Sins.** Wow! This question writing must be serious stuff if it has deadly sins, but we see them committed all of the time. Avoid the temptation to write "all of the above" and "none of the above questions. Neither stands up as a valid testing tool. "All of the Above" questions provide the student with more than one right answer. In fact each answer is correct and we are asking the student to pick a "more correct" answer. "None of the above" questions are not valid testing tools because they don't really test over the knowledge. Because we fail to provide a proper answer it doesn't really test over whether the student knows the right answer or not.

As we said, writing test questions requires more than most people realize. Major testing services validate their tests. We would suggest that if you are writing your own tests and quizzes you should validate them as well. Keep track of the most commonly missed questions and the questions which no one ever gets wrong. Chances are that they both need to be reexamined in terms of their structure and their content.

If you track individual test questions missed against a student's overall score you also will gain insight into the validity of your questions. For example, if students who score high on the test are getting the question right and a lot of others are missing the question, then it probably is just a difficult question, but may be valid. If on the other hand, students who score well on the test overall are missing the question at the same rate as those who scored lower, then the question is probably invalid, has structural issues or is written poorly.

Getting Creative in the Evaluation of Student Knowledge

We believe that if your course requires a final (Gee, that sounds terminal doesn't it?) examination then it probably justifies intermittent quizzes leading up to it. Pre-license classes which contain intermediate quizzes or periodic review examinations tend to build stronger student retention. Repetition wins when it comes to standardized testing preparation. It also helps to build the learner's self esteem, individual self-assessment and familiarization with the testing process to remove or diminish some of the fear always associated with a final examination. We would offer some creative approaches to the evaluation of student knowledge during the tenure of a course.

Varying our approach to periodic evaluation of students throughout a course allows us to appeal more directly to the different learner profiles discussed in Act II and probably allows us to have a more accurate assessment of how much the students truly have learned. There are lots of formats for assessing student learning, multiple choice just tends to be the predominant method of standardized tests. We probably won't see any of the following adopted for standardized tests, but they should be considered by instructors in crafting intermediate quizzes and review exams leading up to the standardized test.

Alternatives For Review Exams & Intermediate Quizzes

✓ **Multiple Answer Questions.** Multiple answer questions are different from multiple choice questions. Multiple choice questions have one answer; multiple answer questions have more than one answer. We believe it is a better more comprehensive type of question to utilize when students have to group certain terms or memorize lists of common elements. This type of question tests the student's knowledge more broadly and also leaves them with a more complete answer. Here is a good example of a multiple answer question:

Which three actions listed below must an Internet service provider take to qualify for "safe harbor" protection under the Digital Millennium Copyright Act (Public Law 105-304)? (Circle Three)

1. Accommodate standard copyright protection measures. *
2. Act against clients who post illegal copyrighted material.
3. Approve client content before permitting content to be posted.
4. Monitor the content of client materials posted through its service.
5. Post compliance representative contact information on its website. *
6. Register a notification agent with the U.S. Copyright Office. *

✓ **Matching Lists.** Students can be given two lists of topics and asked to pair up the items on each list that go together. Many of us have seen these kind of matching lists used with children drawing the connecting lines between each item.

✓ **Mini-Reviews.** Shorter more frequent tests are more effective than longer, end of the course reviews. For example if the end of your class contains a 25 question quiz, it would probably be more effective and interesting to the students if you broke the exam up into five groups of five questions each and spread them throughout the class. Not only is this probably more enjoyable for the students, but it has the additional benefit of inserting the questions closer to the material to which they pertain.

✓ **Rank & Order Questions.** We seldom see rank and order type questions used, but they have multiple applications when students are asked to learn a process or a standard series of steps. Here is an example of a rank and order question.

Place the following steps in the correct order, i.e., the order the technical support representative will direct the customer to follow:

A. Enter a user name
B. Launch the program
C. Create and save an m.pth file
D. Check the sound function
E. Edit and save the drive.var file

✓ **Fill-in The Blank Questions.** Most often these are not used on standardized tests due to handwriting issues and the difficulty in grading, but they are effective in building student retention. We know of many instructors applying this concept to their student materials and firmly attest to its ability to engage the student and hold attention during the presentation.

✓ **Engagement & Games.** All of the engagement exercises discussed in Act VIII can be transformed into review exercises. The games that were discussed, incorporation of social media and group activities can all be brought in as additional tools to vary and enhance review exam activities.

PostClass Reviews & Feedback

If we are not collecting student evaluations at the end of every course we teach we should be. How can we expect to improve as instructors if we don't solicit accurate feedback from our students as to what we did right and what we did wrong? Class surveys don't need to be long nor detailed. There are really only three questions we need to ask each student at the end of a class:

1. **What did you like the most?**
2. **What did you like the least?**
3. **How can we improve?**

The mistake that many of us make is that we wait until the very end of class to distribute the evaluations. We are fortunate when we do that to get 50% of them back. If they do get completed then, we are often diluting student attention to the last portion of the course as they are diligently filling out evaluations. We are big believers in ending a class strong. Think the "Great Endings" we discussed earlier in this book. If we simply move the distribution of evaluations to the time period right before the last break, it solves this problem. More evaluations get returned and we don't diffuse attention at the end of the class.

There are technological ways to gather student feedback, input and constructive criticism following a presentation. Sites like SurveyMonkey.Com allow us to create a post class survey and of course we can also funnel such solicitations for feedback to facebook and twitter feeds where the student comments and ideas might just generate some interest in other classes as they are viewed by non-participants in the class. We are so trained in class due to GAPE to thank students for their contributions, ideas and comments. We are less trained to respond or send a note in regard to an evaluation that a student turned in at the end of a course. Want to generate more loyal students? Want to demonstrate that you truly care about what they had to say? Take a moment and write the student a note and an email thanking them for their comment. Your students and the future of your teaching career will thank you for it. It's one of those things that most other instructors will never take the time to do. We can already hear Sugar Ray Leonard in our ear, "Just do one thing every day that your competition is not willing to do!"

Curtain Call

"Why Should Instructors Pursue a Credential?"

George Bell, Chair of the National Real Estate Educators Association DREI Management Committee

George Bell has taught nearly 500,000 people in various real estate courses and seminars. George has dedicated his career to the practice of real estate, with much of it being in the area of teaching and writing. He is the author of two books on North Carolina Real Estate and is a past president of the Real Estate Educators Association. He holds multiple speaking designations including DREI, CSP(from NSA) and the REALTOR'S® Instructor Training Institute Certification. He is the owner of G. Bell Productions, Ltd. Winston, Salem, North Carolina. You can reach George at George@GeorgeBell.com

In the professional world in which I live and function, the alphabet is not A B C D, etc., but rather DREI, CSP, ITI, CRB, CRS, ePro, etc. And I suspect you are adept at reading my alphabet!

At the tender age of 21 and while in college – and knowing that I knew everything about everything – I entered the world of real estate. But with less than six months experience as a REALTOR® I was thrust into the classroom to teach 80 eager adults about how to get a real estate license. What did I, as a 21-year old recent college graduate, teach these 80 adults? A whole lot less than they taught this – still wet behind the ears – farm boy from NC!!!

The event depicted above occurred the year prior to the time a group of well-versed individuals were organizing REEA in Chicago (1979). In 1981 I attended the first ever real estate educator's conference in NC. A few years latter NCREEA was organized and I immediately became immersed in the REEA and NCREEA culture.

241

And what has this meant to me? In short … A LOT. But first…

What is REEA?

The Real Estate Educators Association is a society of real estate education stakeholders (instructors, trainers, regulators, schools, authors, etc.). REEA's challenge is to continually give its members the latest tools and techniques for effective adult education. REEA's goal is to make sure REEA members meet and exceed the high standards demanded in real estate's rapidly changing legal and professional environment. Annually, REEA hosts a national convention where educators can meet and talk one-on-one with the people who write the textbooks, design the computer systems and develop the teaching methods used to launch novice students toward successful careers. The award-winning Biannual REEA Journal focuses on specific business and classroom issues confronting the modern educator. Every quarter, REEANews updates members on what's happening in the industry, separating "trends" from "fads," and "problems" from "opportunities." And every day, REEA members can communicate with each other via REEAline where topics routinely range from the ordinary to the extraordinary, all in a spirit of fun and sharing.

REEA is where the nation's most respected real estate educators meet.

What is the DREI?

By way of analogy, I would like to think that you would fear seeking medical advice from a doctor that did not continually seek new methods for treating his/her patients, or advice from an attorney that failed to keep abreast of new laws and regulations. Similarly, why wouldn't any adult who wishes to seek a new or higher level of knowledge regarding real estate seek to do so from one who continually demonstrates his/her willingness to stay abreast of new techniques – both teaching and industry related?

To this end, one who "teaches" real estate, wherein most students of such are adults, should seek to achieve a level of knowledge and ability that is "second to none". In the real estate teaching arena, arguably this desire for such 'accreditation' will lead one to the Distinguished Real Estate Instructor (DREI) designation as offered by the Real Estate Educator Association (REEA).

The DREI program is designed to demonstrate that the holder of the DREI designation has demonstrated to a peer group that their comprehension of the field of real estate and their ability to 'teach adults' meets the standard set forth by REEA. The standard that is evaluated and which must be met includes, among other things, the passing of a written examination of real estate topics, a written vita relating to both work-life and teaching experience in the field of real estate, and a peer review of a live presentation by the candidate.

The oversight of the DREI program is the DREI Management Committee of REEA. Detailed information about the DREI program may be obtained by visiting www.REEA.org and clicking on the DREI link or emailing MemberCare@reea.org.

Why should one seek to achieve the DREI designation?

For those involved in the real estate industry, there is no mystery that many REALTORS® seek to set themselves apart from their competition by earning designations. Real estate educators should seek to do no less. However, there is a difference between many of the REALTOR® designation programs and the DREI. Namely, in order to be awarded the DREI designation one must *verify* a proven track record in the classroom as a real estate teacher/educator and demonstrate such ability before a group of peers. Thus, to be awarded the DREI one must possess and *demonstrate* experience and ability as a teacher/educator of real estate.

Thus, "Why should one seek to achieve the DREI designation" – in short, to prove that he/she has *proven* that he/she has earned the right to rise above the norm. The DREI is the only designation for real estate educators and, as such, is used as a measurement by many of the real estate Commissions when considering approval or renewal of instructors.

Pride aside, why would one not desire to demonstrate to their clientele (students, in this case) that they (the client/student) are worthy of the best?!

And so … to digress – What has the DREI meant to me?

Earlier I stated – "A LOT" – and I stand by this! I was fortunate to have been the first DREI in the state of NC and one of the first 25 in the USA. As such, early on I was able to "stand above" many of the other very knowledgeable, experienced and most worthy real estate educators in my home state – many of whom followed suit and earned the DREI.

On several occasions I have been hired (over other very qualified instructors/educators) just because I held the DREI designation. In fact, one state regulatory agency (not NC) hired me as their sole educator to present a series of programs in twelve markets, over a span of several months, across their state because I held the DREI designation. As the Executive Director of that state's real estate

Commission stated, "We knew that since you had the DREI we did not have to ask you to prove that you were good, we already knew you were good."

In conclusion, I am one who has never understood why one who expects to be paid for providing a service to or for another is unwilling to do that which is necessary to better prepare them self in order to better serve others. As an instructor/educator, if you are worthy of the student's attention, time and money, then the student is worthy of you being the very best you can be! And as a real estate teacher/educator, working toward earning the DREI – even if you fall short of earning such – is such a demonstration of desire to be the very best you can be. Your adult students deserve no less of you!

Curtain Call

"The Transformations in Real Estate Education"

Marie Spodek, DREI, CDEI
Professional Real Estate Solutions

Marie Spodek is a nationally recognized real estate trainer and author who contributed to Don Levi's book, "How To Teach Adults." Marie is the author of the Course Development Workshop offered at a number of REEA conferences. She has authored and co-authored a series of continuing education books published by Dearborn Real Estate Education. She received REEA's coveted John Wiedemer Award and awards for best course of the year and several best Journal articles. She is the owner of Professional Real Estate Solutions offering "Real Estate Seminars for Real People." You can find out more about Marie at MarieSpodek.com

A number of years ago, a reporter asked the famous baseball player, Hank Aaron, "Why do you think that you've hit so many home runs?" Aaron pulled from his hip pocket a tattered, worn-out pamphlet entitled, "The Little League Guide to Batting" and replied, "I think it is because I have never gotten away from the basics." While this may be an apocryphal story, I think that it illustrates an important point as to where we are today in real estate education. Perhaps we should not be in such a hurry to find dramatic changes. While most of my comments relate to live classroom instruction, several might be useful for even on-line asynchronous courses as well.

As a DREI, I am required to document 10 hours of education per year, a requirement that essentially can be met by attending a REEA conference and/or an instructor workshop. Over the years, I have made it a point to attend classes and to participate as a student, in order to learn best practices that I can duplicate in my own classrooms. I've also learned things that I vowed I would never do to my students. I always advise new instructors to do the same when taking my classes as well.

From my own experiences, as a student, I value the following:

1. **Instructors who tell us upfront when we can expect breaks.** Honestly, the mind can absorb only what the seat can endure. Many states permit 50-minute hours, meaning that the other 10 minutes of the hour is meant to be used for the restroom, to return phone calls, to have a cigarette, or to just move around. We ask a lot from very busy people to sit quietly for long stretches of time while we instructors get to actively move around. I have found it useful to ask the participants to let me know when/if I go past the time for a break.

2. **The use of a timer on the screen with count-down minutes for not only breaks but also for break out discussion groups.** It is all too easy during breaks for one or two students to monopolize the instructor's time, and a timer keeps everyone on track. Similarly, very often, I will observe a student in a small group notice the timer and get the group back on track with the assigned discussion.

3. **A skilled instructor who ensures that groups form circles of 4-6 participants for breakout sessions.** Break out groups are extremely important to clear up misunderstanding and to encourage creative thinking. A skilled instructor plans for at least one interactivity per hour and creates the best environment for an active exchange of ideas not only with clear and precise instructions but also ensuring an encouraging physical environment so that participants can clearly see and hear each other. Simply saying, "form into groups" is not effective because most people will sit there and talk to only one other person. (The most effective and quickest way is to ask every other row to turn around and face those directly behind them, and then form into groups of 4-6.)

Other observations from reading altogether too many evaluations over the years:

Little value in pep talks. My first training "boss" told me that ending a class with a motivational talk would not alleviate fear. He said that students don't need a pep talk as much as they need to be reassured that they have made progress towards their goal, which in pre-license is passing the state exam. Therefore, I use pep talks first thing in the morning and right after lunch. At the end of each major segment of time, i.e., before lunch and at the end of the day or evening, I use an oral quiz to reaffirm to the students what we have learned up to that point.

I suppose that in an ideal world, students read the material ahead of time, and come to class wide-awake and ready to discuss the topics they didn't understand. It has not been my experience in the last 20 years. My students are rushing from one commitment to another with very little time for homework.

Regulators told me that as pre-license requirements moved from 30 to 40 to 75 hours and more, pre-license instructors were expected to introduce practical applications that included more "hands on" exercises. Unfortunately, all too often, instructors felt that the extra time gave them license to tell more "war stories" about their own experiences in the field. Let's be honest: classroom stories will never take the place of actual practice.

The value of memorization. Students cannot successful respond to any type of application question, even a multiple choice much less an essay question, unless they know the precise meaning of key terms and phrases, not always an easy process. They must memorize definitions! A well-written course and a well-prepared instructor will encourage the use of flash cards and provide matching exercises, and even possibly fill-in-the-blanks to assist in reading the text.

In an instructor development workshop, a number of participants argued with me when I encouraged the use of flash cards. A man stood up and said the following:

> *I am a former state regulator; many of you know that I am now attending law school. As a classroom instructor, and as a regulator, I reassured students that as long as they read their assignments and participated in class, they would pass the test. However, I would never have made it through the first year of law school IF I hadn't used flashcards. Now I am a firm believer.*

A few years ago, the school with which I was affiliated participated as a beta site for one of the very first "computer" pre-license courses. What we learned is this: anyone who sat through 60 classroom hours, loved their classroom instructor (me!) and received their certificates of completion and had about an 80 percent pass rate on the state exam. Not bad! However, nearly all of those who "successfully" completed all modules on the computer disk (i.e., having achieved 90 percent correct responses on all quizzes) passed the state exam on the first attempt. To be honest, I am not at all unhappy about that. On-line instruction requires a high level of reading ability and is not necessarily the best way to learn for poor readers and/or those for whom English is a second language.

Continuing education. Twenty years ago, during the debate about introducing continuing education, one regulator told me that all of her research indicated that additional education did not deflect unwise conduct; what did diminish unlawful or unethical conduct was increasing the number of auditors and meaningful penalties. She expressed fear that required continuing education would only "dumb down" the course offerings. Twenty years ago, licensees paid for classes that enhanced their skills that would help them become more successful as real estate licensees.

Today, more often than not, licensees consider educational requirements as something that must be endured, and they look for the least expensive courses that take the least amount of time. Unfortunately, this is the reason that so many licensees prefer to find "packages" of required CE hours, whether or not they actually can use the information.

They often display the same attitude in the classroom. I am dismayed when I follow instructors who care so little about their material that they agree with their students to "cut out" breaks, and who manufacture fake "discussions" over lunch so that all can leave the classroom several hours earlier than scheduled. This does a great disservice to those who attend the class in order to learn and it may be a violation of state law regarding attendance.

Low bar of entry into real estate. As noted in the preceding text, a beautician spends more hours for her license than does a real estate licensee. However, it's important to note that the majority of those hours are spent actually cutting and styling hair in a very controlled environment under the direct supervision of school instructors. Likewise, dental students spend much of their last year of dental school filling teeth and fitting braces under the direct supervision of skilled instructors.

Simply adding to the number of classroom hours without hands on participation does not ensure better application in the actual marketplace. There is a limit to how much retention new licensees can retain as they move from classroom to real world.

I liked the transitional licenses in South Carolina, now discontinued. After going to class and passing the state prelicense test, SC applicants received a license that was effective for 12 to 16 months permitting them to work under the direct supervision of their broker-in-charge. Near the end of this period, to receive their permanent license, they had to retake a higher-level pre-license course and become proficient in closing statement concepts. They retook the pre-license test and completed a closing statement in detail. Approximately 60 percent chose to let their provisional license lapse, and that was just fine!

Ultimately, have the Internet, PowerPoint, YouTube and smartphones transformed real estate education? As much as changed, so has much remained the same.

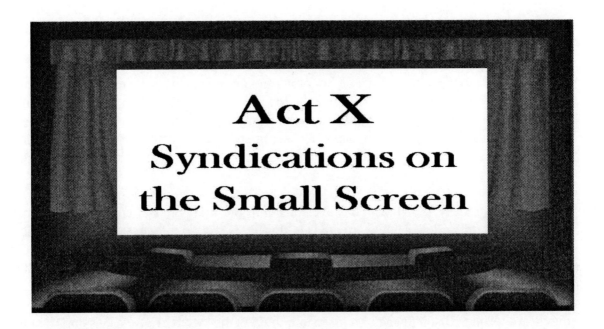

Distance Learning Principles & Tools

The advent of technology brings competition, challenges and opportunities to the world of education. The concept of distance learning covers a lot of territory. The best definition we have found for distance learning is:

The process of transferring knowledge to learners who are separated from the instructor by time and/or physical distance and are making use of technology components.

Before you weigh in as either an opponent or a proponent of distance learning we want you to reread that definition. It means that your Kindle is a distance learning tool, for that matter so are the tutorials on your phone, the educational television programs you watch, the talk radio stations you listen to and the internet you visit every day. So many live instructors are quick to dismiss distance learning because they have too narrow a definition of it. Sometimes when we hear "distance learning" we translate it into "poorly done online classes." This is not what distance learning is all about and reframing our understanding of distance learning will help eliminate the "we" against "them" mentality that exists sometimes between live instruction and online instruction. It really is not a "we" against "them" world. Both distance learning and live instruction require good course developers, good instructors and material that is delivered to the students at high quality applying the concepts of GAPE.

GAPE Meets Distance Learning

GAPE applies just as much to anything online as it does to live classroom instruction. The availability of software, hardware and technology to today's students creates the ability to learn anything, anytime, anywhere. One blatant truth remains: someone still has to teach it. The manner and method in which that teaching is done requires a knowledge of subject matter, an understanding of adult learners and presentation skills.

In 1976 Steve Wozniak and Steve Jobs built the first personal computer (PC) in a garage in Silicon Valley. They were advised that PC's were a nice novelty, but that they had no practical application. Today, Apple, the company started by these two men is still posting impressive statistics more than three decades later. Their "little novelty" is a $200 billion business. It turns out that the MAC, iphone and ipod had some practical application after all. At the 2008 REEA Convention in Coconut Point, Florida, we overheard some distinguished real estate instructors (DREI's) discussing online education. It was an eerie echo of the conversation from the Silicon Valley garage in 1976. Those instructors said, "Well, distance education makes the Generally Accepted Principles of Education (GAPE) a nice novelty, but they have no real application to online education." With that comment they virtually dismissed GAPE as irrelevant to today's online educator and the online student.

The Generally Accepted Principles of Education were not written or created by REEA. They are not a set of standards which only real estate instructors should adhere to, nor are they principles which apply only to live classroom instruction. GAPE offers adult learning principles and fundamental precepts that have been tested over time, validated by research and provides guidance about how best to teach to adult learners.

Though the personal computer, the ipod and the iphone have changed the method and manner in which information and material is delivered, the basic communication and education precepts remain the same. This is particularly true of newer educational delivery systems. Adults learn best under conditions where we apply the basic principles and those principles remain the same whether we are teaching live in a classroom or using distance learning technology.

In Act II we outlined the educational teaching concepts of GAPE, spread over 5 categories: knowledge, andragogy, speech, teaching aids and learning environment. Distance education succeeds or fails for precisely the same reason that live instruction sometimes fails, when we do not apply GAPE to the delivery of the education.

The Translation of GAPE to Distance Learning

Many of the concepts of GAPE translate easily into online course presentations. Whether live or by distance learning tools, instructors should always:

- Provide current information
- Present alternative viewpoints on material when there is not a single position that is accepted industry wide
- Clearly identify opinions as the instructor's opinion
- Build a proper foundation for each major element of a subject
- Deal with all key elements of a subject
- Cover the material adequately in the allotted time
- Focus on students gaining knowledge, not on impressing the students with the instructor's knowledge
- Present new ideas by relating them to pre-existing knowledge held by the learners
- Teach at the learner's level
- Show in a specific way how new material will benefit the learners
- Use a variety of teaching methods
- Use concise, simple, and normal speech patterns, use simple terminology
- Not read to the class
- Keep the topic flowing
- Enunciate clearly without being overdone

Internet Library by jscreationszs
Freedigitalphotos.net

We think you get the idea. Some GAPE concepts which may not have been applicable to the first generation of distance learning courses is now applicable to instructors in the same fashion as it is in the classroom. This is particularly true when we are dealing with webinars and formats of synchronous education where the instructor is online with the students at the time the material is delivered. In these formats we must:

- Use visual imagery when possible to enhance written words
- Deviate from the material only to meet specific needs
- Use color
- Call learners by name
- Involve learners in the learning process through planned activities
- Teach to all participants, not just those who show interest

- Show tolerance – both to ignorance and disagreement thus avoiding confrontations and argument
- Encourage questions and motivate involvement

Today's distance learning tools allow instructors to incorporate and share video. Not only must we wear professional attire and speak loudly enough to be heard by all, but now we must also be careful to avoid becoming a "talking head." Talking head instructors in online courses no more fulfill GAPE principles than the instructors who stood rigidly behind the lectern in traditional classrooms. Instructors of distance education have to incorporate appropriate gestures and physical movements for the same reason that we do these things in classroom settings. It turns out that the instructors who gesture too wildly or have annoying physical habits are just as annoying in distance education as they were in the live classroom. In a live classroom we wouldn't read students page after page of textual material. We wouldn't give them pages of text to read. We shouldn't do that in distance learning either.

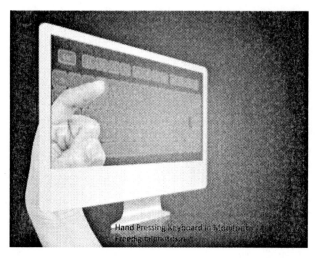
Hand Pressing Keyboard in Monitor by
Freedigitalphotos.net

Some of the GAPE principles may need to be applied more creatively. We may need to think of the GAPE requirements for gestures and classroom movement as the animation of slides and the flow of material on a computer screen. We may have to convert our environment thinking from the classroom to the computer monitor, but the same questions still exist. Is the screen free of distractions? Are there physical objects on the screen which act as barriers to the student's learning? Is the format conducive to the presentation of the information? Will the template arrangement and screen layout make the student feel comfortable or is it overcrowded, cramped and confusing?

Even when the learning is asynchronous (without the instructor present) we can still use GAPE principles to engage and motivate the students. We can involve them in activities and we can still address their questions by anticipating them in advance and leading into discussions with phrases like, "Perhaps you were wondering..." "You may have been asking yourself......" "One of the questions which students typically ask is..."

When talking pictures were invented, the silent film stars worried about their careers being extinguished. For those who remained silent their careers did end. When television was invented, the movie producers and live Hollywood actors feared the worst. Two things happened. Some of them made the transition into the new mediums and others found ways to increase the quality and attraction to the old mediums. Technology never erases anything. It only expands the options. It may mean we need to recraft or reinvent ourselves, but quite honestly, if we are not doing that every day in the current world our careers were in trouble anyway. The advancement of technology and increased competition also tends to force everyone to get better at what they do. Education is no different.

Whether we want to admit it or not, distance learning has been with us a long time and it will continue to grow and expand. It is convenient, cost effective and too popular to ignore. Instructors who offer their skills and knowledge in distance learning formats can apply GAPE concepts and breathe life into online courses just as they bring their passion and skills into the traditional classroom. In the end, distance learning doesn't mean abandoning GAPE, it means applying those principles in new and innovative ways. It's all okay if students decide to join us on the small screen, it's all acting, it's all theater and it's all teaching.

The Role of ARELLO

ARELLO® is the Association of Real Estate License Law Officials and it is comprised of the official government agencies and other organizations around the world that issue real estate licenses or registrations in addition to regulatory real estate practice and enforcing real estate law. The organization has existed since 1930 and began as a national organization. In 1993 ARELLO® was expanded to reach beyond the borders of the United States.

Most of the Association's early years were limited to the informal sharing of ideas relating to administrative practices, the development of license laws and attempts to create reciprocity amongst various real estate regulatory jurisdictions. Over the years ARELLO® has interacted with various government agencies as well as state and national REALTOR® associations to provide answers to industry issues, develop education and create standards in the real estate profession. The Association's mission statement is to support jurisdictions in the administration and enforcement of real estate license laws to promote and protect the public interest.

One of ARELLO's main products and services is the certification of education classes, particularly in the area of distance education. The organization has created standards and a system for course certification. Today, all but 10 states either require or recognize the certifications issued by ARELLO® as part of the course approval process.

Synchronous & Asynchronous Education

There are a lot of different forms and venues of distance education. It is conducted across a multitude of platform in a multitude of forms and incarnations. An ongoing debate exists about the value of synchronous vs. asynchronous distance learning.

Asynchronous e-learning: learning which occurs through technology without the instructor being immediately available or interacting with the students online. Most real estate continuing education classes so far are asynchronous meaning that the courses exist for students to take at their leisure and though the material was prepared by an instructor they cannot interact with the instructor in real time.

Synchronous e-learning: learning which occurs through technology where the instructor in real time leads the students. The students can directly interact with the instructor and multiple students are usually engaged in the learning at the same time so that they can interact with each other. Think live webinar.

Laptop by Gregory Szarkiewicz
Freedigitalphotos.net

There is no debate that many people participate in distance education because it can be asynchronous. Converging family, job and education obligations allow students to take a course when it best fits their schedule, not when it happens to be scheduled or when the instructor is available. Just because the delivery of the initial material may be asynchronous, it does not necessarily mean that the student does not have access to an instructor or the ability to ask questions. Many of the platforms being used allow the learner to text or email questions or concerns which they might have while they are taking the course. On the other side of the debate are those who believe that course material should always be delivered, supervised and monitored by an instructor in real time even if the education is online.

Most of the initial studies done regarding the benefits of the two forms of distance education tried to determine which medium works better for the students and the studies couldn't identify any significant difference. As time progresses it would be our deep suspicion that in regard to some topics and learning objectives synchronous will be a better choice and that on other topics and learning objectives, asynchronous learning may be the better method. In fact there are a ton of options for how distance education is delivered.

A Brief Guide to Distance Learning Technologies

✓ **Learning Management Systems.** A Learning Management System (LMS) is the software application for the administration, management, tracking and reporting of online courses. In situations where credit hours are made available to students involved in distance learning most regulatory agencies require tracking, management and reporting of student activity online. Though the requirements of jurisdictions vary the most commonly tracked and reported items include:

- Identification and recordation of students taking the course
- Time spent by the students taking the course
- Quiz and test scoring
- Completion times for students in covering the material

There are many different types of LMS systems. Each has its own distinct features and most of them use the parameters of SCORM (Shareable Content Object Reference Model) for providing the information online to students. SCORM contains the technical specifications that govern how online information is created and delivered to learners.

Instructors and educational providers need some type of LMS to deliver online education effectively. Some educators design or purchase an LMS system and some use internet based LMS systems (a couple of the most popular are Moodle and Articulate Online). Another option is to deliver courses through some type of collaboration agreement with an entity already operating an LMS system. Which system works best for you will be based on the mandates of the regulatory agency governing your courses and the features that you would like to provide in distance education. Ryan K. Ellis, Editor of Learning Circuits for the The American Society for Training and Development (ASTD) has created a *Field Guide to Learning Management Systems* which you can find online.

✓ **Articulate.** Articulate is a software program that encompasses and empowers us to use the PowerPoint platform for distance learning. It allows for the addition of narration, the insertion of videos, quizzes and interactive activities and packages the material for online delivery. Articulate also provides an LMS on which to manage and track the courses for those who are not connected to a separate proprietary system. The bottom line is that if you can create a PowerPoint presentation then you can easily convert it to a distance learning format.

✓ **Webinars.** Web conferencing allows for the sharing of information between users in different locations. Webinars may involve the sharing of audios, videos, slide presentations and even the display of computer monitors. Most of the webinar systems and software allow for interactive sharing between the webinar participants and the instructor. GoToWebinar is one of the most common internet sites used for the hosting of this type of distance learning. Because the webinars can be recorded and played by students later they may occur as either synchronous or asynchronous education.

✓ **Podcasts.** Podcasts and webcasts contain series of digital media files, in either audio or video format that are released episodically and then downloaded through web syndication services. The technology differs from standard internet access because they are usually subscribed to by the user and then downloaded directly to the subscriber and loaded onto their system. Podcasts and webcasts generally are not interactive with the users and are also usually of shorter duration that webinars and other distance learning programs.

✓ **Packaged Technology Products.** Not all distance leaning occurs through internet based technology. Distance learning education can also be offered in the form of packaged technology products such as DVD's which are purchased and shipped to students. Current technology allows for the content on the DVD to be interactive. For example, the Articulate program allows you to produce the learning program for an LMS, for online or as a DVD/CD product.

✓ **Mobile Learning Technologies.** The future is in mobile technology. With the advent of smart phones, iphones and Droids, consumers are used to getting all types of products and services on their phones. Distance learning programs and products are just beginning to access this market and format.

Meeting the Challenges of Distance Education

Distance education creates new opportunities for instructors to deliver education to more students in more locations with more variety than ever before. Distance education also brings new challenges to the virtual classrooms. Regulators and administrators have their own sets of challenges associated with such education.

We find it interesting that most of the "new" issues that individuals raise as to distance learning are not any different from the challenges faced in all forms of education in all venues. We thought it would be fun to share with you a dialogue between the skeptic of distance education and a DREI (Distinguished Real Estate Instructor) who understands the nature and process of education:

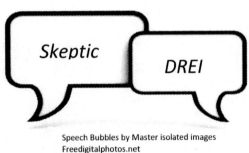

Speech Bubbles by Master isolated images
Freedigitalphotos.net

Skeptic: How will we know for example that the person taking the course online is really the person who is getting credit for it?

DREI: Usually we just have them sign in.

Skeptic: That will never work, they could sign in online with someone else's name.

DREI: They can do that now in live classes.

Skeptic: We can't have that. We are going to need to make online students verify with a thumbprint screen I.D. or a scanned copy of their driver's license that they really are that person.

DREI: Wow! I better let my live course students know they are going to be fingerprinted when they come in the door. Do you think I should remind them in my ethics class that they can't be there if they are pretending to be someone else?

Skeptic: Signing in is only the start of the problem. How can we force them to pay attention to the computer monitor?

DREI: You know, now that you mention it, I have noticed that sometimes in the classroom they look around too. I've never thought about punishing them for not staring at the screen. I always thought it was my job to make the material interesting enough that they wanted to watch.

Skeptic: That's an interesting approach. I'm just not sure it will work. If they are online they could be doing something else rather than paying attention to the class.

DREI: You mean like doodling on their handout, daydreaming about the upcoming weekend or staring out the window?

Skeptic: That's exactly what I'm talking about. They need to pay attention and be listening to and watching the instruction.

DREI: I've always thought that was a good idea. Why don't you try engaging them online?

Skeptic: Well, they might not respond. They could choose to just sit there and do nothing.

DREI: I've noticed that too. Welcome to education. You have to be creative in your engagement and have material that causes them to want to respond.

Skeptic: Response really isn't the point. The questions is how do we make them learn?

DREI: That's a really good question. Maybe you should think about having them swear that they will learn something when you get their I.D. and fingerprints.

Skeptic: We could give them a test. But they might just take the test and be able to pass it without paying attention to all the material.

DREI: You mean if they are smarter than the instructor and the material and they already know it then they shouldn't' get credit for taking the class?

Skeptic: Well, the point is we want to make certain that they cover all the material and spend a certain amount of time with it?

DREI: I thought the point was making sure they knew the material and had learned it. What if they are a fast learner?

Skeptic: Look, we can't be giving people credit for stuff they already know. If they do it faster we just can't give them credit.

DREI: I once read a book in two days that most people take a week to read.

Skeptic: You were supposed to spend a minimum of 10 days on that book.

DREI: Do you want to see my notes? I learned a lot.

Skeptic: Well, you are going to have to have to stop learning so quickly. Slow down when you read.

DREI: I'm sorry. I'm confused. Are we giving students credit for education or are we giving them credit for the time they served?

Skeptic: We have to give them credit for the time they served.

DREI: I thought you wanted them to learn something. Now you are making them sound like inmates. I think I know why you wanted their fingerprints.

We don't mean to poke fun (yes, we do… in an educational way) at the objections we hear all of the time, but to us it seems that the focus of the questions is out of line with what we fundamentally believe about teaching, instruction and the education of adult learners. Distance learning has had a way of bringing to the forefront of our industry meaningful discussions about the nature of adult education. That is a welcome debate.

We understand that "time in the seat" is as easily measurable, objective way to fulfill compliance with administrative mandates. The impostion of mandated education and required courses has gotten our industry to this point. We are just not certain that much was ever gained by forcing a student to acquire education because they had to do so. We are certain less has been gained by instruction that was delivered simply because the instructor was forced to do so.

Busy Senior Business by Photostock
Freedigitalphotos.net

The problem with mandated "time in the seat" is that it focuses on the wrong end of the student. Can you imagine a world where students came to class not because they had to, but because the course and the instruction held out promises of providing something that the student truly wanted and needed to learn? Courses would have to be designed that were interesting, engaging and delivered "items of value" to the student. Instructors would need to continually improve their skills, tools, knowledge and the delivery of material in order to attract students into the classroom. Can you imagine that? We can.

Research and work done into the nature of distance learning students would confirm the need for all of this. Jill Gulusha at the University of Southern Mississippi, created an Abstract, *Student Barriers to Distance Learning.* In the abstract she notes that more so than traditional students, distance learners are more likely to have:

- Insecurities about learning
- Fears about lack of experience and training
- Feelings of isolation and alienation
- Concerns about self-esteem
- Lack of motivation and interest in the material

DREI instructors have been using the GAPE concepts in live classroom settings and know how the application of the concepts can minimize these issues in the traditional classroom. That leaves fertile ground for instructors to take and apply these skills and talents to tackling the current problems in distance education. Distance learning has created a whole new world of opportunity.

When we think of distance learning we should think much bigger than pre-licensing and approved continuing education classes for credit hours. Those certainly are part of distance learning, but the platforms, tools, expanse of delivery and the cost effectiveness of the delivery ought to have us asking intriguing questions of ourselves such as, "Exactly what could be placed in distance learning that would benefit the students and increase our efficiency and profitability?"

Out of the Box Distance Learning Strategies That Add To Effectiveness & Profitability

✓ **Economically Justifiable Classes -** A lot of material got passed over in the age of live classroom instruction simply because it couldn't be justified economically. Let's say for example a great class was written for property managers of single family residences. The course may have had great material, but the best audience we could expect was 10 people per month. By the time we covered expenses and paid for the course instruction each month, the rate of economic return on the course as a business didn't justify teaching it. That was particularly true when we could have been dedicating resources like classroom space and instruction to more profitable courses. As a result only the most popular courses could be offered, although there have always been students on the edges of our industry in niche markets, their needs have been largely disregarded due to economics.

With distance education that 10 person class could be taught once online and then take up no resources and we have gained an additional 120 students a year. When we add in the fact that the course can now be offered over a very wide geographic spanse at no additional costs then the breadth, depth and detail of classes can be expanded in this format. What classes have you not developed because you needed to have a larger audience to justify them?

✓ **Administrative and Orientation Type Information.** Often a lot of time is spent on administrative or orientation type information in the classroom. In a typical sales pre-licensing class we are spending lots of time on review exams, orientation material, test preparation information and other things that could have been delivered to the students in a distance learning format. Particularly if it was informational in nature, we can allow ongoing access to the material so that students can come back and review it should they have further questions.

Even in states that do not permit distance learning for pre-licensing instruction there is a lot of ancillary material that could be provided to the students at low cost using distance learning technology. Time in the classroom could be allocated to more demanding issues and we could reallocate classroom time more productively. Distance learning segments could even be developed to share with students how to use your website, familiarize them with staff and instructors and to discuss administrative policies.

✓ **Ancillary & Enriching Classroom Segments.** A broader view of distance learning to encompass more than just "online continuing education" would open our eyes toward thinking how we would use distance learning platforms to enrich and supplement classroom presentations. Can a live classroom segment be followed up with a more in depth online presentation for the students who are interested in further study?

The gurus of real estate education, Joe Stumpf, Brian Buffini, Tony Robbins and others made fortunes following a model where they would do presentations in order to encourage people to attend a larger more expansive and expensive event. Many of us many not have had the luxury of the time or money it took to travel to all of those different venues. We can be in different venues with distance education. We should be thinking about how we would employ the model. Is it a series of live classes to draw people to the distance education event or is it a series of distant education events to draw people to the live classroom?

We are positively certain that no matter what subject matter or level your teaching may currently be at, there is a way to supplement and enrich those courses with ancillary and supplemental distance learning.

✓ **Short, Useful & Practical Material.** We get into mindsets based on the regulatory atmosphere that surrounds us. In most instances no one mandates that classes must be of a certain length. What is mandated in most states is a total number of hours a student must complete, not the length of specific course times. It would never have made sense for students to leave their office, drive across town, park their car and come to class for 30 or 60 minutes, despite the fact that it would have been easier and more convenient for them to spend 60 minutes than 3 hours.

Distance education makes teaching in these size segments practical and cost effective and probably more convenient for the students as well. What short, useful and practical information could you deliver in 30 minutes that would be of value to students? The price will be low, the economies of scale good and the profitable rate of return on your investment great.

✓ **Non-Accredited Training.** All of us have great ideas for information that business people need to be successful, but that might not fit into the traditional categories or requirements for approved credit hours with a regulatory agency. All of this material could be created and placed on distance learning platforms.

It seems to us that distance learning is not only here to stay, but it will continue to expand and grow. You may have heard us say in a class or two, "business is business and sales is sales" well "teaching is teaching." Many of the same skills that are required to succeed in the classroom are necessary to succeed in distance learning. The only question is whether we can transfer our creativity and skills to those new platforms.

Laptop & Digital Books
By digitalart, Freedigitalphotos.net

Curtain Call

"Leveraging Classroom Experiences to Compete With Distance Learning"

Joe McClary, **Executive Director of the National Real Estate Educators Association**

Joe McClary is the Chief Operating Officer for the Association of Real Estate License Law Officials and directs the ARELLO Education Certification and International Distance Education Certification Center. He also currently serves as the Executive Director of the Real Estate Educators Association (REEA). You can reach him at Joe@Arello.org.

Approximately 50-60% of real estate and appraisal professional education is delivered at a distance today. Many professional licensees in industries such as real estate, appraisal, insurance and mortgage brokerage have found that their educational needs are best met by taking courses at any time and any place via their computer. But while distance learning courses can offer legitimate educational learning experiences, I often find them less than ideal for the continuing education of experienced licensees who need more sophisticated content as opposed to reinforcement of basic concepts. Online courses are often statically designed, meaning the content is set and you get what you get. A statically designed course cannot change direction should the student require it nor can it take advantage or exploit to its fullest potential information the student already knows.

A number of schools have closed their physical doors because of the exodus from the traditional classroom. However, does this mean traditional classroom education is going away? No, not if traditional classroom educators take advantage of strategies that can only be performed best in a classroom and students still demand high caliber educational experiences. To get a view of how classroom courses compete with distance learning, let's consider a few of the most popular teaching theories.

Three of the predominant teaching theories that exist today: 1) **behaviorism** 2) **cognitivism** and 3) **constructivism**. While we cannot offer a thorough treatment of each of these theories here is a quick description of each.

Behaviorism holds that motivation for learning comes from external sources. When students "learn" they are actually learning to "behave" in a particular way. Teaching becomes associated with behavior modification. For example, requiring a student to sit in class for X hours is a behaviorist strategy. If the student sits in the chair and listens to a lecture from an approved outline, then is required to pass a test and retake it if he or she fails, this theory says learning is simply successful behavior modification. The role of the instructor in a behaviorist environment would be that of a "sage on the stage" espousing what they know to an audience and expecting the student to assimilate knowledge as a part of that process.

Cognitivism says learning is accomplished by students who are internally motivated and is primarily achieved through cognitive exercises such as drill and practice. For example, instructors who provide worksheets or other exercises that the student must think through would be considered a cognitivist learning strategy. Through cognitive development of the neural networks that allow us to remember things, learning takes place. The instructor's role in a cognitivist environment focuses on the administration of relevant learning exercises that the student participates in to foster cognitive activity that pertain to the course objectives.

Finally, **constructivism**, like cognitivism, says learning is internally motivated. Students must construct new knowledge and attach it to what they already know. For example, in the process of teaching a new concept, a teacher asks a student, "What significant event happened in the United States on July 4, 1863?" This starts a process by which the student must answer the question by searching his or her internal memory networks of preexisting knowledge. A student can only answer this question, or learn something new by attaching (constructing) the answer to something that he already knows. For example, the student may have previously learned in history class or from reading a book that this date is the final day of the Battle of Gettysburg during the American Civil War. However, what the student may not have known, that may be new, is that this is also the day Vicksburg fell to General U.S. Grant, breaking the Southern supply lines crippling the rebel cause. Both happened on the same day. While you may have known one event that happened on that date, you have subsequently attached new knowledge to preexisting knowledge to learn something new. Constructivism says that students must take new knowledge and assimilate and accommodate it themselves.

Constructivist learning strategies involve social learning through peer groups, case studies, role playing, mentoring, cooperative learning groups, etc. Constructivism plays an especially strong role in adult learning because adults come to the learning environment with a lifetime of experience to share. Much of what adults learn must be learned through their experiences, including their bias, and predispositions. Regarding the role of the instructor in a constructivist environment, as opposed to being the "sage on the stage", the instructor in a constructivist environment would serve as the "guide on the side." Instructors stand by and guide the learning experience and do not micromanage it. Constructivist learning strategies also better answer the student's question, "What is in this for me?"

Now, what does this all have to do with classroom and distance education? Without question, distance education offered in business related professional education programs provides predominantly behaviorist and cognitivist environments for learning. While technologies can facilitate constructivist learning at a distance, it is rare in the world of business related professional education that these strategies are heavily used. I have personally reviewed thousands of distance education courses offered for professional education, in the real estate, appraisal, insurance and mortgage industry, and only a very small percentage incorporate constructivist strategies despite their overwhelming effectiveness and popularity when employed. Constructivist learning strategies such as group discussion, role play, cooperative learning groups, can easily and cost effectively be successfully used in a classroom. This is one huge advantage for classroom educators that can be capitalized on if classroom educators are going to compete with online experiences. Again, online experiences usually do not make use of constructivist learning strategies because they aren't easily automated and aren't considered to be cost effective in most cases.

In the real estate industry, a new educational phenomenon has been growing rapidly among groups who want constructivist learning experiences. Groups holding "REBAR Camps" which are essentially constructivist learning groups that get together face-to-face and share common experiences about a particular topic, in this case, real estate. There are no set speakers but a group of people who want to learn from each other. Some will be experts in something, while others will not. Groups are often facilitated by a moderator who serves as a "guide on the side" to lead discussions and maintain a productive collaborative environment. Learning takes place from what the student constructs and pursues with the group. (More information on REBAR camps can be found at rebarcampsa.com). Regulators typically do not award professional credit for such constructivist events because regulators can only easily regulate behaviorist and cognitivist educational plans. This is unfortunate and is something the regulatory world should think through and find new ways of providing or accepting relevant educational experiences that are outside the typical box of what has been done in the past.

Finally, constructivist learning strategies are not being employed, with a few exceptions, in most professional online education programs in industries like real estate, appraisal, insurance, and mortgage brokerage. Instructors serving as "guides on the side" as opposed to "sages on the stage" can capitalize on the in-class environment that is sought after by students seeking meaningful learning experiences, not rote online courses that rehash the same basic material that an agent learned in their pre-license course. Using creative approaches to engaging students with constructivist strategies should help ensure classroom education maintains an edge in the marketplace. However, the danger for in-class educators is if they continue to use only behaviorist and cognitivist strategies for a generation of students that are more and more identifying with the value of constructivist learning experiences. If in-class educators fail to meet students' needs, students will simply take their course work online and get the credit as fast and as cheap as they can.

Keep in mind; good instructors balance their instructional strategies between each of the three major teaching theories. In other words, good instructors incorporate behaviorist, cognitivist, and constructivist approaches to learning based on the needs of their students. Right now, in-class instructors have essentially a monopoly on constructivist education strategies that they should use to their advantage in competing with courses offered via distance education.

In summary, as long as there is a need for high caliber, dynamic professional improvement, classroom education isn't going away. Distance learning courses certainly have filled a need and many online courses do a good job of approaching the instructional design from the behavioral and cognitivist side. At this time, classroom education is the only cost effective way to provide some of the experiences a new generation of students is looking for. If classroom educators can show students that it is worth their time and energy to attend a class to get something they can't get anywhere else, we should see a growing market if nothing more than by the laws of economics. If in-class instructors offer the same traditional educational experiences offered in statically designed distance education courses that have little or no meaningful interaction or collaboration, such instructors may expect a decline in those attending their classes and schools.

Curtain Call

"Why Education is Important to Real Estate Professionals"

By Dan Adler, Team Leader
Keller Williams Southern Arizona

Dan Adler is the Team Leader for Keller William Southern Arizona. He has worked his way through the real estate industry as an agent, a broker and as the foce behind the Dan Adler Team. As a managing broker Dan has completed several leadership and productivity training seminars and coaches and leads an office of nearly 150 agents. He is also an instructor and trainer with Course Creators. Dan was recently named as one of the "40 under 40" most influential people. You can reach Dan at Dan@KW.com

The highest function of the teacher consists not so much in imparting knowledge as in stimulating the pupil in its love and pursuit

Author Unknown

As a student of history, economics and real estate I can passionately say we are living in incredible times. Never before has the role of a real estate professional been so multi-faceted. While the license may say licensed real estate "salesperson", the reality is our fiduciary duties have almost nothing to do with sales.

I always teach that the most successful real estate professionals are the ones that educate their buyers and sellers before, during, and after the transaction. In what should be a largely referral based business, only those that master their fiduciary duties for their clients will survive their first two years in the industry. The national real estate picture has been shifting and re-shifting since 2004-2005. The agents who are still standing tall and are profitable today understand the requirement to be learning based. As Gary Keller would say "Get real-get right"; in other words, you shift with the market or the market leaves you behind. There is no option to bury your head in the sand and say "I don't need to learn short sales, REO's and BPO's, because they will be gone in 3 years". Your clients need specific help and the agent's fiduciary responsibility requires that they represent their client's best interests in a proficient and knowledgeable manner or refer that business to someone who can.

I was visiting recently with one of the top agents in my market center whose business was up over 100% from 2009-2010 (a time when tens of thousands of agents "de-hired" themselves as real estate professionals) and I will never forget our conversation. I simply asked her, "What do you attribute your success to in the past 12 months?" She smiled and said "I just went where the business went and my clients came with me". Where the business "went" was to the distressed marketplace and she immediately took every single distressed property course available, some she even took twice!

As a classroom educator I often take note at who my attendees are. In almost every class I teach I will attempt to introduce myself to everyone in the audience during some point in the day. Here is what that exercise has taught me. The majority of the agents that come to my classes are top producers. The majority of agents who are top producers are education "junkies" and they "get it" at a very high level! In my local marketplace 58% of real estate professionals did one transaction or less in all of 2010. Now that is a distressed market and makes for some stressed agents! Yet, when you look at the number of classes top agents participate in versus those that are struggling, the top agents take three to five times more education courses than everyone else.

What is the lesson learned? The market shifts with you or without you. It's nobody's fault and it's not unique to real estate. Look at the medical field, procedures that only 2-3 years ago were major inpatient surgery today are outpatient procedures performed by robots! Those medical professionals shifted with the market or were out of business!

Top real estate professionals have a visionary mindset. That is to say they don't allow themselves to get caught up in a single transaction or a "transactional" mindset. They understand that through education, training, models, systems and tools that there is plenty of business to be had so that spending time in the classroom is truly an investment and not an expense. They see the business that will be there in weeks, months and years as a result of their newly learned skills and don't spend two seconds thinking "I don't have time to take a class".

The real estate profession can be competitive and most top producers love some healthy competition. When an agent gets a new designation, REO account or a million dollar client, everyone in the office knows about it and they should! Some agents decide not to be outdone and the launching pad of their pursuit often starts in the classroom.

Winners understand the power of language. Agents who are failing will often ask "why". Agents who are surviving will often ask "how". Agents who are succeeding will often ask "when or what" and agents who are thriving will often ask "who". So apply that to the agent when provided the opportunity to learn a new skill in the classroom. The failing agent asks "why would I take that class". The surviving agent asks "how do I take this class". The succeeding agent asks "when do I take this class" and the thriving agent asks "who is going to help me while I am at this class". That simple change in language impacts their mindset in a powerful way.

Top real estate professionals also tend to be very high energy and systematic in their approach to the business. From time to time this high energy can be drained by the day to day activities of the business. As with any business the opportunity to go learn a new skill or trade motivates and inspires and brings that energy level up and motivation soars to new levels.

Education has never been more important to the real estate professional than it is today. Not only to keep agents on "the pulse" of their industry but also to earn their clients trust, loyalty, referrals and future business. Education is also the best source of prevention for lawsuits and errors and omissions claims. The face of real estate shifts almost daily and will remain in this state of constant flux for the foreseeable future. When the market stabilizes, new challenges will surface and the agents who are learning-based will once again find themselves on top!

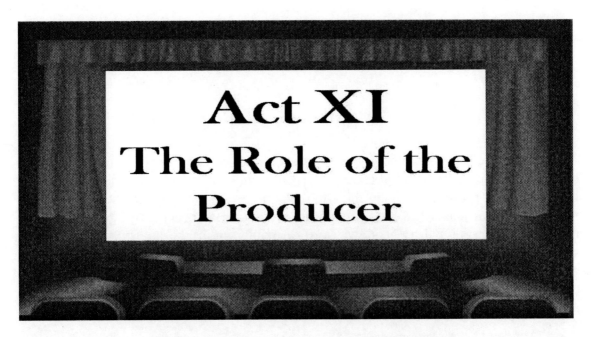

Act XI
The Role of the Producer

Promoting & Advertising Courses

"If a tree falls in a forest and no one is there to hear it, does it still make noise?" Yes, we would say based on still hearing the echo of our voices bouncing off the walls in classes where no one showed up. There we said it. By the way, all that nonsense where people say, "If you talk about it, you will feel better," doesn't really work. It's still painful, but at least it's on the table now. If you have never had to cancel a class or you have never scheduled a class and had poor attendance, please call us. You apparently have information we should have included in this book.

Every great movie producer knows that they can spend months on a project, hire the best actors and use an award winning screenplay, but if they don't promote the picture then all is lost. As instructors we sometimes overlook the importance of course promotion and even the promotion of ourselves. We tend to operate in the "Land of Oz & Blinders." Hey, we are great instructors, this is incredible material...they will have to come." No they don't. More importantly, they won't; at least not without proper marketing and publicity of the courses.

Fortunately, today we have many avenues and venues to promote courses and while they all involve time and effort, the out-of-pocket costs of course promotion have been greatly reduced by technology and social media tools. We also have to recognize that as instructors today we are marketing and promoting courses, not just to students, but to clients like brokerages, associations and sponsors. In this Act we will deal with various types of promotional activities. Before we delve into the specifics we have to address the general promotion of the instructor or the course provider. Many of us have been telling our students that they must promote and market themselves and the same rules apply to us as instructors.

Creating a Presence & Getting Known

Developing a presence as an instructor and getting known is an incredibly important part of the business of teaching. It is not simply a matter of building a network. It is a complex process involving the tying together of many different philosophies and tools. Most of us just taught long enough that over time we became recognized as good instructors, speakers and trainers and word of mouth within the industry and from our students helped to gradually build a reputation. We happen to believe that there ways to cause that recognition to happen rather than waiting for it to happen so if you have not done so already, here are some key concepts to build the proper foundation for a career as an educator.

Building A Foundation for Presence & Promotion

✓ **Craft A Mission Statement** – Why is it that you want to teach? What do you want to teach? How will your teaching or approach to subjects be different from other instructors? Do you have strengths in a particular area of expertise? All of these are good questions. All of us should take the time to analyze how we would answer these questions. A good mission statement will accomplish a number of objectives: including:

1. Motivating you because of what you do
2. Assisting you in the development of a business plan
3. Assisting you in the development of a marketing plan
4. Helping you differentiate yourself in the marketplace
5. Initiating your branding activities

272

Ultimately we would hope that your mission statement, your branding and your message will be crafted with the student in mind. We devoted a lot of thought to the development of a mission statement at Course Creators. We knew that the courses which we enjoyed teaching the most were those geared toward the delivery of useful, practical information for practicing agents and business people. We also knew that there was market for courses which helped people succeed in their careers as opposed to just completing hours for the sake of renewal. That's how we end up with a mission statement that says:

"Get It, Use It, Become More Successful Because of It!"

Once you have crafted a mission statement, be prominent about it's use. It belongs on everything that you do. Make your mission statement one of the ways that people recognize you.

✓ **Determine What You Want to Teach & Why.** Most instructors have areas of specialty that they teach, usually it is because that is where their greatest experience lies. Even if you have a plan or goal of expanding into other areas it is a good idea to start with your area of expertise. We teach best when we can teach from what we know and our own experiences. Because real estate is an area of growing complexity most people would find it difficult to teach a room of commercial agents when they themselves have no commercial experience. When people are thinking about a career in writing, the most common advice given by editors and other authors is, "Write what you know." We would say the same thing about teaching.

When we ask you to examine why you want to teach it is more though than identifying areas of expertise. If you have a strong interest in helping people with sales skills, then a pre-licensing class may not be the best venue for you. If you have a strong desire to help people understand basic concepts and grasp complex issues in an industry with which they have no familiarity, then pre-licensing may be the proper fit. So much of the time teaching requires us to bring passion, excitement, energy and enthusiasm to an audience. It's possible to know something, but not be very passionate or care about the subject matter. Take the time to discover your passion and where your true enthusiasm lies. Your teaching will be better for it, you will be better for it and so will your students.

✓ **Identify the Things In Your Background That Are Important to Your Teaching Ability.** When you analyze your background forget about employers names and even job titles. Instead analyze the skill sets that you developed because of that experience and then articulate and identify why those skill sets are important to your students and what they allow you to bring into the classroom. Doing this exercise is incredibly important and it will help you immensely. As an example you may have been the Vice-President of Product Development for the ABC Widget Company, but everyone else is thinking so what? On the other hand, if you explained what you learned in the position because you were required every day to give board and employee presentations that would be identifying a skill set meaningful to your role as an instructor in education. If you then communicate that you know how to deliver engaging and enlightening presentations you are identifying a benefit to the students who come to your class. Work on crafting both your job experience and your educational experience in this fashion.

Later in this Act we are going to address social media sites including facebook, Linkedin and YouTube. All of these sites allow you to complete a personal profile. Use the above information to develop a profile that let's your student know what's in it for them when you describe your background, credentials and education.

✓ **Analyze What Other Instructors In Your Area or Market Are Doing.** As with any business you have to be aware of what is occurring in your market and what other instructors are doing in your area. To this day, we attend other instructor's classes every chance we get and it is difficult to think of a time when we didn't learn something by doing so. We can't walk by an education flyer without picking it up and we review other people's marketing material all of the time. We don't think of it as spying. It is a standard practice used by all types of businesses and it is called "competitive intelligence." How can you compete in a marketplace if you don't know what's in the marketplace? Today more than ever the teaching profession is a business.

✓ **Get Involved In Quality Organizations & Networks.** You can't build any business without a network. Build a database and a sphere of influence. We will show you some easy ways to get started with that in social media later on this Act, but the traditional organizations and networks shouldn't be overlooked. We have told many of our students that if you want to be successful, then do what other successful people are doing. Who are the best instructors that you can associate with and learn from in order to be in a state of constant improvement?

That brings us to the subject of the Real Estate Educators Association (REEA). No other single association has meant as much to our teaching career and our personal development than being involved with REEA. They hold regular national conferences and share information on a regular basis. Many of the relationships we have across the country, several of our teaching opportunities and much of our knowledge about education came through REEA. It also has been a source of a lot of close personal friendships. Want some proof? As we were writing this book we reached out to several of the people we met in the organization and asked them for their input, insights and contributions. You have been reading the "Curtain Calls" at the end of each Act that they voluntarily and selflessly wrote to help you get a better understanding of education and be a better instructor. See that, they reached out to help you and they may not even know you yet. It is a group of sharing, friendly and helpful people. We guarantee your teaching career will be better and your success greater because of your participation in the Real Estate Educators Association. You can find out everything you need to know about joining at REEA.Org, but here is their contract information.

REEA Headquarters

2000 Interstate Park Drive
Suite 306
Montgomery, Alabama 36109

Telephone: (334)625-8650
Fax: 334-260-2903

✓ **Leverage the Power of Testimonials.** We collect testimonials from students all of the time in the form of evaluations. We read them after class to see how well we did and many instructors receive glowing recommendations. We also receive thank you notes, emails and cards from students thanking us for our help or a particular class. Most of these testimonials can be found in desk drawers, file cabinets and sitting on credenzas. Testimonials are the most powerful form of marketing and promotion. We know that people trust advertising 17% of the time and we know that they trust the recommendations and comments of their peers 73% of the time. Create a system to get the testimonials into your promotional material, onto your website and built in to your social media profiles. We believe that we get more business and more students from the prominent display of testimonials from former students than we do from any other form of marketing in which we engage.

We also would invite you to contact us if you have any questions or concerns. We wrote this book because we are passionate about education and teaching and we will do anything to help you with your success. You can locate us through our website at **CourseCreators.Com**. If you wish to speak with either of us directly you can contact us at:

Course Creators

Len@CourseCreators.Com
TheresaB@CourseCreators.Com
(520) 360-0280

Ways to Establish Yourself With
Social Media & Technology

We are very fortunate to be teaching in the age of social media and technology. Today, a business presence can be built faster than ever before. Networks that would have taken years to create can be built in a couple of months and all of that exposure and marketing potential is at our fingertips with little or no cost.

Although there are multiple social networks in existence we believe that the basic building blocks for promotion exist on two key sites. One of those is facebook and the other is Linkedin. We both teach an awful lot of technology courses. We teach them to real estate professionals, business professionals and instructors. If we were to attempt to teach our *FaceBiz* course (focusing on facebook) our *Get Linkedin* course (okay take a guess) our *WebBiz* course (on creating your own blog) our *Catch the Wave* course (overview of social media) our *VideoBiz* course (teaching how to create videos) our *Video Transaction Guides* course (how to use videos in real estate) and our two day hands-on *InstaTekkie* course (on video and internet marketing) we would be covering 39 hours of live technology material. We're not certain how many written pages that would take to write up and add into this book, so let's just say a bunch.

Not only would we not put you through any of that, but as we said in the beginning there are much better ways to teach than through a textbook and that is particularly true in regard to technology. So instead, we are just going to highlight the most popular tools. We know there are many others, but this is not a technology book. We are simply going to approach them in the context of this Act with creative ways that instructors can use these sites for the promotion and marketing of courses and education. If you are not familiar with any of these sites, we have provided a list of technology training products at the end of the book which will show you exactly how to use these tools effectively and efficiently.

10 Things
All Instructors
Should Do
With Facebook

1. **Connect With Your Students.** Most of them are there. With the mobile applications that exist today, they are probably on facebook during your class if you haven't been paying close attention. Facebook isn't about the number of friends; it's about the quality of the contacts and the relationships that you build once a connection has been made. Students have favorite instructors and their favorite instructor is someone they know, like and trust. Connecting with them on facebook allows you to build that relationship faster and maintain it longer. While you are at it you might as well be networking too with instructors, industry leaders, education directors and subject matter experts.

2. **Create a Business Page.** You need both a personal page and a business page. The business page will allow you to more easily promote classes and discuss business. It will also help you separate the classroom from your personal life. Business pages provide analytics that will let you see what items are being read on your education page, the demographic makeup of your students and other important information.

3. **Post Items of Value for Your Students.** It is easy on facebook to post up links to industry news articles, videos, and other information that may be important to your students. The more you provide industry information and news, the more you become the source of information for your students. We often times get asked in class for a particular website link or the source of some particular information. We usually tell the students we will post the link and the additional information to our facebook page. It has the effect of driving them to our page and it is seen by other prospective students on facebook.

4. **Start a Discussion Prior to Class About Class.** The easiest way to start a discussion is to ask a question. It could be as simple as, "In the upcoming class about....what would you most like to learn?" It could also be a question particular to the content of the class, for example: "Has anyone ever had a client who obtained an FHA 203(k) loan?" The question creates a response and a point of contact. Each point of contact strengthens the relationship and provides you with the opportunity to draw another student (or more from those simply watching) to class.

5. **Post up Invitations to Class.** Facebook makes it easy for you to post up course announcements and discussions on your business page. You can link to registration information and other promotional material associated with the class.

6. **Thank Students for Attending Class**. Go to facebook after a class and post up a general thank you for the students who attended. It not only is the socially respectful thing to do, but it will generate interest in your teaching. We cannot tell you the number of times that we have done this and had students respond on facebook that they missed the class, but would like to know when we are going to teach it again.

7. **Start a Business Page or Group for a Particular Class.** You can start an unlimited number of fan pages, business pages or groups. You can even create a page for a particular class. It is a great way to allow the students to connect with each other should they so choose and both the instructor and the students can continue to share information after the class.

8. **Start a Testimonial Collection.** Students will comment about your class on facebook. First of all, as instructors we should be responding to all student comments and questions in social media, just as we would if the student were sitting in class. Collect the testimonials. Don't just let them appear on facebook and then gradually fade away. Find a way of capturing these powerful marketing statements.

9. **Post Up Photos of Students In Class.** One thing we know that people do pay attention to and that is photos of them. With today's smart phones we can take a photo in class and post it immediately to facebook. We would recommend that you get your students approval to not only post pictures of the class, but to use them in your promotional material. This can usually be done with a simple line on the sign in sheet that says, "By signing in students give the

instructor consent to use photographic, audio and video recordings during the class for promotional purposes.

10. **Use Facebook Notes as Blog Posts.** Facebook has a "Notes" feature which allows you to write a blog post and save it in your Notes. They can be articles including links, videos and photos and they remain indefinitely. You can add to a discussion from class, after class and provide additional "items of value" to your students through the use of notes.

10 Things All Instructors Should Do With Linkedin

1. **Connect With Potential Clients.** Instructors who teach for brokerages, conventions and associations need to be on Linkedin. As the most professionl of the social media sites, Linkedin's members tend to be industry leaders, company executives and the movers and shakers in business. You can reach out to these people and build contacts easier than on facebook. Linkedin allows you to search out its members by company name, geographic location or profession. Think about searching "education directors", "managing brokers" and others with whom you would like to develop future business.

2. **Add Your Courses As Publications.** Your Linkedin profile has a section for "Publications". Most people just think of books, but if you have written industry articles, contribute to newsletters or have been published in the REEAaction Newletter or the REEA Journal these are publications too. Consider adding the courses you have written or created as publications. You have the ability to include information about them.

3. **Post Links To Your Classes on the News Feeds.** Linkedin's news feed tends to be very business oriented, direct and to the point. You can include links to your classes, to your schedule and to other items on your website when you post an update. We recommend that you use links often.

4. **Gather Recommendations.** Linkedin makes it easy to gather recommendations and make them part of your profile. While you can always ask for recommendations, we believe that the easiest way to get a recommendation is to give one. Start recommending others, solicit recommendations on a regular basis and build your credibility and trust as a professional.

5. **Join Groups That Feed Your Business.** There are lots of groups on Linkedin that can help you build your business and your skill as an educator. Each group has a news feed where you can engage in the comment and discussion and post links. You can join industry or subject specific groups in an effort to gain access to potential clients and students. You can also join instructor type groups, such as REEA, to build your skill as an instructor, gather teaching tips and network with other educational professionals.

6. **Emphasize Your Real Estate Education & Training**. Linkedin asks you to provide your education. Many instructors in completing this information stop at their high school, college and doctoral degrees. What education is really the most relevant to what you do? Include your real estate training, your professional designations, courses that you have taken to specialize in a particular area, focused continuing education classes and your involvement in instructor development workshops and train-the trainer programs. Your clients want to know that they are hiring someone with knowledge in the industry, yet we seldom see these qualifications listed in social media instructor profiles.

7. **Use Website Links for Specific URL's.** Linkedin profiles allow you to use specific URL's not just generic websites. Rather than simply referencing your website, make it easy for the client to see what you do and get in touch with you. Link them to the specific pages, content or material that you want them to find easily.

8. **Post Updates Regularly.** We think there is a big difference today between advertising and marketing. Marketing requires you to have a top of mind presence. Use the updates to continually put your name and face in front of your potential clients and in front of your potential audience. Linkedin allows you to increase your visual presence on the internet.

9. **Use Slideshare and Connect with Linkedin.** You can link to just about anything in your Linkedin posts, including presentations that you decide to

create on Slideshare. In fact, Linkedin interfaces with Slideshare so that you can show off your presentations to your prospective clients.

10. **Utilize Linkedin's Power as a Contact Management System.** Linkedin is more than just a powerful networking tool. It allows you to track your activities and contacts with your prospective clients. You can create notes about each client and add more detail on contract screens than most people realize. Learn how to put the full power of Linkedin behind your building of a sphere of influence.

10 Things All Instructors Should Do With Videos & YouTube

1. **Gather Course Testimonials.** Testimonials are the most powerful marketing that we have. In a technology world we ought to be capturing our student's testimonials on video and then using that to promote the next class. The testimonials are easy to shoot with the Flip or Kodak Zi8 cameras, can be edited easily in Moviemaker or iMovie and can be shared and distributed with YouTube.

2. **Create Course Promotion Videos.** The creation of multimedia pieces help sell a course. We believe that students pay more attention to them than flyers and they can be shared across social media sites with comments once they have been uploaded to YouTube.

While posting of a video on YouTube will easily allow you to email a link you cannot email the video directly. Most videos consist of too large a file size for email servers to handle efficiently and there is always the accompanying problem of compatibility. If you want the ability to email videos directly and embed them in emails with your branding, contact us. We use a program called *Talk Fusion*. It is not free, but it is a great investment. The program allows you to send your videos directly in an email (no link to YouTube) and they appear in a custom designed screen format that is appealing and unique. We can help you understand how it works and show you the most cost effective way to get started so that you don't waste a lot of money.

3. **Gather Industry Expert Videos.** In order to establish ourselves as the industry experts we have to be constantly positioning ourselves as the source of high quality expert information regarding the industry. The good news is that we don't have to be that expert; we just have to be able to videotape the experts and relate the videos to the courses we are teaching. Having a mortgage expert talk about the importance of FHA financing and using part of that video interview as a lead-in to a financing class both validates the importance of the course and the resources of the instructor.

4. **Create Your Own TV Channel.** Once that a free YouTube account has been established, it is important to complete the profile and background information for potential students and clients. YouTube will empower you through your account to set up your own channel. It can be customized and branded to your particular marketing strategies. The real benefit of creating a YouTube Channel is that it creates one single place where you can consolidate material for your clients on YouTube.

If you want to see what a YouTube Channel looks like and how it functions search YouTube for the Course Creators Channel. There are lots of videos there and you have our permission to use any of them or any portion of them and make them your own. We were also instrumental in helping to create REEATV. See what REEA has to offer on their YouTube Channel.

5. **Organize Your Videos into Playlists.** Once you have a YouTube Channel you will have the ability to group your videos into playlists. Playlists allow us to place videos into categories for ease of access by students.

6. **Create Informational Videos That Your Students Can Use.** Being the source of information has become important to your clients and students beyond classrooms. They are looking for material that is easy to pass on to their clients. If we create material that students can readily use in their business then it heightens the benefit and value of the course. Instead of creating

everything with the student in mind, try creating videos with their end client in mind so that they can save time, money and effort and simply pass the material along in a way that allows them to take credit for it and use it as their marketing material.

7. **Be Consistent in Titles, Tags & Descriptions**. When you are uploading videos on YouTube you have the opportunity to title them, create descriptions and add tags (keywords) that assist a user in finding the videos in a typical YouTube search. Words that you use in the title, description and tags should have some consistency. For example, every video should contain your name as the instructor. We know that when it is placed consistently in all three of these locations that the search engine capacity of YouTube and Google are maximized.

8. **Promote Your Students Videos.** As instructors we all know that the more you give, the more you get and the more that you promote others the more that you promote yourself. It doesn't cost anything for us as instructors to promote the videos of our students, use their best videos as examples in class and recognize them when they have done professional and creative video work. We have always gotten more out of promoting others than we ever have out of promoting ourselves.

9. **Create a Speaker Bio Video.** Remember it's not just about promoting courses; it's about promoting yourself as well. Each of us should create a video that helps students get to know who we are, what we believe about teaching and answer the question of why they should come to a class that we are teaching. Remember to keep the students viewpoint in mind. They want to know what they get out of coming to a class that we are teaching. They are less interested in our education, backgrounds and credentials.

10. **Capture Snippets From Your Courses.** Word of mouth has always been beneficial advertising and so has the presence of students in class who then spread the word to other potential students. Today we don't have to depend on the fact that someone heard about the class or talked to someone from the class in order for them to understand your teaching in the classroom. By taking snippets of class and posting them on YouTube we are exposing our skills and talents better than we ever could in words.

The Creation of a Website or Blog

Today real estate instructors as well as our professional business students are not building websites to support their business. They are creating blogs. Blogging has become prolific because of its ease in disseminating information and the exposure that blogging creates. We should all be blogging. Before you run screaming for the door voicing objections to technology and trying to assess your time commitment let's reset our mindsets about the entire concept of blogging.

Blog on Target Board by digitalart
Freedigitalphotos.net

What if we were to relabel blogging as "article writing"? That's really all blogging is and you don't have to be a technological guru to engage in blogging or leverage its power in your business. We would all agree that we have thoughts, ideas and concepts we want to share with learners. That's the foundation of teaching. We also ought to appreciate the need within any industry for students to have access to accurate, immediate information that they can trust and rely upon. Blogging enables that. In the old world if you wanted to distribute an article on the internet about some aspect of the industry in which you teach you had to know html language or you had to engage the services of a webmaster to take your content, convert it and place it on the internet for you. Neither of those were very attractive options to instructors or the students they taught.

Blogging allows us to create information and articles in simple text, add in links to multimedia, internet sites and include photographs and graphics with simple clicks. The vast majority of internet users are reading blog post articles (blogs from here on out) regularly. Blogs are picked up and indexed more heavily by search engines, which means their content elevates your position on sites like Google. In order to get a better understanding of the power of blogging and the nature of it we would encourage you to visit Technorati.com. Technorati is to the blogging world what Google is to the rest of us. Technorati indexes blogs, provides tips on blogging and even has platforms to help you get started.

While you can create your own blogging site and we recommend that you do (something we will discuss in just a moment), you don't have to start at that level to begin blogging. There are many existing blogs that you can contribute to and use. You can blog as we mentioned earlier, by using the "Notes" application in facebook. Trulia and Zillow, two well known national listing databases that real estate agents and their consumers frequent, have locations where you can write a blog post. When you are writing a blog post keep some basic fundamental principles of journalism in mind:

- Titles are key. The headline is the attractor that gets people to read the blog post.

- Shorter is better. Blog posts can be a paragraph or a couple of paragraphs. The more you write, the more compelling your content must be to hold the interest of the reader.

- Use bullets and summarize. People don't read anymore. They skim (Have you wondered why this text contains so many bullet point sections and so many checklist sections?)

- Use links and incorporate multimedia content. Videos, photos, graphics, internet links all add to the value and appearance of your blog. Use them as often as you can.

As you progress in your blogging experience we have no doubt that you will see the power and convenience of having your own blog site branded with the information that you create. We believe that the best site for this is WordPress. At WordPress.com you can create your own custom blogging site for FREE. WordPress will even give you a domain name for FREE to get you started. The tools and ease of using WordPress as a blogging platform are phenomenal and there is virtually no limit to what you can do. Many of the instructors who contributed to this book have their own blog sites and many of them were created on WordPress.

If you go to CourseCreators.com our entire site is a blog. You may think it looks like a html based website. It is not. It is a WordPress blog. That means we can add content to it, edit it and redesign it all without the help of a computer programmer. (Okay.

We use a programmer when we get in over our heads. Sometimes that happens a lot. **Thank you George from JensenConsulting.com for all you do for us!)** We don't have to pay any hosting fees or monthly charges. You owe it to yourself to know how to blog and to create a blogging site that allows you to promote yourself and your courses.

Power in Language & WIIFM's

What do our students care most about? If you answered themselves, you are probably correct. If you answered the instructor then we think you are probably delusional, need to get out more or send us your secrets. Our only consolation here is that students care even less about administrative agencies and what an education director thinks may be good for them. Students want to know what's in it for them.

Asian Woman Pressing Like Button
By Kittikim Atsawintarangkul
Freedigitalphotos.net

Therefore, the crafting of promotional material for courses distributed to students must address what the benefit is to them of attending the course. This is initially done with the title we choose for the course and is secondary done by the course descriptions and promotions we craft as instructors. We suppose that we could title a course, "Summary and Review of Agency Principles and Concepts," but we know the course will be better attended if we just retitled it, "Using Agency Principles to Get More Clients.' Make no mistake about it, we have to deliver on the promise to provide the material that is suggested by the title. We never want to mislead students simply for the sake of better marketing.

We are also very aware of the statutory obligation of most administrative and regulatory agents to approve courses that promote and protect the public interest. Despite our knowledge and teaching of social media, we don't know that a course that is focused simply on using technology tools and that is entitled "How to Use Google" has a place in the approval process for credit hours in continuing education. We are pretty certain that there is lots of room for a course entitled "Using the Internet to Better Protect and Promote Client Interests" that is fine, so long as the course content accomplishes that objective.

We could all probably benefit from being advised to take a look at our course titles and descriptions and look at them not through the eyes of an instructor or an administrative agency, but instead through the eyes of our clients, practicing professionals with competing demands on their time and attention.

Here are a few examples of promotional material reworked with the student WIIFM in mind:

BEFORE	AFTER MODIFICATION
Fair Housing Case Updates	What To Do To Broaden Housing Opportunities for Your Clients
Learn RESPA Law	Building Relationships and Affiliations That Really Work
Understanding the New Contract	Become a Better Negotiator For Your Client & Your Pocketbook

We tend to use words all of the time like "understand" "learn" and "know" in the titles to classes. That's because to us as educators those seem like pretty big WIIFM's. We want our students to understand, learn and know. Understanding, learning and knowing often result in a "so what?" in the minds of our students. They ask how the information will benefit them, their business or their client. They want to know they will be able to do something useful with the information. English author Francis Bacon, once wrote "Knowledge is power." Maybe our students are smarter than us as instructors and smarter than Francis Bacon. They remember and understand the modification that Albert Einstein made to Bacon's quote:

Knowledge is not power. Knowledge by itself is worthless, it doesn't become powerful until it is applied."

Curtain Call

"How To Fill Seats at a REALTOR® Association Event On A Limited Budget"

By Doug Divitre, CIPS, e-Pro, , CRS, ABR

Doug Devitre is an international speaker. He has spoken extensively throughout North America and other countries worldwide. He is a master at technology and has also been acknowledged as a Business Leader of the Year, Entrepreneur of the Year and has been inducted into the National Association of Real Estate Buyer's Agent Council Hall of Fame. Heavily involved with the St. Louis and Missouri REALTOR® Associations, Doug helps students and clients master social technology. As the owner and President of Doug Devitre International, Inc., you can contact him at DougDevitre.Com

Just because you can do something doesn't mean it is worth doing. I see many event planners doing multiple tasks to find out that very few have registered and they have to pick up the phone and beg others to attend. Why won't people attend?

We as a society are bombarded everyday with advertisements that can easily be filtered, ignored, and overlooked. That is why meeting planners have challenges in getting people to attend.

If the message is to be received then it must address the **value proposition.** Is the cost of money and time worth the investment to spend the day learning/networking/sharing with others who have similar challenges? Personally, in choosing which sessions I will attend, I'm more concerned about the time I invest rather than the money spent because the money can be made again. The time away from business, family, and fun activities cannot be replaced.

As a marketer of events here are 27 things you can do each time:

- Create a Facebook page
- Create a Facebook event
- Create a Linkedin event
- Design and distribute a flyer
- Create an EventBrite page
- Send out an email to top brokers
- Send out an email to membership
- Create a QR code to place on a flyer
- Tweet the registration link to your followers
- Pick up the phone and call
- Create a podcast interview with the speaker
- Film a video interview with the speaker to share at a future event
- Design and send out a postcard
- Advertise in the local and state publications
- Write a blog post about the event
- Create a promotional video for the event
- Share the promotional video on YouTube
- Embed the promotional video into blog/website
- Email the link of the promotional video
- Ask the speakers to send out a message about the event to their database
- Create a PowerPoint presentation that talks about the event
- Upload the flyer to Dropbox to send the link out using online marketing
- Shorten and customize the URL using http://bit.ly or http://budurl.com to include in online marketing so others can remember how to find it
- Send out a SMS to member cell phones with the registration link
- Send out an electronic broadcast fax with the flyer to members

Do you yourself have the time to do each of these?
Do you rely on other team members to accomplish these tasks?
Do you have the technology to support these actions?

To fill seats for an annual meeting presentation, CE class or conference I recommend the following:

Be Clear About What Attendees Will Receive. Melynn Sight of nSight Marketing says that unless your speaker is a celebrity you will want to start your marketing message with what are the top 3 things that audience members will receive as a result of attending the session, instead of who the speaker is and and what they have done in the past. No one cares about a speaker's resume. They care more about what actionable items they can take away and implement that will save them time, save time and make more money.

Create Shareable Content. A blog post is the best way to send out information to as many people as possible with the least of amount of time, money, and energy. The blog post should include the following in this order:

Catchy Title

If the title is boring no one will read it. Create a title in 8 words or less that pops off the page. Sam Horn, author of *POP!* Has a great book on how to make names POP! off the page.

Description

This is where you include the list of the 3 things people will be able to implement. Focus on the pain of the target audience and how attending this session will be able to solve the challenges.

Registration link

This is the sign up form that attendees will fill out to register. This could be a site on the existing website, Eventbrite page or PayPal payment link. This registration link will be more effective if it is a picture of a button that links to the site that says "Register Here" rather than just the link itself. If you don't have the time to make a picture of a button the link itself will have to do.

Multimedia

The YouTube video is the most effective for capturing attention because most would rather watch a video than read. If the video isn't captivating after the first few seconds then viewers will exit and move on to something else.

Use Windows Movie Maker or iMovie to make a video that transitions text every 5 seconds with 6 or less words on each transition. Include each of the 3 takeaways as a single transition on a blank screen or in front of an existing video. I like iStock videos to play behind the 3 takeaways. Next, include the sponsor name and logo as a transition with the subtitle "presents". Include a picture of the speaker with credentials and website following the sponsor transition. End with transitions that include the event location, date, time and shortened registration link. You can shorten the registration links at http://budurl.com or http://bit.ly.

When you upload the video to YouTube be sure to optimize the Title, Description, and the Tags. The description should start with the registration link. This way, viewers can click on the link from the top instead of scrolling down to the end to register. Also include it at the end of the description as a friendly reminder. Copy/paste the 3 things along with any verbiage used to the market the event into the video description under the registration link. This could include the marketing remarks, learning objectives, and time/date/location.

Identify Your Local Influencers. Find your local social media influencers. The reason why Inman's Agent Reboot program has been so successful at filling seats is because they find the agents who are the best at social media marketing and give them free registration, hotel stays, plane tickets for outsiders, and the opportunity to share their expertise live on stage. You may not have the budget to pay for these expenses, however, if you can tap into the local talent leaders in the association you will find yourself doing less work and receiving more registrations.

To wrap it up, just because you can do something doesn't mean it's worth doing. I know you only have so many minutes in the day and can't do everything. Prioritize your own list to determine what is feasible with your existing schedule. Determine how much time and money it takes to accomplish these tasks and measure the results from them. Take the time to see what marketing methods are working and improve on them each time. Otherwise you will find yourself overwhelmed and working much harder than you have to in order to produce the same results.

Curtain Call

"What Education Directors Look For In Selecting Instructors & Courses"

Annalisa, Moreno, Education Director of The Tucson Association of REALTORS®

Annalisa is a valuable member of the Tucson Association of REALTORS®. Her position requires her to prioritize and arrange educational opportunities for TAR members. Annalisa is an avid participant in industry events, regional seminars and national conferences. She was asked by the National Association of REALTORS® to share her thoughts on the hiring and selection of real estate instructors and courses that would benefit association members. You can reach Annalisa at Annalisa@TucsonRealtors.Org.

There are MANY factors that go into selecting an instructor. It's not just a matter of who looks good on paper, but really who is the right fit for the membership. Every Association is different and they operate with great diversity. Therefore, I speak from my own personal experience and what has worked for the Tucson Association of REALTORS®.

There is always a list of things to consider when hiring a speaker. Here is a brief insight into what an Education Director examines. What are your qualities as an instructor? What sets you apart from your peers? Will you meet the specific needs of the membership? Do you have concrete tangible tools to offer the members that will make a difference in their business? Do you incorporate a local perspective into your presentation? Are you energetic? Etc. And ultimately, why should we hire you?

There are multiple facets to the process, but here are a few top things considered when hiring a speaker: budget, networking. personal relationships, recommendations, referrals and approach. Here are some helpful tips for instructors who seeking opportunities:

BUDGET:

Of course other than speaker qualities, the number one factor considered when hiring someone is BUDGET. Can we afford to work with you? Education departments are often held to the restraints of their budgets. Further, most associations' budgets can change each year. It seems that most instructors are aware of this and are willing to work with associations. This is helpful! There are times when we would like to hire you, but simply cannot afford to. Also, associations prepare their budgets at least six months in advance of the coming year. Therefore, if your goal is to get hired by XYZ Association, it is best to approach them early!

NETWORKING/ PERSONAL RELATIONSHIPS:

Network, network, network! Get to know your Education Directors locally and across the nation. Attend national conferences like RAPDD, REALTOR® Association Professional Development Directors. This is a wonderful opportunity to showcase your talents and get to know Directors. I have met and befriended some wonderful instructors across the nation and have been able to bring them to Tucson, Arizona. Further, I work with other local associations across the state. Therefore, if I am bringing out an instructor, it is a good possibility the other local associations will want to hire them as well. This is one way to help share the cost of the instructor as there is only one flight involved. This is a win-win opportunity, as the instructor will have more work and the associations will have less cost. Many other states also operate in this fashion.

RECOMMENDATIONS/ REFERRALS:

First hand recommendations are often helpful when selecting a speaker. Providing testimonials and referrals can be assistive. Also, Education Directors will consult with each other from time to time to review instructor performance. Who better to receive a review from than a fellow peer? Morale of the story…be nice to Education Directors. ;)

APPROACH:

How are you currently approaching or "soliciting" associations to get business? Your approach is a key element to the success of booking a speaking engagement. Education Directors are typically busy people whom often juggle multiple tasks and wear more than one hat. An aggressive approach will not always lead to the best result. It is one thing to be persistent and another to be pushy. Keep that in mind when pursuing job opportunities. Your best approach is to think of this as building a partnership and not just landing the "gig". Education Directors will often continue working with instructors, so work on building a partnership. From personal experience, I appreciate an email or mail first followed up with a phone call a couple of days later. This allows time for me to review what you're offering and determine if there is a need for you to fulfill.

It may not always work out initially, i.e. timing or budget, but there is always hope for future engagements.

Copyright & Intellectual Property

The areas of copyright and intellectual property are complex topics and are about as full of myths and legends as you can possibly get. They are areas that take on increased importance in the social media, multi-media world in which we currently teach so we just didn't feel that any text on the education of adults would be complete in this day and age without addressing such an important issue. Here is our disclaimer before we begin:

> ***Nothing presented in this section is to be construed as legal advice. As with all legal issues you should seek the advice of counsel and are encouraged to do your own research when dealing with copyright, trademark and intellectual property issues. The information contained herein is offered purely for educational purposes. Now that we have made the proper legal disclosure, you must raise your hand and promise, "No matter what, I will never respond to a lawyer, judge or the owner of a copyright and begin the sentence with Len and Theresa said…"***

With our legal disclaimer out of the way let us share with you what we know based on our research and legal backgrounds. Copyright law exists because the U.S. Constitution gives Congress the ability…"to promote the Progress of Science and useful

Arts, by securing for a limited time to the authors and inventors the exclusive right to their respective writings and discoveries." Therefore, all of U.S. copyright law and patent laws grow from this one brief passage in the Constitution.

There are fundamental principles at the heart of copyright law that help us understand its application in any given situation or circumstance:

1. Copyright law was meant to protect the commercial and monetary rights of the creator of certain permanently affixed works.

2. Copyright law was intended to promote and encourage the free flow of information and ideas and not impede creative expression.

3. Copyright law was intended to foster the creation of learning and education and the expansion of knowledge, not limit it.

Because there are so many myths and misconceptions about copyright law we thought that a logical place to begin would be with the correction of those misunderstood principles. We believe that there are at least five fundamental myths and misconceptions about copyright.

Correcting Myths and Misconceptions

Myth #1 – Copyrights Must Be Filed and Are Only Valid on Works and Material that is marked with the traditional ©

Everything that you create is copyrighted automatically. Copyright attaches at the moment of creation. Please notice that we said "creation" and not "idea". You can't copyright an idea, a thought or a plan. You can only copyright items that have become "permanently affixed." That means that your work must be created and actually exist in some type of physical form whether it be an article, a book, a song or in today's world a blog post. There's a good reason to write everything down. For years we have written out things on the backs of scraps of paper, envelopes and napkins. Now we know why it was important to write it down and transform the thought into a "permanently affixed work." Create an original drawing on the back of a bar napkin and you have a copyrighted image.

Everything that you create and transform into a permanently affixed work is copyrighted. You don't need to file anything and whether or not it contains the traditional © is immaterial. However, we do this because it indicates to serve notice to the world that the information is indeed our original work and we seek to protect it. The use of the symbol is a "notice" act, not an act that is required to make the work "copyrighted."

Myth #2 – Copyright Means That We Can't Take & Use Anyone Else's Stuff

Copyright law never meant that we could not use someone else's original work. It was meant to keep us from taking someone's original work and depriving them of the proprietary gain or value that the work had while we stuff the money into our own pocket. Just understanding that basic concept will differentiate you from many people who misunderstand the nature and basis of a copyright infringement. Here's the theory, if a popular song writer takes the time to create a brand new song we are not in copyright violation because we are humming it while we are walking down the street. That activity in no way affects the ability of the artist to sell their work in the manner in which they had intended and we are not harming their proprietary or monetary interest in any way. By contrast, if we went home and played the song on our guitar, recorded it onto a CD and headed back to the street to sell the discs we are directly interfering with the artist's proprietary creation and we are depriving them of earning income in the way that they probably most intended.

In addition there are lots of exceptions to copyright protections. There are uses and applications which are not protected by the copyright. We will outline those in this Act, for now, just know that it's not illegal to use someone else's material, it's illegal to deprive them of the economic interests associated with the work.

Myth #3 – So Long As We Give the Original Creator Credit We Don't Have to Worry About Copyright

If you are infringing upon someone's economic and proprietary interests and using something they created and have copyright interests to, giving them credit hardly solves the problem. The whole point of copyright law is to give the creator control over who uses their permanently affixed work. It is not about giving them credit, it's about giving them control over what they have created. While it is true that the owner of the copyright can give you permission, using copyrighted works without authorized permission and giving the creator credit, is sort of the equivalent of yelling, "Hey, look over here...I am the one who stole your stuff." Can you imagine the burglar who thinks they are not in the wrong because they said, "I would like to give Mr. & Mrs. Jones credit for allowing me to take all of this stuff from their house!" As instructors and trainers we should all know how clearer we can make things by way of comparison and analogy.

Myth #4 – So Long As We Use the Material for Education There is No Copyright Violation

Using material for educational purposes is an exception to copyright protection. However, it is not a blanket exception and it depends upon how we have used the copyrighted material and the nature of the material that is being utilized. Let us give you an example. Including a quote from someone's material and using it in teaching a class generally is not a copyright violation. However, if we took your class outline and student materials, copied them and began teaching the class in the building across the street from you, we would likely have some copyright issues. We are certain you would feel that your proprietary and monetary interests in the work have been threatened. To understand just where the line gets drawn, we are going to have to understand more about the educational and fair use exceptions to copyright law.

Myth #5 – If We Found It on the Internet We Can Use It Because the Material is Now Part of the Public Domain

If this were true we should all be running to the public library to copy the books and resell them because they clearly have been placed out there in the public domain. The misconception about public domain gets confused with the broadest exception to copyright law having to do with the fair use doctrine. We can't use everything we find just because we found it. The fair use doctrine has been subject to a lot of court case interpretations and it is a complex area of which we will need to understand a lot more before we know what we can use and what we can't. Just because the creator of something made it publicly available doesn't mean we are free to use it all the time in all circumstances. There are restrictions and limits on the fair use doctrine and we will explore that at length in this chapter.

The Source of Copyright Law

We live in a rapidly expanding sharing social media world. Every day the debates rage about copyright, fair use, the public domain and the use and spread of information on the internet. It would take volumes to explore the intricacies and details of copyright law. If you are interested in the complete and full analysis of the history and evolution of copyright law try reading *Copyright Law, The Complete Treatise* assembled by Robert Gorman and Kenneth Gemmill, Professors Emerti at the Pennsylvania School of Law. One of the country's leading experts on copyright and intellectual property issues is MIT Professor, Keith Weinstein, and he has created an eight hour video lecture series on the issue which is available on YouTube.

As we mentioned, the authority for copyright law was initially granted by a short statement in the United States Constitution. In this country the first copyright law was the *1909 Copyright Act* which is no longer in existence. However, it is often used as a basis for understanding the purpose and intent of copyright laws and the protections that they afford. It was replaced by the Copyright Act of 1976 which took over 15 years to create. The law went into effect in 1978 and today still forms the bulk of copyright law in the United States. It was codified as *Title 17 of the U.S.Code* and contains 1332 sections. In 1998 Congress amended certain provisions of *Title 17* with the *Digital Millenium Copyright Act*, sometimes referred to as the DMCA. Both the 1976 Act and the DMCA now comprise the provisions of *Title 17.*

Many court cases have been litigated under *Title 17* alleging copyright or intellectual property violations. They help us interpret the law and aid us in understanding just what a copyright violation is and how one occurs. The combination of statutes and cases also provides us with an understanding of just what can be copyrighted and what cannot be copyrighted. Copyright protects the authors of an "original work of authorship" *Title 17 U.S. Code, §106.* Copyright protects literary, dramatic, musical, artistic and intellectual works and gives the owner the right to control all of the following:

- Reproductions of the work
- Derviative works based on the work

- Public display of the work
- Peformance of the work
- Sale of the work

In order for the work to be protected it simply has to exist as a permanently affixed item in tangible form. *17 U.S.C. §106* no longer requires that the work have been published, but it must exist in physical form and you can't copyright any of the following because they are not "permanently affixed works of authorship"

- Titles, names, short phrases, slogans, symbols or designs
- Ideas or thoughts
- Processes, systems, methods or concepts
- Principles or discoveries

A bit of clarification and application is probably in order here. All of this means that you can use without fear the names facebook, Twitter, Coca Cola and General Motors in your presentations. You can even freely use the logos. They may be subject to trademark limitations, but they can never be copyright violations. There is a possibility that they could be trademark infringements, but unless you are relabeling a product similar to theirs and selling it under their name you probably don't have a trademark violation either. It's really good news when you understand that when talking about copyright you don't need permission to reproduce the copyright symbol. The symbol can't be copyrighted. You are probably already beginning to see that copyright law differs from most people's understanding. Nonetheless there are items which can be copyrighted which may affect classrooms and teaching. All of the following could be subject to copyright protection:

- Every textbook and other written work you have ever seen
- Every photo, drawing or diagram
- Every song, piece of music or original arrangement
- Every video or movie that has been created

That doesn't mean that you can't use any of these things, it's just that all of the owners could potentially claim a copyright violation. Whether or not a violation exists will depend on the exceptions to copyright law and how and in what manner you use copyrighted material.

The Role of the U.S. Copyright Office

The 1996 Digital Millenium Copyright Act removed the requirement that anyone needed to file or register their work in order to preserve copyrights. Copyright is automatic and attaches the moment the work is created. It sort of leaves us wondering why then is it necessary for a U.S. Copyright office to exist, it's not like the patent office where creators and inventors are forced to file in order to be entitled to protection of their work.

The U.S. Copyright Office has existed since 1897. It is an office of public record and it furnishes information about the provisions of copyright law to both the general public and Congress. The office works with a number of agencies on amendments or changes to copyright law and the office does record copyright registrations. The registration is not necessary in order to have a preserved copyright interest, but it does serve to provide public notice and while not mandatory there are reasons why it is beneficial to file a copyright registration. You can bet that the authors John Grisham, Dean Koontz, J.K. Rowling and Stephen King as well as major movie producers and record producers have registered their copyrights. Most of us and most other people don't. The reasons why people actually register a copyright are because:

- Registration must be filed before a copyright infringement lawsuit can be filed

- Without registration prior to an alleged copyright violation, damages in court are limited to actual damages, no attorney fees may be recovered

Keep in mind that there are no copyright police. There is no federal agency charged with the enforcement of civil copyright violations (we'll talk about the FBI criminal investigations later in this Act) and the U.S. Copyright Office does not get involved in such issues. If a violation is believed to exist by the owner of the copyright, it is up to that owner to secure legal counsel and pursue the offender through a lawsuit in federal court. That is the only option for civil enforcement. If the owner of the copyright didn't file a registration prior to the alleged infringement then the only remedy they are entitled to is actual damages and that means that they are paying all court costs and legal fees out of their own pocket, win or lose.

Exceptions & Exclusions to Copyright Protection

Just because something may be of the proper subject matter to be copyrighted does not mean that others can never use the work in any way. Copyright law is full of exceptions and exclusions of uses and applications that don't violate *Title 17*. Fortunately for you, we are not going to attempt to recreate the 250 page treatise of Forman and Gemmill and we are not going to outline in painstaking detail all 1332 Sections of *Title 17*. Our purpose here will be to identify the exemptions and exclusions that an owner's copyright protection does not extend to, because many of them apply in the educational arena. These exceptions are detailed and complex and sometimes various judges in various jurisdictions interpret the provisions differently since they are the ones who enforce the law in federal courts. Once we have discussed some of the exceptions and exclusions we will also discuss a few of the recent court cases, particularly those involving social media and some of the tools that we utilize in the classroom

The Fair Use Exception

The Fair Use Doctrine is the most significant limitation on the exclusive rights held by a copyright owner. To understand "Fair Use" we first have to understand that the overriding purpose of copyright law is not to restrict the flow of information or education, the purpose of copyright law is to protect the owner's proprietary and monetary interest in the work that they have created. The principle of "fair use" first appeared in an 1871 court case from the Massachusetts Supreme Court called, *Folsom vs. Marsh*. The case involved someone including quotes from others in a biography. Justice Story opined that it is proper to include the commentary and quotes of others in limited form so long as you are not diminishing the value of the original author's quoted work by reproducing large sections of it.

When Congress enacted the 1976 statutes which became *Title 17*, they actually made the "Fair Use" concept part of the law. *17 United States Code §107* now states:

Notwithstanding the provisions of Section 106, the fair use of copyrighted work for purposes such as criticism, comment, news reporting, teaching, scholarship or research, is not an infringement of copyright. In determining whether the use of the work is a fair use the factors to be considered shall include:

1. The purpose and character of the use;
2. The nature of the copyrighted work;
3. The amount and substantiality of the portion when compared against the work as a whole,
4. The effect of the use on the potential market value of the copyrighted work

Fair use is the reason that Universal Studios lost their case against Sony Television pictures in 1984 in the United States Supreme Court. *Sony Corp. of America vs. Universal Studios, Inc.* 464 U.S. 417 (1984) The Court held that it is not a copyright infringement to videotape copyrighted movies or television shows for home viewing at a more convenient time. Fair use is the reason that TIVO and ON DEMAND systems can be sold and used today. By contrast in *A&M Records vs. Napster,* Napster loses when it creates a site for the wholesale downloading of songs to private servers and promotes a service that directly impedes A&M's ability to sell records.

In a classroom when we utilize a photo or a portion of anything, it can logically be argued that the application clearly falls within the fair use exception. The use of bits and pieces as we so often do hardly ever rises to the level of taking such an amount and substantial portion of the work that we are impacting the potential market value of the original copyrighted work. If you understand it is about the proprietary impact on the owner of the work then it becomes very clear that we can quote from text books, provide resources, play pieces of music, utilize clips from movies or videos and be entitled to protection as fair use. Copying the entire textbook so students don't have to buy it from the publisher or putting the MGM movie on a disc and distributing it probably are not protected activities and probably are copyright violations.

The Media Education Foundation (MEF) has done a great job of explaining and demonstrating just what fair use means. Their video "A Fair(y) Tale Use" hangs on YouTube. After a disclaimer that the video was made without the express written consent of Disney and that the film is not authorized by, associated with and should not be confused with anything produced by Disney, they use Disney music, characters, drawings and scenes to teach the concept of fair use. Yes, Disney has copyright claims to Cinderella, Beauty & the Beast and Snow White. Don't copy the movies and distribute them through your website. Don't transcribe the dialogue in its entirety and try to sell them. You are interfering with Disney's proprietary interests and you are affecting the potential market value of their copyrighted work. Want to use a image of Cinderella? Want to play a short clip from the movie? In all likelihood that is fair use. The Media Education Foundation apparently agrees and so do many court decisions.

The Educational Exception

Section 110 of Title 17 specifically exempts a variety of public performances and displays, typically in the context of educational and other non-profit uses. The language of subsection 110(1) exempts face-to-face classroom performances of copyrighted works for teaching purposes in a non-profit educational institution. We realize that most of us are not in the area of non-profit education. However, the educational exemption has been expanded in a modification to the law that occurred in 2002. Congess amended §110 with the TEACH (Technology, Education and Copyright Harmonization Act) and allowed for the use of coyrighted works in "digital distance education" while attempting to protect

the copyrignt owner against the hazards of losing the proprietary income from such works. The law now exempts "reasonable and limited portions of any other work" while limiting the use to that which is "typically displayed in the course of a live classroom session." It has never been the goal of copyright protections to impede or limit the free flow of information and ideas in the classroom or other educational venues.

Sometimes even legal scholars claim the education exception in §110 contains the language "non-profit" and therefore, if you are getting paid to teach the class you don't get educational purposes exception from the copyright law. (By the way teachers in non-profit institutions do get paid to teach and students often pay for the classes). Just because money was made from the education does not mean that instructors and schools are not allowed to use any copyrighted material. Section 107 specifically lists "teaching" as one of the applications and uses that is to be considered in determining fair use and under that particular section it doesn't matter whether you were making a profit or not.

However, we should understand that just because the use was for "educational purposes" does not give us a free pass from any and all potential copyright claims. It depends on whether the use was a "fair use." If you quote or use an example from someone else's material, that's probably "fair use" If you copy their entire textbook on the photocopier and hand it out to students you are probably committing a copyright violation and saying that it was for the classroom is not going to protect you.

Satire, Comment, Parody & News

Where copyrighted works are utilized for purposes of satire, news and commentary they are specifically exempted from copyright protection. When Saturday Night Live and NBC were sued by Elsmere Music, *Elsmere Music Inc. vs. NBC*, 482 F. Supp 741 (S.D.N.Y. 1980 aff'd 623 F.2d 252 (2nd Cir. 1980), over the creation of a skit that parodied the song, *"I Love New York,"* the court held that such applications are beyond the scope of copyright protection. Section 107 of Title 17 is where we find the exception for such uses and the courts have given them broad expanse.

Much of our use in the classroom may fall under this exception, particularly when we are utilizing the material or quoting it simply as a source, much like the evening news and offering the material up for commentary and discussion. Copyright was created to add to existing dialogue and knowledge, not to limit the free expression or exchange of ideas.

Transformative Uses

Copyright protection also does not extend when portions of copyrighted material are collected and gathered together to create an entirely new original work. We pretty much believe that is what educators do when they collect bits and pieces of information, rearrange it, organize it and create their own original presentations. It is a process the courts have labeled a transformative use outside the protection of copyright law. In a 1994 case, the Supreme Court in *Salinger v. Colting*, 641 F. Supp. 2d 250 (S.D. N.Y. 2009) emphasized that transformative uses are at the heart of the fair use doctrine. Whether the material has been used to create something new or merely copied verbatim and utilized as the original copyright holder's work is an important issue.

The court noted that purposes such as scholarship, research or education are often transformative uses because the original copyrighted material is the subject of review or commentary. The court suggested that in analyzing whether or not a copyright violation has occurred we should examine two key issues that sound a lot like education and educators to us:

- Has the material you have taken from the original work been transformed by adding new expression or meaning?

- Was value added to the original by creating new information, new aesthetics, new insights, and understandings?

Here is a great example. If we take a photo and use it as a background on a PowerPoint slide in the classroom; add titles and information to it and use it to explain agency concepts we are engaged in a transformative use. A court would likely ask, "By using the photo, creating a PowerPoint slide, adding titles and new aesthetics, displaying it in a classroom in association with a discussion on agency principles, has the instructor destroyed the artist's commercial and proprietary rights to sell their original work? (We are trying to figure out if a home decorator or an art gallery might be interested in our PowerPoint Slide as an alternative to the artist's work?) We probably have not in any way affected the artist's ability to profit from their work or photo.

Copyright Cases in a Social Media World

To demonstrate just how broad the application of fair use and transformative use has become, in 2007, the ninth Circuit Court of Appeals decided the case of *Perfect 10 vs. Google,* 487 F.3d 701, (9th Cir. 2007). Perfect 10, an adult magazine, sued Google over the reproduction and indexing of its photos from a private subscription based website. To make a long story short, Perfect 10 lost their claim for copyright violation. The court shot down Perfect 10's claim that Google was using their images without permission and in violation of copyright law. The Court took into account the public benefit that search engines provide, discussed Google's transformative use of the photos and found that Perfect 10's ability to prove actual revenue losses and damages from the distribution of the photos was highly speculative. Here is what writer, John Paczkowski, had to say about the decision in

Digital Daily:

Finally, the court also rejected Perfect 10's attempts to turn web surfers into pervasive copyright violators. Specifically, Perfect 10 had claimed that Google users who looked at photos in their browsers were infringing on copyright because their computers automatically "cached" a copy of the photo in memory. Thankfully, the ruling today affirmed that any such copying is a fair use and cannot be infringing.

In the meantime the *Viacom vs. YouTube* case for copyright infringement is on its way to the U.S. Supreme Court. Viacom claims that YouTube is displaying some movies and television shows in violation of copyright law. So far all the wins have been for YouTube. Viacom lost their copyright infringement claims in the Court of Appeals with the court citing provisions of the Digital Millenium Copyright Act (DMCA). That particular case may or may not have much of an impact on us as educators in the classroom, it depends on the language and principles with which the Supreme Court decides the case. The YouTube case has more to do with intentional, knowing and willful violations of copyright when it comes to wholesale displays on the internet of the entire movie or television show and the safe harbor provisions of the DMCA.

If you want to know more about social media, the evolving litigation and copyright law there is a great article on social media and its relationship with copyright law written by Jonathan Darrow and Gerald Ferrera in the *Northwestern Journal of Technology and Intellectual Property, 6 NW. J. Tech. & Intell. Prop 1 (2007)*.

What Does It All Mean for Education?

Try as we might we were unable to uncover a single copyright infringement case against an instructor or an educational institution. We know there are those who say that there are claims and infringements but they are settled out of court. That is a business decision made by those who may have received a violation notice. The fact remains that instructors and educators are not losing or even defending copyright violations under the law. The reasons that no cases exist are many, including:

- Instructors and educators are not the YouTube's and the Google's of the world with huge resources for the owners of copyright claims to target;

- Most copyright holders have not registered with the U.S. Copyright Office, an action that is required prior to the filing of a lawsuit;

- The pursuit of a copyright violation is an expensive proposition in the federal court system and unless the copyright was registered the holder of the copyright would have to pay their own legal fees and expenses even if they win;

- Most copyright holders cannot prove actual damages that they have incurred as a result of the copyright infringement;

- Educators have many defenses to alleged copyright violations because it is more likely than not that their activities fall under one of the exceptions or exclusions for copyright protection.

We believe that all of us have moral and ethical obligations to respect the work of others. We shouldn't be using other people's "permanently affixed works," that are

protected by copyright without their permission. That's more a matter of ethical and moral standards than it is copyright law. Whether we can get away with something is never a good justification for carrying out the act. Maybe it's time for a commitment to education that highlights our ethical and moral commitments while still acknowledging as instructors that we have more protections under copyright law than we have threats from it.

A Pledge to Ethical & Moral Standards Relating to Intellectual Property

✓ **The Fostering of Education.** We believe in the free exchange of ideas and the education of individuals. We support the principles of the U.S. Constitution..."*to promote the Progress of Science and useful Arts, by securing for a limited time to the authors and inventors the exclusive right to their respective writings and discoveries.*"

✓ **The Crediting of Others.** We believe that when we use quotations, statistics, charts and other such resources for our students that we ought to credit and cite the source of the information so that our students may use that information for further study and the expansion of their knowledge. If someone believes that we have used their work without permission and asks us to remove it, we will do so immediately out of respect for their request and a desire to protect their creations.

✓ **Fair Use.** We retain our right to fair use and the ability to provide our students with additional information from outside sources. We promise to be mindful and aware of copyright statutes and cases and to pay attention to the method and manner in which we are using material. We will be cognizant of the amount and the substantial nature of the material that we use and we will refrain from engaging in activities which have an adverse effect on the potential market value of the copyrighted work.

✓ **Transformative Use**. We recognize that we are engaged in the continual transformative use of material as educators. We pledge that when we utilize material from an original work we will endeavor to transform it by adding new expression and meaning. We will always endeavor to add value to the original material by creating new information, new aesthetics, new insights and new understandings.

The Use of Royalty Free & Public Domain Items

Sites exist that promise royalty free photos, music and the use of public domain items to avoid the issues with copyright law. The public domain is a matter of time expiration, not whether the work was available to the public in many places. Works pass into the public domain when the copyright has expired. Anything created since 1978 will not pass into the public domain until 2048 (and probably longer, depending on how long the owner of the copyright lives). That's because the current length of the copyright is the life of the author plus 70 years. So 70 years after we die you can photocopy this book and give it away for free to your students. Until then, please buy a copy. Nonetheless you can quote portions of the book, use parts of it and take our ideas and concepts and use them freely.

Works published prior to 1923 are all in the public domain and can be used freely in any manner. In case you are wondering how much Disney paid to the family of Hans Christian Anderson and other fairy tale authors for the rights to stories like Cinderella, Snow White, Beauty and the Beast…the answer is zero. Those stories were already in the public domain.

Everything in between 1923 and 1978 was protected for a total of 95 years from creation. This means that John Steinbeck's Pulitzer Prize winning novel, *The Grapes of Wrath* will pass into the public domain in 2034. It also means that the Beatles hit song, A Hard Days Night, created in 1964 will arrive in the public domain in 2059 which means that it won't do most of us any good.

We shouldn't be fooled into believing that there are any contemporary photos, music or videos that are in the public domain. These sites do not contain free, public domain material. What these sites hopefully have and are giving you is either the work of artists and authors with whom they have an agreement or else they are giving you their original work. It isn't that the material isn't subject to copyright. It's that these entities hopefully have the power and agreements to give you proper permission to use the work. As you might expect some of the people selling such services may have the right to give you permission and others may not. We should research them carefully.

Because it is a grant of permission, not the providing of public domain material you should review the permission you are receiving fully. Many of these "permissions" are limited to personal use, one time use and other such restrictions. Sometimes they are just providing the material and requiring that the material be utilized for "non-profit education," "fair use" or instructing us that we must engage in the transformative use of the material. Sites such as this are not giving us any more rights than we normally would have, they are just telling us how to use the material so that we comply with copyright restrictions. Make certain that you have read in detail what the terms of use are for the site and that they really are providing something of value.

Classic & BestSelling Books That Just Passed Into the Public Domain (Printed 1922)

  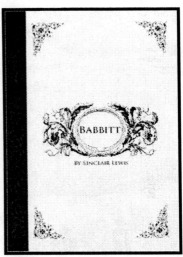

The Velveteen Rabbit
By Margery Williams

Ulysses
By James Joyce

Babbitt
By Sinclair Lewis

Terms of Use & Their Enforcement

Part of what causes all of the confusion surrounding copyright law is the overlap with other intellectual property rights. Earlier we distinguished between copyrights and trademarks. Copyright protects the creation, trademarks protect the marketing or "trade" of a product or service in connection with a certain "mark." They really are about two different things.

There are also a lot of people running around claiming that something is a copyright violation when it is not. Just because someone sent a letter or just because someone claimed that a copyright violation has occurred does not mean that one has been committed. The only person who can tell you that you have violated copyright law is a judge and a jury in federal court. Can it be a crime? Yes, but only under certain circumstances if the infringement is willful and for purposes of commercial advantage or private financial gain. *18 USC §506(a)*. If the offense consists of the reproduction or distribution during any 180 day period of 10 or more copies having a retail value of more than $2,500, the offense is a felony, otherwise it is a misdemeanor *18 USC §2319*. Still the fact remains that only a judge and jury can determine whether a crime has been committed.

While the FBI can investigate cases, they are very few and far between and usually reserved for the likes of Julius Chow Lieh Liu, a 55 year old El Cerrito man, who was sentenced to four years in prison on June 11, 2010 for violating copyright laws. Through his company, SuperDVD, he had engaged in the large scale infringement of thousands of copies of Symantec software, music CD's and movie DVD's over the course of  several years. He replicated and sold thousands of counterfeit copies of Norton's Anti Virus software, Beatles CD's, and the movies Crouching Tiger and Hidden Dragon. The conviction came after a three year long FBI investigation.

Many people label a violation of a "Term of Use" a copyright violation. It is not. Again they are two different things. If you utilize certain sites such as YouTube or Flickr® those sites have "Terms of Use" that we agreed to follow when we signed up for the service. Independent businesses have the right to control how their business operates and they can suspend an account or take other action. For example, YouTube is permitted as a business entity to enter into an agreement with BMG Music to protect the intellectual property of BMG's music. You may be entitled to use a portion of the song under any of the copyright exceptions or exclusions that we have discussed. In other words your use of the song may not be a copyright violation. However, YouTube may send you a notice saying that they believe "any use of the song" is a copyright violation and disable links to the song or your ability to download it. They have that right. It is incorporated in the terms of use for their site. It does not mean we have violated copyright law.

Be cognitive of other people's rights. Don't use other people's material in a way that violates copyright law. Most of the time, if someone feels that their rights and interests in intellectual property have been interfered with, they will send a notice. Sometimes it takes the form of a cease and desist notice, sometimes a more cordial letter asking us not to use certain material. We are all best served by respecting each other and doing what we can to protect interests in intellectual property. If you receive such a letter the best thing to do is to remove the item.

Copyright law is an important concept. We have great interest in copyright as instructors. It was meant to protect us, both in regard to the creation of our own "permanently affixed original works" and in our desires and quests to spread information and education to the public and our students.

Fundamental Questions to Ask If You Are Accused of a Copyright Violation

✓ **First – Offer to Remove the Alleged Violation.** Courts and lawyers are expensive and it is easier most of time to simply remove the item that is alleged to be a violation. Notification is required under the Digital Millenium Copyright Act (DMCA) and removal creates a 'safe harbor' from litigation in a lot of instances. Most of the time removal will solve the problem and it's cheaper than hiring a lawyer, even if you are right.

✓ **Ask for Proof of Copyright.** It is only the holder of a copyright who can claim damages. This means that they will have to prove that they actually own the copyright and prove when the material was created. They are going to have to demonstrate that they are the legal owners of the copyright in order to bring any type of claim. It is too easy in today's world for entities to generate letters, claim to be the copyright holders of something and demand money when they may not even be the legal owners of the item. We could log on to the internet right now, copy pictures from someone's website, then send the picture back to the website owner and claim we are the holders of the copyright for the picture and make a demand for payment. Make certain you know with whom you are dealing and that they truly are the owners of the item.

✓ **Ask if the Copyright is Registered with the U.S. Copyright Office.** Copyrights do not have to be registered with the U.S. Copyright Office, but proof of such registration does demonstrate that the person with whom you are dealing is the copyright holder. Registration is required prior to the filing of any lawsuit for violation. If he holder did not register the copyright prior to your alleged violation they will not be able to recover anything except their actual damages which must be proven.

✓ **Ask Why the Holder Believes that Your Use is Not Subject to Fair Use.** Fair use covers a lot of ground. Unless we have copied someone's work in its entirety, using a portion of it may be permitted under fair use. Fair use is a defense to copyright claims and courts have been very liberal about applying this exception and exclusion to copyright claims of infringement.

✓ **Ask the Holder Why They Believe Your Use Was Not for Educational Purposes.** Much of the language in copyright law promotes and protects educational uses. There are limitations on educational purposes and the circumstances under which it applies are set forth in Title 17 U.S.C. §110 (read it in conjunction with §107) and courts interpret the fair use doctrine in light of the purpose for which the work was used, even if it does not fall under the specific language of the educational exemption.

✓ **Ask the Holder Why They Believe Your Use Was Not a Transformative Use.** Much creative work is transformative in nature. It is likely that any use made of certain alleged copyright material was part of a larger whole that you created and that the creation of the whole transformed the work into a new copyrighted work with insights, commentary, new expressions and meanings.

✓ **Ask for Proof of Monetary Damages.** In order to prevail in a federal district court lawsuit the holder is going to have to prove actual damages that they have incurred because you used their copyrighted work. Before you pay anything find out what actual damages can be proven. This is extremely difficult for most entities to do.

Even major companies like Perfect 10 in their lawsuit against Google had difficulty trying to prove that they had actual damages.

We strongly recommend that these responses and questions should be done in writing. Keep a copy of everything. Understand that if you write a check you should get a release of any and all liability and we would always recommend that before you write checks to someone who is allegedly claiming a copyright violation that you get the advice of an attorney who is well versed in the area of copyright and intellectual property. We believe that when violations occur the copyright holder is entitled to remedies. As instructors we should not become victims to those who are claiming copyright violations that cannot be proven and may not even exist.

Curtain Call

"The Role of Education Directors in Real Estate Brokerages"

Sharon Montague, Education Director, Beverly-Hanks & Associates

Sharon has been a national and regional trainer for two major franchises teaching in the United States and Canada. She previously owned a private real estate school in Asheville, North Carolina and taught pre-licensing, appraisal courses and broker courses. She has been active as a member of REEA, and served as President of the North Carolina Real Estate Educators Association. Sharon has won awards for the "Most Outstanding Program of the year. Today she supervises the training and education for the prestigious Beverly-Hanks & Associates firm in Asheville. You can reach Sharon at Sharon@Beverly-Hanks.com

EDUCATION COSTS MONEY, BUT THEN, SO DOES IGNORANCE. Today's real estate market is fraught with legal liability and frivolous lawsuits making real estate agents easy targets. Which, to me, begs the question; how can you afford NOT to provide ongoing in-house education?

I am fortunate to be associated with a company whose culture includes a strong belief in education for its agents, consequently, the company and the entire Leadership Team recognizes the cost, versus the value, for a full time professional dedicated strictly to education. It's amazing to me that in this day and age, many companies still hire new licensees and offers them no training, or limited training at best.

Your in-house training program should cover a broad spectrum of educational opportunities. We provide over 100 classes per year, which of course includes a new agent training series as well as required training for experienced agents new to our company. Additionally, we sponsor professional designation classes, technology classes, continuing education classes, local experts on specific areas of expertise and lots of one on one coaching. Include in your training budget at least one national speaker a year with a topic that is totally pertinent to the current marketplace. During my 15 years as an Education & Training Director for a major company, we have provided speaking professionals like Steve Harney, Pat Zaby, Tom Lundstedt, Course Creators; Len Elder and Theresa Barnabei, Walter Sanford, Terry Watson and many more. Providing this high level of education to your agents at no cost to them solidifies in the agents' minds the company's commitment to their individual success.

Every company has lots of untapped talent in their own leaders and agents. Use agent guest instructors that you have interviewed and coached in being a well prepared good presenter. Be thoughtful and careful here. Why do they want to teach a class? Is it for the right reasons? An old saying goes: Ego. Do you have _it_ or does _it_ have you? A healthy ego is vital to being a good presenter, however, if IT has you, then the performance will be self-centered instead of caring more about the learner's objectives in attending the class.

Most presenters know the principles of GAPE and that's a good thing, however, a classroom of students respond most to instructors who teach with enthusiasm, empathy and from the heart. Students can "hear" how you really feel, regardless of the words they are hearing. Zig Ziglar's definition of "Communication" is: "The transference of a feeling, a concept or an idea from one person to another that brings results." Instructors should ask themselves…. "Did I just cover the material I need to cover OR did I move the learners to take action….to believe they could accomplish something based on what I just shared….did they believe I cared?" If there is no subsequent action by the learner we did not truly communicate. As an instructor you are always "on stage". Will you get a "thumbs up?" or a "thumbs down?"

In preparing this *Curtain Call* I wondered if I was truly objective regarding the advantages and the value of in-house training so I queried the agents. The agent response I received from my query astounded me so much that I decided to let their comments talk to you about the agent's perception of the value of a full time in-house educational program. Their words are far more valuable to you than mine. Here are a few:

> *I like…convenience, risk management by having someone monitoring trends and providing courses to address those issues, team building and unity.*

> *The training has been very important to me. After 36 years in real estate it is still important. With all the changes made in forms, rules, etc. I feel that in-house training is so easily accessible and keeps us on our toes.*

I have worked in the real estate industry for 11 years, first in a small independent firm and then with a large franchise firm. When first with this company I was a very experienced top producer and reluctant to attend the in-house training. I was pleasantly surprised by the amount of information I received in the training classes which were introduced in a professional and relaxed atmosphere and easy to ask questions and get answers from the trainer; unlike the online courses of my previous big company. I now look forward to the in-house educational opportunities that hone my professional skill set.

I would say that training of agents is directly proportional to the value of the agent to the company. The in-house training saves agents time and money because it is always within easy access. It creates a "win-win" scenario for agent and company.

I came to this company for the in-house education. I know the company will keep us abreast of the important necessary things we need to know and learn to be more successful. In-house training is an added plus regarding cost and travel distance.

From the day I joined the company 15 years ago I have been aware of the value of the in-house training. The convenience is without question, to say nothing of the time savings. Other important issues are the rubbing of elbows one gets from attending these sessions, getting to know our fellow agents pays dividends in the long run. Of greatest importance is the knowledge we all get from these sessions. I don't know how other companies handle their training but I do feel that no one does it better.

The initial new agent training was amazing to me because it gave me the tools I needed to start building my business. I would have been lost without these live interactive classes. I continue to attend the many other education opportunities offered and benefit from asking questions and listening to other experienced successful agents.

One thing that we know for certain: agents want, demand and need good high quality instruction. When it is done in that fashion they do participate and they do appreciate it.

Curtain Call

"Real Estate Education Through the Eyes of a State Regulator"

Ryan Adair, Education Director, Alabama Real Estate Commission

Ryan Adair is the Education Director for the Alabama Real Estate Commission and a board member of the National Association of Real Estate Educators (REEA). Ryan previously served as the director of an adult program in the College of Business of Faulkner University as well as the Director of Education and Board Services for the Alabama Association of REALTORS®. With an M.S. in Human Resource Management from Troy University in Montgomery, Ryan has distinguished himself as a regulator dedicated to excellence in the delivery of education throughout the real estate industry. You can reach Ryan by email at ryan.adair@arec.alabama.gov.

What comes to mind when you think of a state regulator? What is your impression of the real estate commission? I am afraid we are too often seen as the guys in the black hats. We have the reputation of wanting to catch someone violating license law like state troopers who strategically position themselves behind a highway divider with a radar gun trying to catch speeders. We are viewed as being obsessed with "seat time" requiring instructors to actually say, "You can't get out of your chair for another 2 minutes and 13 seconds if you want CE." Actually, it is quite the opposite. Even though regulatory bodies exist to serve and protect the public, the vision of the Alabama Real Estate Commission is to ensure excellence in the real estate profession. A huge part of a licensee achieving excellence is quality education. Therefore, we are just as passionate about quality education as the instructors who are offering it. So, here is the question. What does a state regulator do to make sure that real estate education is what it needs to be? I have identified three areas to address and the first one may surprise you.

Relationship with Instructors

If the common goal of real estate educators and the Real Estate Commission is quality education, then it only makes sense to work together. This is why it is so beneficial for regulators to be members of educator groups such as the Real Estate Educators Association (REEA) on the national level and any similar associations on the state level. Alabama, along with other states, also uses an Education Advisory Committee made up of instructors who assist the Commission in working on special education projects such as the development of new courses, the improvement of existing courses, and the collection of resources that can benefit all instructors. This allows Education Division staff to interact with instructors with the goal of creating education offerings that benefit both the educators and the students. Education audits for both instructors and schools work well in not only identifying potential problems that need to be addressed but also providing time for face-to-face contact with instructors where beneficial conversations can take place, questions can be answered, and information can be shared. Building and maintaining healthy relationships with instructors is a great way for the Real Estate Commission to ensure quality education is being offered.

Training of Instructors

Proper training is important in any discipline. Therefore, you especially need to make sure that the trainer has been properly trained. Our newly approved pre-license instructors are required to attend a New Instructor Orientation where they learn basics such as Bloom's Taxonomy, writing proper learning objectives, and using various teaching strategies. They are also required to give a 20 minute presentation for evaluation by Education Division staff before receiving the green light to step into the classroom. This is very important for some new instructors who may not have much teaching experience. After the evaluation, they know exactly what the Commission is expecting when their courses are audited. Instructors are then required to get 12 hours of instructor training every two years. Topics range from general IDWs to specific areas such as Technology, License Law, Course Development, Ethics, and Instructor Branding. It is a very beneficial day when you can get 40-50 instructors together to learn not only from a very knowledgeable nationally known presenter but also to learn from each other. Realizing the importance of continued training and development, Education Division staff members even attend training at various conferences and get certifications such as the Certified Distance Education Instructor® (CDEI) to stay current.

Levels of Education

As regulators, we deal with education for individuals on many different levels...from someone just getting into real estate who knows nothing about it to someone who has had a long career in real estate and is an experienced instructor. We need to make sure the level of education is appropriate for each person. For example, the Salesperson Pre-license course must be taught at a level that is basic enough so the individual will be prepared to pass the licensing exam and considered to be minimally competent to be licensed. The Post License course is where the licensee is actually taught how to use that license and begin listing and selling under the guidance and direction of a qualifying broker. Therefore, it is taught at a higher level than the Salesperson Pre-license course. Eventually, a salesperson may choose to become a broker and will be required to take the Broker Pre-license course. Once again, a higher level of education is required here since this individual now has at least two years of experience and is looking at supervising other licensees. When you look at continuing education courses, the levels of education will vary based on the topic and content. For example, a Fair Housing Made Easy course will be taught at a much lower level than Financial Analysis for Commercial Investment Real Estate. This is an important realization for instructors in order to guarantee all students get the most from each course. Not being prepared for varying levels of knowledge runs the risk of some students being lost or other students being bored. This is a big challenge of continuing education courses since instructors do not always know who is going to attend as opposed to the pre-license and post license courses where all students are at a similar level of knowledge.

These are just three areas that are addressed. There are more concerns and we do our best to communicate those to our instructors. There is much more to the regulation of real estate education than making sure licensees take their required continuing education and instructors follow their approved course outlines. Education plays a major role in ensuring excellence in the real estate profession and we want to ensure that the education that is offered is of high quality. Finally, we know that educators understand all education is valuable…even if there is no continuing education credit associated with it. Our goal is to try to convince licensees the same. We know that may be wishful thinking, but according to former Los Angeles Dodger Steve Garvey, "You have to set goals that are almost out of reach." This goal will require a great deal of reaching and stretching, but it is worth the effort.

Act XIII
The Future of the Theater

Previews of Coming Attractions

Through all we have shared with you in this work, by now YOU should be able to write the last Act. Let us be even more direct about that: YOU must write the last Act. The last Act will be written and it will exist. The only choice that gets to be made is whether it will be written by default or by design. Nothing that we say about the future, the direction or the possibilities for real education mean anything without YOU. The future of our industry and our profession will be exactly what YOU make of it. It won't be dictated by markets, administrative agencies, education directors or appreciative students, it will rise and fall based upon what YOU do with the opportunities ahead.

A lot of people gave freely of their time, effort, energies and passion to put this book in your hands. It contains the story of real estate education and that story comes from a long and distinguished past. There have been contributions to the story by those whose names have been lost in that history; they taught in classrooms for decades and worked to refine and hone the craft of teaching. There are researchers, regulators, school officials, students and mentors who all contributed to this work more than they realize by the things they taught us in our journeys in education. All of them made those sacrifices for this moment. They did it for YOU. They have left YOU with a legacy and a promise to fulfill. But make no mistake about it, this has been and was always intended to be a book to help YOU be a better and more committed instructor. With all of that said, let us share with you a few things that lie beyond the final curtain and outside the content of this work.

The Evolution Revolution

We speak often of the evolution revolution and we truly believe that now is the most exciting, opportunistic time ever in education and the real estate industry. We are on the cusp of seeing traditional adult education reinvented and morphed into something that previously did not exist. From the technology tools available, to new educational theories and insights to new teaching venues, it really is a brave new world.

Alvin Toffler, the noted author once said, "The future belongs to those who are willing to learn, relearn and then learn again." We think that is true. It's true of our students who are business professionals and it's true for us as instructors as well. Now is no time to stand still. The world moves far too fast and leaders must be constantly advancing to leverage and teach in that changing world. You did know that the teachers should lead didn't you?

Fireworks Exploding by foto76, FreeDigitalPhotos.Net

The evolution revolution is upon us as we recraft ourselves continually and find new ways of doing old things better. If the statistics and numbers are true (and we happen to agree with them) about the amount of technical information doubling every two years then that means for our students one-half of what they learn today will be replaced in twenty four months. Seven of the top ten in demand jobs did not even exist ten years ago. It forces us to teach to people whose jobs were just created using technology only recently invented to try and solve problems that we don't even know exist yet.

All of this means that the demand, that the need for education, training and good quality instruction has accelerated beyond our wildest imaginations. "Embrace the revolution," we say, "It's where all opportunity is created."

Fractualization of the Theaters

More venues exist for teaching today than ever before in history. We do believe that it broadens the opportunities and the outlets for education. We also believe that the traditional business models of strong localized proprietary schools built of brick and mortar is at risk. We have seen a number of them close in recent years, a number of them have consolidated and those that are left are trying to reach beyond their walls to new venues and forums such as distance education.

The causes for this transformation are many, but part of it lies in the specialization and distinctive needs of students based on the areas in which they practice, the geographic areas of their business and even the brokerages and companies with whom they are aligned. Agency law is different in Colorado, than it is in New York, than it is in Arizona. Within any given state the policies and procedures are different from one brokerage to the next. For an agent to learn the proper way to do things it makes more sense to attend a course customized to their brokerage than it does to attend a generic agency class where little of what they learned may be transferable to their business practices.

Also contributing to changes in educational venues is the fact that many of the benefits that REALTOR® associations and brokerages traditionally used to attract agents have been washed away by market conditions and technology. Such entities previous offered websites, today agents create those online on their own for free. They offered desk space which is no longer needed. They offered networks that can now be built on a host of social media platforms at no cost. What can associations and brokerages offer as a true benefit to being associated with them? It must come in the form of education and training. Education and training is one of the few differentiating factors left. Associations and brokerages will continue to offer more in-house courses and use the promotion and hosting of educational opportunities as a means of differentiation. We have witnessed many brokerages and associations forming their own schools. They have revenue from other sources so the education can be offered at less cost and more efficiently than the traditional proprietary institutions.

We think it is reasonable to assume that there will be more creation and formation of "schools" by these players in the future. We also think that makes the opportunities for instructors broader. It probably will not make economic sense for these associations and brokerages to build full staffs of faculty and that means more demand for independent contractor instructors. These entities can all be clients and the custom crafting of education for them will in all likelihood continue to grow.

The Insatiable Appetite for Content

As more and more entities enter the education business, as online platforms expand there will be (and already is to a large degree) a sharp increase in the demand for content. We can't exist in a digital world where content is being consumed at a phenomenal rate and not expect demand for more content to go up.

Woman Opening Refrigerator by Ambro
FreeDigitalPhotos.Net

New schools, outreaching educational entities and associations are going to demand more and more content. The audience of real estate professionals is hungry for it. Practicing and producing agents know with the rapid changes occurring in the profession that they have to keep learning to stay ahead of the curve and stay on top of the market. It will result in a lot of education providers looking into the refrigerator and asking what do I serve next? What else is in here? Maybe I should go to the grocery store. We have the opportunity to be their "SuperMarket."

The content is going to come in a variety of forms. It will come in the nature of more and varied courses. It will be delivered both live and through the distance learning platforms that we discussed in this book. It is going to be tailored to meet the needs of agents at different levels of practice, different geographical areas and different areas of expertise.

Mastery & Skill Based Learning

Up to this point the vast bulk of education has been knowledge based education. To a large extent we have been stuck at the lowest level of Bloom's taxonomy. That means that courses and instructors were simply trying to convey principles, concepts, theory and laws to learners. We would expect that over the next several years one of the major fundamental changes will be the shift from knowledge based education courses to skill based education courses. More and more educators will try to provide knowledge in a way that students "Get It, Use It and Become More Successful Because of It!"

Our students today parallel the attitudes and needs of today's consumers. The shift in attitude seems to be developing along the following mindset:

"I have a specific task I am trying to accomplish. Tell me the best way to go about it. Don't bother me with a lot of theory and detail, just tell me what I need to know in the shortest possible time in the most direct manner and show me how to apply the knowledge."

When we analyze this mindset in the world of real estate education, it manifests itself in a number of ways. Perhaps you have heard something similar in your classes and as feedback from the students you are currently teaching.

"Don't teach me agency principles, show me how to have an agency discussion with my client."

"Don't read me the paragraphs of a purchase contact, teach me how to overcome specific client objections."

"Don't tell me about the general impact of social media. Show me where to go and what I should be doing."

All of this means that training and education will become more skill based and stress more than ever before the practical application of the learning. It has always been in the practical application that students struggle the most and they will look for innovative classes and instructors to help them integrate knowledge into practice. These demands will go hand in hand with more pressure from students for educators to guide them forward from their current position of practice and knowledge. In the past, we were much more likely to offer a variety of courses, in no particular order, with no hierarchy and allow the students to choose the class they thought they should attend. We believe we will see more packaging of classes into defined series so that a student can appropriately plug-in. It will require more thought on the structure and organization of classes, but the students are looking for educational direction not only of which classes they should take, but in what particular order. Education will be much more than simply taking a class in a particular category just to get a certificate to renew a license.

We believe that the easiest way this will be accomplished will be through the introduction of "Skill Based Ladder Mastery" and although the following is simply one illustration of how that might occur, we believe it will provide insight into what lies ahead.

With "Skill Based Ladder Mastery" students will be able to pick a particular skill which they want to improve and then will select a learning track series of classes that guide them toward obtaining that objective. For the most part, in the past we have simply packaged classes into knowledge based categories as renewal packages and they have been structured to meet the needs of an administrative or governmental entity for purposes of licensure or renewal, not based upon the skill needs of the real estate professionals.

The opportunities to create various arrangements and packages of classes into these skill based learning ladders has only just begun but we expect it to accelerate as dictated by the demands and needs of students. We presume that social media and technology have given the students more of a voice than ever before. Education is about to be dictated from the bottom up and not so much the top down. The industry will increasingly be driven by what the students want and need to learn. We will all get better at helping them assess their knowledge and skills and pointing them in the direction of improvement.

The Art of Blended Learning

These increased demands on learning will also force educators into worlds of combining tools. Until now we have asked questions like: Is the class live or online? Is the class synchronous or asynchronous? What we have failed to realize is the formats are not mutually exclusive of each other. Why can't a class involve both live and online portions? Why can't a class on distance learning have a synchronous module completed with the instructor in real time and then transition students to asynchronous modules that they can explore on their own?

We have always known that different students learn best in different ways, at different speeds with different mechanisms. Why not broaden that approach? There is no reason for example that a pre-licensing course couldn't be broken down along the following lines. We understand in sharing this example that we have vastly oversimplified a pre-license course, but we think it makes the point about the blended learning approach:

Orientation & Information About Getting a Real Estate License	**Asynchronous Education Offered Online**
Introductory Principles of Real Estate	**Synchronous Education Offered Online**
Real Estate Principles Applied Mortgages, Appraisals & Escrow	**Live Classroon Education**
Introduction to State Laws, Statutes & Real Estate Regulations	**Asynchronous Education Offered Online**
Practical Applications of State Laws Statutes & Regulations	**Live Classroom Education**
Exam Review & Test Preparation	**Synchronous Education Offered Online**

There is no reason that continuing education and non-accredited courses couldn't be offered in the same format. We could teach a live classes that covered three major topics and then offer to the students further distance education that allowed them to select and choose the area that they are most interested in learning more about.

We predict that you will see course developers and instructors exploring the concept of blended learning. Similar courses will be offered in different formats creating more choice for the student to select their method of learning and both schools and instructors will be able to teach more students more efficiently with blended learning approaches so we think that economics alone will cause a proliferation of blended learning classes.

Increased Instructor Collaboration

Older established education models were based upon the establishment of proprietary schools. An instructor taught for this school or that school, not multiple schools. The proprietary location model was important when we needed a physical location to teach. Someone had to pay for the overhead, the staff, the classroom, the materials and the corresponding demand was that an instructor had to remain loyal to a particular school. Teaching for a competitor has been strict taboo in many areas.

Teamwork by jscreationszs
FreeDigitalPhotos.Net

Today locations are everywhere. When education can be offered online, through brokerages, through associations and presented with the use and support of sponsors on a regular basis, the need for a physical fixed location classroom diminishes greatly. It leaves instructors in a world of free-lance. We transition the industry from teaching to students to teaching for clients. If this sounds a lot like the world of corporate education in business, then you would be correct. We are witnessing the real estate profession move closer and closer to the corporate business world where it should have been along anyway. It's just that this time the agents are driving the train with their demands and needs for education.

When we view this in light of the increased demand for content, blended classes and the expansion of distance learning, instructors are going to find more and more ways to collaborate in the creation of educational programs. You might be an expert on developing a sphere of business, someone else might be an expert on the Real Estate Settlement & Procedures Act and still another person might be an expert in developing an online presence. Doesn't logic dictate that these three instructors together would offer the "Ultimate Sphere of Influence Building" course and leverage their respective talents and abilities to bring new products to the marketplace? Sure, they could travel together and deliver live classes, but they much more efficiently could put together a distance learning program that incorporated synchronous and asynchronous tools.

Because of the technological advances, we won't see this collaboration occurring just along subject matter lines, we will see more collaboration occurring based on instructor talents and skill sets. Perhaps you are the best at research, but someone else does amazing PowerPoints and then there is that person with the golden voice just made for audio recordings in an Articulate program. We can see it already. Guess what it looks like ? The movie credits at the theater.

Course Design & Concept By:

Audio & Voice Recordings By:

Powerpoint & Visuals Created By:

Research Provided By:

It never made sense in the previous world because proprietary schools could not afford a course development team that looked like this and independent contractor instructors couldn't either. You had to do it all yourself. That's simply not true with today's technology and various delivery modes for education. We think that this movement is really good for everyone. We can all play to our strengths, we can pool our ideas, we can brainstorm together. Can you imagine how much we can all teach each other in an educational world based on collaboration where we are not in competition with each other, but associated with each other so that we can try and figure out how to create win-win relationships? We can.

Of Bits & Bytes

We would expect learning segments to get smaller. That doesn't mean that there will be less education, as we have already stated there will be more. We just expect it to be broken down into smaller bits and bytes in the manner and form in which it is offered. Maybe that will occur because we live in a time pressured world and students will find it easier to allocate shorter, but more frequent blocks of their time to education. Maybe it will occur because of the advent of mobile technology. It's easy to pick up 15 or 30 minutes of education on our iPhones, Droids, Kindles and iPads. It's a little less convenient

Data Network by jscreationszs
FreeDigitalPhotos.Net

for us to try and do a three hour class on these devices. Maybe it will occur because nearly every one in business today grew up with 30 to 60 minute television shows.

Part of what will drive the trend is simply our students' desire in professional environments to seek out what they need to know for that particular moment. Just give me a library of education and let me pick to find out what I need to know right now.

Beyond Limiting Beliefs

The greatest barrier to our success and future as educators is not the markets, the students or regulators. It is our own limiting beliefs about what is possible and what we can achieve. In the movie, *Coach Carter*, Tino Cruz shares some insight which has been attributed to many including Nelson Mandela and others:

> **Our deepest fear is not that we are inadequate**
> **Our deepest fear is that we are powerful beyond measure**
> **It is our light, not our darkness that most frightens us**
> **Your playing small does not serve the world**
> **There is nothing enlightened about shrinking**
> **So that other people won't feel insecure around you**
> **We were all meant to shine as children do**
> **It's not just in some of us, it's in everyone**
> **And as we let our own light shine**
> **We unconsciously give other people permission to do the same**
> **As we are liberated from our own fear**
> **Our presence automatically liberates others**

When we continue to do or decide not to do something because "that's the way it's always been done" "that's the way they told me to do it" or "they said that won't work" we immediately limit our perspective and the possibilities. We hope this book has opened new worlds of perspective and excitement for you. Prior to 1954 the leading researchers, scientists, doctors and physiologists concluded that man could not run a four minute mile. They claimed that our bone structure was all wrong, that our lungs were inadequate, that our hearts could not withstand the strain and that men would die if they tried. Roger Bannister refused to listen to any of them.

On August 7, 1954 at the British Empire and Commonwealth Games in Vancouver, B.C., Bannister ran for England. The race was billed as the "The Miracle Mile." Bannister crossed the finish line in 3 minutes, 58.8 seconds. So much for the belief that it couldn't be done. The amazing part and moral of the story is not that Roger Bannister achieved something that everyone thought was impossible. It is the fact that following Bannister's shattering of the perceived ceiling, many others broke the barrier as well. To date 955 runners have broken Bannister's record a total of 4,700 times. That pretty much proves there were no physical barriers only psychological ones. All Roger Bannister did was remove the limiting beliefs.

Remember what Shakespeare said, "All the World's a Stage!" So whether you want to think of it as scripts to write or productions to create we are all right here to help you. Whether you choose Alexandra Scott as your mascot to create a nationwide presence and legacy or whether you want to be Roger Bannister and remove some barriers and break down some walls we are here to help you do that as well. Maybe we all can just band together in a circle, no one in higher ranking than the next; might for right, right for might and just call ourselves the Knights of the Roundtable in the middle of the evolution revolution.

As for us, this book has taken us full circle and we are back on the opening pages with Merlin and we can't help but think:

"What a lot of things there are to learn!"

To us that translates into:

"What a lot of things there are to teach!"

(Curtain)

Your Voice, Comments & Insights Deserve to Be Heard

As a reader of this book, your comments and insights are important. If your name did not appear on the list of Contributing Authors we know you have knowledge and experience that would be useful to share with others. We will continue to update this book and add to the shareable body of information relating to instruction.

In reading this book, if you have a great idea or thought and would like to share please send it to us via our email: support@CourseCreators.Com. You can also post your comments, feedback, additions and insight on our facebook page "OVATION – How to Present Like a Pro." We would also encourage you to share your ideas and feedback on the Real Estate Educators Association facebook page and submit your article for publication in the *REEAaction Newsletter*. REEA is always looking for contributions and ideas for the *Newslettter* from fellow educators. Come & Join the Dialogue:

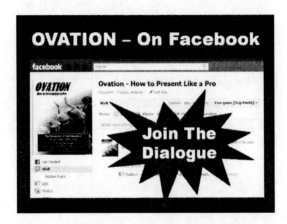

If you respond we will reach out for you as we create future editions and the supplemental material that we are creating to accompany this book. We would love to be a collaborating author with you. Would you be interested in working with us on the future creation of:

What we do is mostly in our name,

"Course Creators"

Causing Colorful Change

At Course Creators we create and develop cutting edge custom crafted courses to help our students, clients and other instructors:

Get It, Use It and Become More Successful Because of It!

We teach. We train. We also write and develop courses for others. You can license our courses or collaborate with us on creating something that you can license to others. Either way everybody wins.

- Workshops or Keynote Presentations
- Give your instructors the right tools to help you succeed
- Get rave reviews and feedback
- Generate more business
- Set high standards for delivery and presentation

You can order copies of the book for your instructors & trainers from Course Creators.com

- Collaborate with us on your dream course
- Create a live and an online version
- Differentiate yourself
- Target your ideal student or market
- Make more money & have more students

- Collaborate with us to turn any business book into a course
- We can revenue share together
- Help you learn to teach it or find instructors to teach it for you
- Show you how to promote it and earn additional revenue
- Generate more book sales

- Revolutionary Pre-License Course: the new generation of licensing
- Innovative concepts to get more students
- Why spend thousands writing when you can license this

Experience the "Ah Ha" of a Whole New World of Business!

Get It, Use It and Become More Successful Because of It!

THE 2 Day "Hands On" Video & Internet Marketing Course

Share 2 Days With Us & You Will Be Able To:

- *Invite students, clients and customers to your TV Channel*
- *Make, edit and post videos on the internet*
- *Invite fans to your Facebook business page*
- *Network and get business from anywhere in the country*
- *Manage your sphere of influence & stay in contact*
- *Market where most consumers and students exist*
- *Succeed in the changing business world of today*
- *Know just where to go on the internet and what to do once you are there*

You can license it, revenue share with it or sponsor it!

Find Out More at CourseCreators.com

ELEVATE THE LEVEL OF YOUR INSTRUCTION
TECHNOLOGY TRAINNG TO GO

Each training DVD-Rom has approximately 3 Hours of Material. Step by step training videos that will have you using these internet tools like a pro in a day. No more wondering where to go and how to use them. Practical applications for business that will get you more money, more students and more profit.

FaceBiz –   Find out what Facebook can do for your business

Linkedin – Grow you business and database faster than ever

VideoBiz- Start your own TV Channel and shoot, edit and post videos

WebBiz – Create your own website and blog

Trulia & Zillow – Know how to market where your clients are

Available in the Products Section
CourseCreators.com